WEARING MY TUTU TO ANALYSIS
AND OTHER STORIES

WEARING MY TUTU TO ANALYSIS
AND OTHER STORIES

LEARNING PSYCHODYNAMIC CONCEPTS FROM LIFE

KERRY L. MALAWISTA, ANNE J. ADELMAN,
AND CATHERINE L. ANDERSON

Columbia University Press 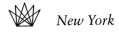 New York

Columbia University Press
Publishers Since 1893
New York   Chichester, West Sussex
Copyright © 2011 Kerry L. Malawista, Anne J. Adelman,
   and Catherine L. Anderson

Library of Congress Cataloging-in-Publication Data
Malawista, Kerry L.
  Wearing my tutu to analysis and other stories : learning
psychodynamic concepts from life / Kerry L. Malwista, Anne J. Adelman,
and Catherine L. Anderson
       p.   cm.
  Includes bibliographical references and index.
  ISBN 978-0-231-15164-1 (cloth : alk. paper) — ISBN 978-0-231-15165-8
(pbk. : alk. paper) — ISBN 978-0-231-52531-2 (ebook)
  1. Psychodynamic psychotherapy. 2. Communication in psychology.
3. Psychoanalysts—Vocational guidance. I. Adelman, Anne J. II. Anderson,
Catherine L. (Catherine Louise) III. Title.
  RC489.P72M3325   2011
  616.89'14—dc22
                                                      2010051579

To our husbands
Alan, Bill, and Eric

And to our children
Amanda, Anna,
David, Isabel, Lynn, Matt, Nate, Peter, and Zoe

In memory of Sarah

CONTENTS

Contents

Part Two: Development

Part Three: Technique

Part Four: Treatment Challenges

ACKNOWLEDGMENTS

We thank Lauren Dockett for guiding us through the writing and publication process from start to finish and for her thoughtful editorial comments and wise suggestions, as well as Annie Barva for her meticulous copyediting of the final manuscript. We are also grateful to Deirdre Salcetti for first encouraging Kerry to write her stories. Along the way, many readers of various chapters offered exceptional insight and critique, including Linda Kanefield, Jenifer Nields, Aimee Nover, Sara Taber, and Robert Winer. Nan Heneson supplied her keen editorial skills. Michaele Weissman gave us many hours of thoughtful editing and suggestions.

This work could not have been completed without the guidance and support of the faulty and colleagues at New Directions. We are especially grateful to the analysts and therapists who taught us to listen to our own stories and those of our patients with sensitivity, insight, and often a bit of humor.

Most important, this book would not be possible without the

many lessons that our patients taught us throughout the years. For that, we thank you.

We are most grateful to our husbands, Alan, Bill, and Eric, for encouraging and supporting us and to our children for tolerating our preoccupation with writing.

INTRODUCTION

Tell me a fact and I'll learn. Tell me the truth and I'll believe.
But tell me a story, and it will live in my heart forever.

—Indian proverb

Think back to your own education. You may remember a poignant story told by a professor, perhaps with humor or emotion, that has remained with you long after the lengthy lectures on various theories, facts, and figures have slipped away. Recalling my own education, I remember drifting away during long academic seminars on complicated concepts that even seasoned clinicians still debate today. Once I began teaching in a clinical program, I was discouraged by the paucity of materials that could fully engage my students' minds and imaginations. It became a challenge to find a creative approach that would bring to life difficult psychoanalytic concepts such as transference, compromise formation, and defense mechanisms.

It dawned on me that I teach through stories. Anecdotes of everyday life are my most effective vehicle for teaching complicated psychological concepts to students and supervisees. Stories fire the imagination. They are loved for their simplicity, and yet they capture a deeper wisdom about human nature that can resonate long after they are heard. I recalled running into former students, some from more than twenty years ago, who reminded me of the influence a story had on their understanding of a concept. In that moment, I recognized that psychotherapy* and personal essays are a perfect union.

In the spring of 2008, while I was attending my final weekend of New Directions, a psychoanalytically oriented writing program under the auspices of the Washington Center for Psychoanalysis, an idea began to crystallize. Energized about the idea of writing a book of personal stories, I approached my colleagues Anne Adelman and Catherine Anderson, who were similarly excited at the prospect of creating a more easily comprehensible teaching tool to ignite their students' curiosity about the complexities of the mind. Working from the belief that "everyone loves a good story" and from our experience that the use of personal vignettes brings theoretically important but conceptually difficult material alive in our classrooms, we began to develop the idea for a shared project. We would demonstrate both the depth and the accessibility of psychodynamic theory through stories. Stories contain universal emotions, which, like life itself, run the gamut from dread to delight.

Our book takes the reader on a journey through stories that range from light-hearted and whimsical anecdotes to gritty tales of challenge and change and, finally, to somber personal laments of pain, loss, and love. Each essay, drawn from our personal and professional histories, speaks uniquely to events in our lives that can be understood in light of certain important psychodynamic concepts. Our stories illuminate how therapists think and work. The vignettes convey developmental or emotional moments that capture the essence of a universal experience. Of course, like any good tale, our stories are borne out of our real lives, although some details and names have been fictionalized. We believe that it is important in work such as ours to write from our own experience, yet the sto-

---

* When we refer to "psychotherapy," we are referencing all of the psychodynamically oriented psychotherapies. We limit the terms *analyst* and *analysis* to those occasions when we are specifically referencing that particular treatment modality.

ries do not portray the entirety of our worldview. They reflect the authenticity of our voices but not the full range of our experiences. Thus, although the readers' personal histories will inevitably differ from ours on the basis of gender, culture, orientation, and other life circumstances, we hope to convey moments that they will readily recognize and identify with. As in real life, we refer to both male and female therapists/analysts and patients.

We paired these brief, vivid stories from our lives with important psychodynamic ideas in a way that helps readers grasp the underpinnings of analytic theory. In turn, our reflections on the stories are our joint effort to ruminate on the meaning of the stories in light of core theoretical conceptualizations. We guide the reader in appreciating how these concepts inform our understanding of the broad range of human experiences. We believe that this approach will help diminish the apprehension that often interferes with the capacity to master material that is difficult and sensitive enough to produce anxiety and confusion at times.

Where appropriate, we address these issues through a developmental lens, offering stories from early childhood through the present, allowing the reader to explore more fully the unfolding of various psychodynamic concepts across the lifespan. We also view psychodynamic theory through a developmental lens in which theories constantly change and expand as new areas of research are incorporated. To enrich the reader's theoretical understanding and breadth of knowledge, we have relied on a variety of psychodynamic theories. We begin with an appreciation of the foundation of Freudian theory and its offshoot of ego psychology. We touch on the influence of Melanie Klein and other British theoreticians whose ideas expanded the field to include earlier and more primitive psychological states. We also include attachment theory, object relations, and relational and self-psychology, which emerged as the field moved from a one-person psychology to a two-person psychology. We also emphasize the importance of understanding the medical and neurological underpinnings of many disorders.

The difficulty in effectively teaching psychodynamic material is complicated by important trends in the field. In education in general, there is an ever-increasing propensity toward reductionism—that is, an effort to simplify concepts, both biological and psychological, by breaking them down into their smallest measurable increment. Not surprisingly, these attempts to clarify clinical theory have sometimes had the unfortunate consequence of obfuscating many of the nuances essential for understanding. For example, in efforts to investigate the complexities of the mind, the beam has been narrowed until only the tiniest brain structure can be illuminated, devoid of the context in which it operates. In this way, we are at risk of not seeing the forest for the trees.

The opposite is also true. Many important concepts—such as "ego," "repression," "Oedipal conflict," and the "unconscious"— are so widely used and accepted as part of our everyday language that they are no longer associated with the deeper truths of analytic theory. Although these ideas are intuitively understood, their absorption into popular culture cannot help but dilute their rich meanings. It is our hope that through the real-life vignettes presented in the following chapters, the complexity and elegance of each theory will speak directly to the reader.

We provide an understanding of these often esoteric and confusing concepts by placing the definitions within the context of accessible and engaging narratives. With this in mind, we have divided this book into five main sections that explore some central areas of psychodynamic education: theory, development, clinical technique, treatment challenges, and themes of trauma and loss. Neither the scope of the sections nor the range of topics addressed within each section is intended to provide a comprehensive overview of psychodynamic thought. Rather, these vignettes create a potential window through which to view the complex and compelling world of psychodynamic thinking. Once the readers' appetites have been whetted by these stories, we hope they will be inspired to continue their exploration through further study.

Part I is an introduction to fundamental concepts that are part of the bedrock of psychoanalytic theory. The six stories contained in this section address the following psychoanalytic ideas: *screen memory, symbolic representation, magical thinking, superego development, dream theory*, and *transference and enactment*. We chose these concepts out of myriad others to highlight how a therapist may think about a patient's musings during a clinical hour. The theoretical reflections that follow each vignette allow us to introduce a variety of other important, related concepts such as *repression, displacement*, and *compromise formation*, among many others.

Part II comprises six vignettes that provide an introduction to some common developmental events. Such experiences include *an infant's first love object, the child's fear of bodily harm, the adolescent's struggle with identity, the young adult's anxiety about leaving the protection of home*, and *adult development and parenthood*. With a developmental perspective on our patients and ourselves, not only do we think about early experiences as retrospective inquiries, but we also can appreciate the maturational context within which those events unfolded.

Part III addresses issues of technique from both sides of the couch. The chapters in this section cover the span of the treatment process. Topics include *beginning the work, creating a holding environment, understanding therapeutic action*, and *ending the treatment (termination)*. The challenges, joys, and sorrows of beginnings and endings are explored, as is the encounter with various primitive and potentially frightening forces within both the therapist and the patient. The stories in this section portray the powerful processes at work in these intimate encounters. Thus, they illustrate the value that we place on a thoughtful psychodynamic understanding of our experiences.

Part IV deals with the treatment challenges that the therapist encounters during the course of everyday work. The narratives contained in these chapters illuminate the gradual unfolding and deepening of treatment from both the patient's point of view and the therapist's point of view, the numerous and powerful pulls of the *transference* and *countertransference* within the therapeutic dyad, and the therapist's struggles to hold the patient firmly and compassionately in mind in the midst of these powerful forces. We chose to address several complex issues in this section—such as the *racial divide* that may be present within any therapeutic relationship, the clinical work with patients who are prone to *self-injury*, and the fallout from *ethical violations* by the therapist—because such topics can be particularly elusive, uncomfortable, and threatening to the treatment.

Finally, our last four stories explore the not infrequent experiences of *trauma, loss, betrayal,* and *psychic dislocation.* Such experiences have a powerful impact on the individual and on future generations, both consciously and unconsciously. We share four narratives of devastation and coping from the perspectives of personal experience and clinical encounters. It is essential for clinicians to listen for and understand the influence of traumatic history as it is interwoven into a patient's—or even the clinician's own—self-narrative.

In this book, we bring together storytelling and psychotherapy, both of which are borne out of the human urge to be known and to forge connection through language. Our own voices reveal themselves to the reader just as the patient's inner world unfolds before the therapist. In the initial stage of the writing process, we attempted to record our ideas and insights freely. We then stepped back, reflected, and rewrote. Likewise in psychodynamic psychotherapy, individuals put their thoughts and feelings into words and, with their therapist's help, reflect back on the process. With each rewrite or retelling, the memory and meaning may change. Indeed, one often finds that where one started is very different from where one ends up.

We invite you, as students, clinicians, and curious readers, to put yourself in our shoes, to come to know intimately how we experienced and processed some events in our work and personal lives. We hope that you will step back, as we have, and join us in reflecting on these stories and what they tell us about the complexity of the mind and the richness of human experience.

—Kerry Malawista

WEARING MY TUTU TO ANALYSIS
AND OTHER STORIES

PART ONE
Theory

I POPPED

A young mother discovers what lies beneath a memory of her older sister's destruction of a cherished toy.

The memory, my first, is crystal clear. I'm two and a half years old. It's early summer, and my forehead is damp with sweat. Elated, I am prancing around the living room in a bathing suit, a yellow tube in the shape of a horse snug around my waist. The horse's face is black and smiles mischievously. I sashay through the living room. My five-year-old sister Sophie scowls at me. A limp paisley apron sags around her middle, her new gift from "Grandma-Up-the-Hill." The more I prance, the angrier Sophie becomes. I got the horse, but all she got from Grandma was a flimsy cloth apron.

Wh...wh...whoa, horsey! From behind, I feel a push. I turn and see Sophie, diaper pin in hand, wearing a victorious smile. I am confused. Why is she smiling like that? I look down and see my horse deflating before my eyes. I am momentarily stunned. Never have I

Permission received to republish parts of this chapter from K. Malawista, "Memory," *Voice: The Art and Science of Psychotherapy* 43, no. 1 (2007): 70–72.

been so wronged. She popped my horse! *How. Dare. She.* . . . I burst into tears. My world collapses. *"Where is my mother?"* I need to tell her what Sophie did. Only she can make the world right again.

At that moment, my mother walks through the door. I run to her and tell her what Sophie did. Mom looks down at me, but she doesn't seem to notice I'm upset. Why is she *smiling?* Sophie popped my horse, but Mom just smiles. Here, the memory ends.

Twenty-five years later I lie on my analyst's couch a few months after the birth of my first daughter. My thoughts have turned to my earliest memory. I once again tell the story of my sister's envy, her attack on my beloved toy. As I speak, however, the memory suddenly shifts, and my perspective broadens. I see the image of my mother, clear as day. And only now can I see what I could not see before: my newborn baby sister, Rachel, swaddled tightly in my mother's arms. My parents have just arrived home from the hospital with the new baby.

Lying on my analyst's couch, free to cast my mind back in time, I remember the strange thought that had entered my two-and-a-half-year-old mind on that long ago afternoon: my mother's stomach has popped. With a rush, I recall the feeling of horror and rage aimed not at Sophie, but at my mother. I feel a familiar hot flush of jealousy spread throughout my body—this is my envy, not Sophie's. Now I understand why my mother looked so happy in spite of my distress.

A smile of recognition slowly spreads across my face. The mystery of this laden memory is revealed, and my long-held hurt begins to dissipate. Over the weeks and months that follow, I begin to understand my fury over the birth of my younger sister and can grasp the complex undercurrents in the relationships among my sisters, my mother, and me.

Analysts Reflect on Screen Memories

Salvador Dali revealed himself to be a perceptive observer of inner life when he said, "The difference between false memories and true ones is the same as for jewels: it is always the false ones that look the most real, the most brilliant." In psychotherapy and psychoanalysis, we listen to our patients' early memories, and we ponder which are the real gems and which are false baubles hiding treasured jewels.

This story of one memory hiding another beautifully illustrates Sigmund Freud's ([1899] 1953f) concept of "screen memory." The idea that we create a screen memory to hide the more important truth is one of Freud's lasting contributions to the practice of psychotherapy. In a screen memory, one memory serves to shroud another. Both memories are filled with powerful emotions, melded together because the two experiences are laden with similar affects. Screen memories contain a composite of elements that form a compromise between repressed or unacknowledged feelings and the subsequent defenses that arise against them.

In our offices, we practitioners often see this phenomena at work. A patient recalls a memory, and though it is true, we sense that he dwells on this recollection in order to protect himself from deeper and more unsettling meanings. The unacceptable aspect of the memory is screened out to protect the ego—that is, the individual's core sense of self. Freud hypothesized that what most often lies behind the screen is the memory of childhood dilemmas and disappointments.

The story of the little girl and her "popped" toy is a good illustration of how screen memories work. Envy probably did drive the older sister to destroy her younger sister's new toy. But the way the narrator unconsciously constructed her memory of that event protected her from recalling that she had suffered a far greater betrayal that day than the destruction of a new but replaceable toy. She could not conceive of her mother as the perpetrator of this terrible injury. Thus, the narrator "chose" to remember her loved and hated older sister, Sophie, as the source of her impotent fury, as she writes, *"Never have I been so wronged. She popped my horse! How. Dare. She. . . . I burst into tears. My world collapses."* In other words, she displaced one event onto another.

Displacement is a common form of psychic protection that shifts bad or dangerous emotions from indispensable "objects" (persons) onto those who are less significant. In this story, the screen memory masks the deeper, more painful awareness of her forbidden feelings of envy. Thus, the child created the displacement because it was too frightening for her to recognize how angry she felt at her mother. This form of psychological defense is a necessary and protective process that functions in the service of facilitating a healthy progression toward feelings of self-worth.

In this instance, the child needed to preserve her mother as the source of goodness and protection. She was baffled by her mother's reaction: "*Mom looks down at me, but she doesn't seem to notice I'm upset. Why is she smiling? Sophie popped my horse, but Mom just smiles.*" Even more profoundly, however, the little girl needed to screen from her own view her "bad" feelings of envy and anger. The adult hid the envy and hurt aroused by her mother's pregnancy behind a memory laden with comparable, albeit less charged emotions. She could not allow herself to remember her own aggressive wishes to "pop" her mother's pregnant belly—doing away with the new baby as her sister had done away with her toy. In other words, she replaced the memory of her own hatefulness with a memory of her older sister's hatefulness. The emotion is similar, but the storyline is drastically different. Thus, the screen memory serves as the disguise for the more painful and ultimately more powerful memory.

In *The Psychopathology of Everyday Life* ([1901] 1953e), Freud describes the unchanging quality of screen memories. We see in our practices how our patients cling to these iconic memories, freezing them in time. The story of her sister's unprovoked attack remained with the narrator until she discovered in analysis the threatening truth that lay beneath the surface. Just as Freud noted his patient's surprise in discovering the real memory behind the screen (45), the narrator was astonished when she recognized the accuracy and importance of the newly restored memory (an "aha" moment). Such is the nature of the dawning of insight.

In many ways, a screen memory resembles the manifest content in a dream where the actual visual imagery disguises the latent meaning of the dream. As in dreams, screen memories unconsciously "borrow" material from a related time period and use it to disguise meaning that exists on a more deeply felt level. The memories are connected, but one masks the other.

A screen memory is an example of a compromise formation—defenses that all of us create to resolve the tension between unacceptable or frightening wishes that we have repressed and the desire to see these "bad" wishes fulfilled. Compromise formations can be viewed as creative attempts to reconcile wishes that are in opposition to one another—one of which is seen as aggressive and "bad," and the other as "good." For example, the writer may have felt, "I hate my mother and want to hurt her because she brought another baby into our home" as opposed to "I love my mother, and I would never ever think of being angry with her."

Just as in a dream, each image or element of a screen memory highlights an aspect of inner conflict. It is no coincidence that a significant element of the memory is the diaper pin that Sophie wielded to destroy the prized horse. Although the memory of the newborn's homecoming was erased from conscious awareness, the diaper pin stands in as a talisman that proclaims the deeper significance of this event.

Like the contents of dreams, screen memories and the elements that link them together also serve as buoys guiding clinicians to listen carefully for hidden meanings. To the practiced ear, a screen memory often has a telltale veneer, as if it has been unconsciously "photoshopped," to highlight certain details and obscure others. The new baby was completely "photoshopped" out of the memory, and other details, such as the deflated horse and ugly apron, were spotlighted. Likewise, the specificity of the offending diaper pin—an item associated with babies—alerts the clinician to pay special attention. Here, the diaper pin is like Dali's jewel. It stands out in the memory as "the most real, the most brilliant," but it ultimately disguises the significant hidden riches of buried memory.

2 PLAY WITH ME

A toddler's symbolic play illustrates her healthy attachment and growing independence.

April was two years old when we moved to a suburb right outside of Washington, D.C. I was several months pregnant with our second child. With my husband tying up loose ends at his old job, the move took place in stages. I was at the helm, charged with the task of settling us into our new life.

Every week April and I drove several hours to our new home to start the process of putting down new roots. The trip was exhausting, and at times waves of fatigue would overcome me. We slept on mattresses on the floor, surrounded by unpacked boxes, dusty furniture, and plastic toys of every shape and size. Most mornings I would load April into her car seat with a quick kiss and head off to the deli to buy her favorite "Eggie-on-a-Bagel." I was so glad she never tired of it because, bewildered by the traffic patterns in my new hometown, I didn't know where else to go.

At the house, efforts to establish order eluded me. Clothes that April had gleefully pulled from suitcases lay scattered on the floor.

I would fold a few and then wander off to do something else. Each day brought yet another exercise in trying to locate the essentials—our toothbrushes, my wallet, the keys—which were as likely to turn up at the bottom of the bathtub upstairs as in a random drawer in the hallway. April's toys and belongings were strewn about the house. Each night we spent frantic minutes searching for her beloved Blue Bear before she could settle down for the night. Everything was in flux, and I had a hard time believing things would ever feel normal again. Yet I tried to minimize the chaos for April, delineating islands of order where she could play.

The day the movers arrived with our belongings, April planted herself on a chair in the middle of the front lawn and watched as they carried furniture, bicycles, and endless numbers of boxes into the house. The very last item out of the truck was her little plastic kitchen. Delight spread across her face, and she leaped out of her chair, exclaiming happily, "My kitchen!" She instantly set to work brewing a pretend pot of tea and flipping stacks of invisible pancakes.

Weeks later her poor little kitchen was still bare. There it stood, in a corner of our real kitchen, forlornly surrounded by half-unpacked boxes. All the toys that had been neatly arranged around her kitchen at our old home—her tea set, plastic plug-in toaster, sack of plastic fruits and vegetables—were nowhere to be found.

One morning, wanting to escape, I made a trip to a consignment shop to trade in some of April's old clothes. There, April fell in love with a red, child-size grocery cart complete with baby seat. Watching her play, I gave in to the impulse and bought it for her. While I paid for the toy, April pushed the little cart around the store, delicately putting objects in and taking them out again. Her joy lit up her whole face, and I promised to play store with her as soon as we got home.

In our living room, April deftly navigated the little cart around the piles of boxes. "Play with me, Mama!" she implored. I mused over what role I could play. Should I pretend to be her baby? Perhaps here was an opportunity to help her imagine what it would be like for her when the new baby arrived. Or perhaps I should be the shopkeeper and fill her empty cart.

But April had other ideas for me. She made it plain that I was to sit back and simply watch. Soon my little daughter announced, "I going to the store now." There she was, pushing her cart along until she stopped, midtrack, hand on her forehead, exclaiming, "Oh, I forgot my keys!" She returned to me, and I handed her some imaginary keys. Off she went, only to stop again and exclaim, "Oh, I forgot my money!" I produced an imaginary wallet and handed it to her. Off she went for the third time, until she exclaimed, "Oh dear, I forgot my phone!" And then, "Oh, no, now where's my baby?" This time she didn't need me to solve the problem. Grasping "Baby"—her favorite doll—firmly by the leg, she jammed the doll into the front seat of the cart, planted a swift kiss on her forehead, and set off again, this time, I hoped, finally well enough prepared to get through her expedition to the store with no further mishaps.

I gazed at her with amazement. Without my ever having noticed it, something had been happening for April all along—in spite of the upheaval, in spite of the changes, in spite of my exhaustion. While I stumbled along trying to create order, she was busy taking me in. Her experience of our relationship, of me trying to hold it all together and somehow miraculously holding her together too, had been absolutely enough for her all along. Watching her play, I felt profoundly grateful that our relationship existed not just in the real space between us, but also little by little in the internal landscape that was flourishing within her.

Analysts Reflect on Symbolic Representation

Play can be thought of as the universal language of children. Children are not taught how to play; they do it naturally, intuitively, and early in their lives. Child therapists believe play helps children learn to integrate new information, to plan and delay immediate gratification, and to experience themselves and others as stable and whole. In addition, play helps children dramatize important aspects of their lives and teaches them to express and manage their feelings.

April's play illustrates how the use of imagination promotes and supports emotional development and growth. Her delight in seeing her belongings "magically" restored by the moving truck highlights the importance of play in resolving difficult or stressful issues. In the midst of family upheaval, April is able to perceive continuity and to hold on to what we call her "representational world": *The very last item out of the truck was her little plastic kitchen. Delight spread across her face, and she leaped out of her chair, exclaiming happily, 'My kitchen!' She instantly set to work brewing a pretend pot of tea and flipping stacks of invisible pancakes.* Symbolic play is rooted in the child's secure attachment and indicates that she has begun the process of psychological separation and individuation.

The process of establishing an internal world develops gradually. The infant's sense of the world is initially global and diffuse, organized primarily around pleasure and unpleasure and in getting what he needs. As development unfolds, the infant's inner world becomes increasingly symbolic, delineated, and richly detailed (Sandler and Rosenblatt 1962; Mayman 1967). The child's emotional tie to a responsive and empathic caregiver provides the bedrock of the child's nascent sense of self. For children such as April, the ability to create an imaginary world of symbolic representation demonstrates a significant psychological achievement. As children develop the capacity to internalize the important people in their lives, a gateway opens to a rich inner world. This world in turn provides a springboard from which to negotiate attachments and the developmental challenges to come.

Margaret Mahler (1972) first introduced ideas about symbolic representation forty years ago. Mahler understood that before play can occur, children must achieve what she called "object constancy"—the ability to hold important people in mind, even when they are not present. She saw the emergence of this capacity in babies' love of peek-a-boo and other games in which objects are repeatedly hidden or dropped and then retrieved. Through multiple repetitions, the baby's "out of sight, out of mind" mentality slowly gives way to the realization that objects and individuals continue to exist even when they are not visible. Thus, the infant gradually develops the capacity to *imagine*, or hold in mind, that the object or person he desires still exists somewhere beyond his immediate purview and can be retrieved.

Mahler and her colleagues went on to posit that the acquisition of object constancy gradually leads to the concept of "libidinal object constancy." According to this idea, the infant gradually comes to see his caregiver as stable and reliable whether that caregiver provides immediate gratification or not.

As babies learn about object constancy, play helps them gain mastery over loss, separation, and frustration. For example, one can observe the infant repeatedly engaging in the universal game of hide-and-go-seek, where the delight in finding and being found again and again reproduces the infant's early pleasure of being held and comforted when distressed. As Anni Bergman has written, "The reappearance after brief disappearance evokes the joy of re-finding, that is, rediscovering mother. Furthermore, the experience of 'making' mother retrieve the lost object enhances feelings of the self as agent . . . at a time . . . when babies are just on the brink of becoming capable of more independent activities, in particular locomotion" (1993, 362).

All these elements are readily visible in April's play: *"There she was, pushing her cart along until she stopped, midtrack, hand on her forehead, exclaiming, 'Oh, I forgot my keys!' She returned to me, and I handed her some imaginary keys. Off she went, only to stop again and exclaim, 'Oh, I forgot my money!' I produced an imaginary wallet and handed it to her. Off she went for the third time, until she exclaimed, 'Oh dear, I forgot my phone!'"*

The developmental achievement of object constancy unfolds alongside the process of separation and individuation during which the child consolidates a sense of self that is separate, stable, and unique. Mahler called the last stage of this process "rapprochement"; it is "the stage in which a unified representation of the object becomes intrapsychically available" (1972, 488). What she means is that the developing toddler begins to build up a somewhat realistic view of those who care for him and slowly learns to trust that if those persons disappear, they will soon return. Bergman elaborates: "With the achievement of a measure of object constancy (which we assume to be achieved as the rapprochement crisis is negotiated at the age of about two and a half to three years), the child begins to be able to take the perspective of the other—one of the hallmarks of the achievement of object constancy" (1993, 363). The individual's eventual ability to tolerate ambivalent feelings toward others relies on learning to "take the perspective of the other."

As symbolic representation emerges at around eighteen months, the child figures out that an object or gesture can represent an absent person or thing. In short, he learns to pretend. A little boy may look in the mirror and pretend to shave his imaginary beard, just like his father, or, watching his mother, he may pretend to put on makeup. Pretending gradually grows more elaborate, as when April pushes her grocery cart around the living room. In this set piece, her imagination is clearly at work. She uses her emerging language skills as well as her understanding of object constancy to represent symbolically a series of important ideas and thoughts. These dramatized moments are about her mother, and they employ her real-life mother as an actor.

Symbolic play can be thought of as developing along a trajectory that begins in earliest infancy and progresses throughout life. In its most rudimentary forms, playful explorations can be observed in very young infants. For example, infants roll on their backs, suck their toes, and wave their arms in front of them or toward their caregivers. According to Albert Solnit, although these early forms of activity are primarily in the service of exploration and discovery, what makes them "playful" is that infants can "seek out repeatedly what gives them pleasure and relief from unpleasure" (1998, 105). These activities can be viewed as precursors to symbolic play because of the pleasurable aspects of the infant's experience. Solnit suggests that play can be understood as "trial thought" (108) and thus as serving as a bridge for the infant between the internal and external realms of experience.

As development unfolds, the child's explorations at the edges of fantasy and reality lead to an ever-greater capacity to move between the two realms. Thus, the world of make-believe is increasingly available for the child to practice, gain mastery, work through conflict, and consolidate a sense of self and other. When all goes right in a young child's world, this process requires no parental intervention. As April's mother notes, "While I stumbled along trying to create order, she was busy taking me in. Her experience of our relationship, of me trying to hold it all together and somehow miraculously holding her together too, had been absolutely enough for her all along."

Children's play serves many different functions and can be understood in myriad ways. As Linda Mayes and Donald Cohen explain, "The child at play makes use of . . . varied mental processes. . . . [He] integrates his past experiences and his current feelings and desires. . . . [He] explores the inner and outer world, investigates hypotheses and possibilities, and moves ahead in personal development" (1993, 1240).

British child analyst D. W. Winnicott (1968) championed the importance of play throughout his career. For Winnicott, play is exciting and magical; it exists in the "transitional space" between mother and infant. Many contemporary writers have expanded this view of play, considering it a cocreation between mother and infant in which each one's role elaborates and expands the meaning and reach of the play. The infant who has a good enough, attuned mother gradually internalizes this relationship, an internalization that, Winnicott maintained, forms the later capacity to be alone. The capacity to be alone, as Winnicott ([1958] 1965a) described it, allows the child to discover a growing sense of self and of his impact on the world and is essential for play.

The toddler's capacity to play arises out of such early experiences of self and others. "Playing facilitates growth and therefore health," Winnicott wrote in 1968, and it leads to "group relationships. . . . [It is] a form of communication in psychotherapy" (593). In his view, the capacity to play creatively requires the presence in a child's life not of a "perfect" mother, but of a "good enough" one living in a "good enough" holding environment. The feeling of "going-on-being," or the sense of the continuity of one's self, relies on the existence of a holding environment provided by the good enough mother (Davis and Wallbridge 1987).

In Winnicott's terms, April's mother is a good enough mother. Had she been otherwise, April's story would have been different. Contemporary attachment theorists suggest that when a caregiver is severely depressed or erratic, the child can be expected to develop what is called a "disorganized attachment." Such a child is stranded, with no model helping him create an inner image of a caregiver (and a world) that is soothing and comforting. The play of a child with a disorganized attachment may appear to be random and lack identifiable patterns or meaning. These untethered children are sometimes unable to use play to work through their struggles and conflicts.

April's play, in contrast, is organized and flexible. She trusts her mother to enrich her play, adding to the fun, but she does not fear her mother's overinvolvement. Left to her own devices, April cheerfully creates a world that is both the same and different from everyday reality. In a psychological sense, she uses her play to re-create with her mother moments of disruption and with her mother's help to forge moments of psychological repair. In fantasy, she is able to represent her mother as a person who forgets belongings but does not misplace her child. With a kiss, this mother can undo instances

16

of forgetting. This happy ending is not an idle wish—it is an expression of April's dawning awareness that even amidst all the changes in her life, her loving mother will not fail to care for her. Thus, her play helps her work through her experience and transform her internal sense of self.

Symbolic play has therapeutic as well as developmental value for the young child. Winnicott conceived of adult psychoanalysis as an instance of "two people playing together" (1968, 591). For children, play is the equivalent of free association. Early child analysts used interpretation to point out defenses and unconscious wishes. However, contemporary psychoanalysts view the child analyst's task very differently. As Mayes and Cohen suggest, "In therapy, as in life, it is sometimes *not* necessary, or even useful, for the psychoanalyst to interpret (in words) the child's play for this facilitation to proceed. . . . The technical issue is when and how the analyst chooses to interpret the content of the play back to the child such that the child's playfulness is sustained even while he and the analyst step briefly outside the fantasy" (1993, 1241, emphasis in original).

Thus, as in the story "Play with Me," sometimes what is needed is only *"to sit back and simply watch."* In the quiet of the therapy room, change occurs under the patient and attentive gaze, interpretive stance, and affective attunement of the good enough therapist. Thus, the space is created for the child to play about conflicts, wishes, and fears and ultimately to deepen his understanding of his internal world and his relationships with others.

April's play touches on a number of developmentally relevant themes. Through her play, April tries to find a meaningful resolution to the changes she is experiencing in her family. The shared pleasure of mother and daughter make the play more meaningful for April. She tests her mother again and again; her fantasy mother is able each time to produce all the "everything" April requires. She wonders, through her play, whether a mother can really "forget" a baby—especially with a new baby on the way—and reassures herself that no baby is left behind, that kisses are always to be had. This abundance of warmth and affection enables her to launch herself. "*Grasping 'Baby'—her favorite doll—firmly by the leg, she jammed the doll into the front seat of the cart, planted a swift kiss on her forehead, and set off again, this time, I hoped, finally well enough prepared to get through her expedition to the store with no further mishaps.*"

3 THE CALLING

A six-year-old parochial school girl worries about sex, God, and the nuns who are her teachers.

As a first grader at St. Matthew's, I loved grilled cheese sandwiches, Campbell's tomato soup, Barbie dolls, and Twister. I spent afternoons building forts and playing doctor. At night, I lay in bed worrying about whether I was going to go to heaven.

Like many little girls in Catholic school during the 1960s, I thought a lot about nuns. To me, they were mysterious, looming figures, wrapped from head to toe in black fabric no matter the weather—women in wimples who wore the most sensible, ugly shoes any girl could imagine. I wondered, what are those outfits hiding? Do they actually even have hair under those wimples? What do they wear when they go to bed at night?

However, my most consuming question was, "How do you turn into a nun?" I feared the answer. I could imagine being a teacher, a mother, a ballerina, or a singer, but never a nun. I thought nothing could be worse than a life as Sister Anthony, Sister David, or any of the other sisters of the Holy Cross. The nuns' austere existence stood in stark relief to the life as a princess I felt certain was my destiny. And why, oh why did they all have boys' names?

The scariest sister of them all was my first-grade teacher, Sister Michael. What stood out most about her was the huge mole on the right side of her upper lip with its three long coarse black hairs sprouting from the center. As hard as I tried, I could not take my eyes off that mole. When Sister Michael turned her fierce gaze in my direction, I was terrified. When she raised her ruler threateningly, my vision narrowed, and all I could see were those three ugly, angrily twitching hairs.

My friends and I would gather on the playground at recess to exchange fantastic stories about the secret life of nuns. We whispered about the atrocities we imagined occurring in their convent. We pictured the sisters being disciplined by a furious Mother Superior wielding an extralarge ruler, doing to our teachers what our teachers did to us. In awe, we listened to an older girl who bragged that she actually had snuck into the brick convent and lived to tell the tale. We would describe, in ever gorier detail, how a child—who I now realize must have moved away—was trapped in the convent and never seen or heard from again.

It was my best friend, Mary Jane King, who dared to ask "The Question." As you can imagine, "Mary" was a very popular name among girls in my class. Parents seemed to feel that naming their daughter after the Virgin Mother would bring them closer to God and perhaps secure them a spot in heaven. By this reasoning, Mrs. King was the godliest woman in our neighborhood. She had twelve children—eight daughters named Mary. Of course, Mrs. King added a different middle name so that all eight wouldn't come running when she called "Mary!" I secretly felt uncomfortable around Mrs. King. My older sister had already told me all about sex, so I figured out that Mrs. King must have had sex twelve times. A huge number. My own parents were embarrassing enough given the undeniable evidence that they had had sex five times. This was apparently an inadequate number because I once heard my aunt Colleen, who had nine children, tease my mother by calling her frigid—a reference I didn't understand for years.

It was in religion class one day that Mary Jane, in her navy blue plaid uniform and new penny loafers, brazenly asked, "Sister Michael, how did you get to be a nun?" I could hear the ticking of the clock on the wall as we waited for the answer. I looked down and ran my pencil along the groove in the desk. In front of me, Mary Margaret giggled. I glanced at Sister Michael, whose nose flared. We all waited to see what torture would be inflicted on Mary Jane for being fresh. We were surprised when Sister Michael drew herself up and replied that it was a "calling from God" to become "a bride of Christ." Bride! I nearly fell out of my chair. "Bride of Christ!" So that's why they wore wedding bands. I tried to wrap my mind around this strange idea. What could becoming a "bride of Christ" mean?

That afternoon I left school feeling absolutely certain that I did not want to receive such a "call." In bed that night, under my pink ruffled bedding, I could not stop obsessing about what would happen if God "called" me.

During recess the next day, after my Hostess cupcake and milk, I summoned up the courage to ask Sister Michael, "What happens if you get the call and you don't want to be a nun?" Eyebrows raised, mole twitching, she replied, "It's a calling from God, and you must accept and be honored that God selected you." Now I really panicked.

As I walked home down Shaler Boulevard, cutting across Mr. Newman's backyard, all I could think about was how to make sure God did not call me or, if He did, how not to be the one to answer the phone. This made my walk home from school more treacherous than usual. In addition to avoiding the cracks so I wouldn't break my mother's back, I nervously searched the skies for bolts of lightning—another sure sign that God was calling.

As I sat tucked into the old green-twilled couch reading *Ramona the Pest*, I was on constant alert. When the phone rang, I darted out of the room. Whenever my mother or one of my sisters answered the phone, my ears perked up. Was it God on the other end? If my mother answered, would she have to become a "bride of Christ"? My mom was already married to my dad—If God called, would she still have to go? What if my sister Abbey answered the phone? Would she have to leave home and become a nun? Abbey didn't strike me as nun material, but it would be nice to have my own room.

With each ring of the phone, my palms began to sweat. On the third day of my religious trial, I used the phone to make plans to play with my friend, Kimmy. When we finished our conversation and I placed the receiver back on the cradle, the phone immediately rang. I jumped back as if I'd gotten an electric shock. Removing my hand from the receiver, I slowly inched away.

My mother, in her usual outfit of stretch pants with stirrups, button-up blouse, and a baby on her hip, asked, "Honey, would you get that?" Frozen, I shook my head no. She repeated, "Pick up the phone." I squeaked, "I can't!" My mother looked puzzled and slightly annoyed. "What do you mean you can't pick up the phone?" "I can't. . . . I-just-can't-I-don't-want-to-get The Call!"

My mother handed me the baby as she picked up the receiver. I slipped out of the room. As soon as she hung up, she called me back into the kitchen. "Why have you been so jumpy lately?" she asked. "Why wouldn't you answer the phone?" I summoned up all of my courage and turned to face her. All the pent-up fear and anxiety of the past few days flooded out of me. "Sister Michael says God calls you to be a nun, and when he calls, you have to take the call and be a nun, be his bride. I don't want to be a nun, I don't want the call, I don't want to marry God, I don't want to wear that outfit, I don't want those shoes, and I don't want to go live with those nuns! I just won't!" My mother, clearly trying hard not to laugh, said, "Slow down, honey. Hold on there. . . . " She sat me down and gently explained that a "calling" just means a strong wish to do something, that it definitely would not come over the phone, and, most important, the call came only to girls who wanted to be nuns.

What a relief! But don't think my religious worries were over. I would soon be making my first confession, and that brought up a hornet's nest of fears about priests in black boxes demanding that I tell all my secrets.

Analysts Reflect on Magical Thinking

Magical thinking is a normal stage of development in young children. Adults sometimes return to this stage, whether under circumstances of stress or alternately during moments of creativity or playfulness. Magical thinking enables children to retreat to the realm of imagination and provides them with protection from the psychic assault of an often overwhelming reality. Betty Smith beautifully expresses the central importance of the child's capacity for magical thinking in her novel *A Tree Grows In Brooklyn*: "The child must have a valuable thing which is called imagination . . . a secret world in which live things that never were. It is necessary that she believe. She must start out by believing in things not of this world. Then when the world becomes too ugly for living in, the child can reach back and live in her imagination" ([1943] 1989, 84).

In "The Calling," the young girl wrestles with the hitherto unknown concept of a religious calling to become a nun. When the much feared nun at her school informs her that religious life is a "calling from God," she interprets this statement both literally and with the unquestioning egocentricity of a young child. She associates the ringing of the telephone with the dreaded "call from God" that will compel her to enter a vocation both tantalizing in its power and mystery and frightening. Her dilemma is resolved when her mother helps her attain a more abstract cognitive understanding of the concept of a "calling."

Young children view the world through the lens of their wishes and fears. Their cognitive development prevents them from understanding abstractions. Nor can they see events from any point of view other than their own.

Peter Fonagy and Mary Target, contemporary psychoanalytic thinkers concerned with the inner world of children, offer us an interesting way to understand magical thinking. They describe a small child's inability to see the world from any perspective other than his own as "psychic equivalency," the expectation that his internal world corresponds without question to external reality. In this "psychic equivalence mode," the child "behaves as though his inner experience is equivalent to and thus mirrors external reality, and that by extension others will have the same experiences as he does" (1996, 219). The concept of the "psychic equivalence mode" illuminates the process of magical thinking, "where feelings and fantasies are experienced as reality and not as mental states representing reality" (Fonagy et al. [2002] 2005, 199).

Until children move from magical thinking into abstract thinking (a much later developmental achievement), they are unable to comprehend another's perspective. Fonagy and Target define mentalization as the "developmental acquisition that permits children to respond not only to another person's behavior, but to the child's conception of others' attitudes, intentions, or plans. Mentalization enables children to 'read' other people's minds. By attributing mental states to others, children make people's behavior meaningful and predictable" (1998, 92). For example, a young child who sees her father in distress may try to comfort him by bringing him her own favorite stuffed toy because this object is what she would find comforting. Everything in a young child's world revolves around her, and her understanding stops and starts with what she can literally see and touch.

In the mind of the six-year-old in our story, the dreaded phone call becomes a concrete representation of God's absolute power: *"That afternoon I left school feeling absolutely certain that I did not want to receive such a 'call.' In bed that night, under my pink ruffled bedding, I could not stop obsessing about what would happen if God 'called' me."*

In magical thinking, children attempt to establish a cause-and-effect link between their thoughts and what actually happens in the world. Such a link enables them to feel powerful and to make sense of what they experience. In magical thinking, events or words that resemble one another or that occur simultaneously are assumed to share a common meaning. When the child in the story is informed that becoming a nun is preceded by God's calling, her concrete understanding of such a call results in the intense fear that God will "call" her on the telephone and compel her obedience.

Magical thinking serves different developmental functions at different stages of childhood. In infancy, the most primitive form of experience can be described as a magical feeling; for example, warm milk and a feeling of fullness follow the baby's experience of hunger. The change happens as if by magic. A cold wet diaper is likewise magically replaced by a warm and dry one. Babies live in a world in which needs are mysteriously fulfilled. They do not fully comprehend the association between their sensory experience and the presence of others. This early state, which revolves around the magical belief that experiencing needs creates their very fulfillment, is referred to as "primary narcissism." The critical early process of experiencing either a safe, predictable world or, in contrast, an unsafe or unpredictable one forms the basis of the attachment pattern that we carry into all subsequent relationships (Bowlby 1969; Main, Kaplan, and Cassidy 1985).

When things go right for babies, their early experiences of feeding become intertwined with the warm feeling of being securely held, smiled at, and spoken to gently. Carefully attuned responses by caregivers result in infants' understanding that their upset state can and will be soothed. Over time and with repeated experiences, the securely attached baby comes to associate the presence of caring adults with the relief of distress and an emergent sense of security.

Toddlers have only one perspective—their own. Their limited view of the world, in fact, protects them from realizing how dependent they are on others and thus how small and vulnerable they are. Try and imagine, for example, how difficult it would be for toddlers to navigate a playground if they possessed an adult's perspective on all the dangers contained in that space. The young child's limited awareness and blithe confidence facilitate his active engagement in exploring the world.

By the age of three, most children can tell the difference between fantasy and reality, but they still operate at the level of magical thinking. As a result, preschoolers are convinced that their thoughts are powerful enough to create the events that happen in their world. Such an understanding encapsulates the powerful mix of wishes and fears that characterizes early childhood.

When children endow their wishes and fears with a belief in their own omnipotence, they sometimes become afraid of the magical power of their own destructive or aggressive thoughts. This fear stems from the fact that small children experience their thoughts and feelings as real events that exist in the world. Fonagy and his colleagues write, "In this way . . . [the] 'psychic equivalence mode'—like with magical thinking—makes the child's own emotions, impulses, and fantasies seem real and hence dangerous" ([2002] 2005, 199). For example, when a child thinks, "I wish you were dead," and then a parent goes away, the child concludes, "I must have killed you."

In his writing, Bruno Bettelheim (1977) shows how children's fantasies, wishes, and fears provide the fuel for their imaginary play. Bettleheim understands that fantasy play allows a child to calm herself by mastering scary feelings. When a little girl calls upon a caring adult—a fairy godmother or a good witch, for example—to rescue her, she is using magical thinking to restore a sense of safety to her world. Children's role playing also helps them begin to develop the capacity to see things from another's perspective, which will help them become empathetic and compassionate individuals eventually.

As development progresses, the child's tendency to view the world exclusively through a lens of magical thinking begins to give way to an understanding and acceptance of reality. Growing up requires that the child relinquish the fantasy of omnipotence and egocentrism while still maintaining the internal flexibility that allows him access to imagination and play. Movement between the contours of reality, on the one hand, and creativity and delight in fantasy, on the other, is a life-long process that at best remains fluid. In contrast, as people solidify their position at either end of the spectrum between the "pleasure principle" (i.e., magical thinking and wish fulfillment) and the "reality principle" (a way of looking at the world that can be cold and hard), the necessary balance among flexibility, creativity, and rationality can be lost.

In "The Calling," we observe the emergence of magical thinking as a response to anxiety, but the same phenomenon in a more limited form is present in the day-to-day lives of many, perhaps most, adults. A professional athlete, for example, may have an elaborate ritual built around the belief that if he doesn't wash his socks, a winning streak will magically continue. Research similarly shows that many of us get well when given placebos that are nothing more than sugar pills. When playing the lottery, we rely on the magical powers of combinations of meaningful numbers—our children's birthdays, for example—even though we know that the numbers we hope to match are randomly generated. We all are magical thinkers in our sleep, where a primary process frees us from our more logical waking minds.

Another form of magical thinking occurs when people believe that their words can directly shape events. This belief can result in avoiding speaking about certain subjects ("speak of the devil, and he will appear"); using euphemisms instead of more anxiety-provoking words, such as "he passed away" instead of "he died"; or believing that to know the "true name" of something gives one power over it (Zusne and Jones 1989). For instance, in the children's fairy tale "Rumpelstiltskin," the dwarf holds absolute power until the princess divines his secret name, thus releasing her from his debt. The residue of this type of childhood magical thinking can be found when family members speak in hushed tones of a relative's getting "the Big C," as if saying the word *cancer* out loud will somehow bring bad luck.

A similar reliance on magical thinking can be found in various cultural norms, symbols, and rituals. According to Freud, people of animistic cultures all over the world and from earliest times see objects of the external world as inhabited by spirits, demons, and souls that are "constructed on the analogy of human souls" ([1913] 1955l, 76). Freud argued that the very idea of a soul or spirit refers to the perception of one's own mental life. He furthermore asserted that magic, like animism, is a fundamentally psychological phenomenon. According to his definition, "Magic reveals in the clearest and most unmistakable way an intention to impose the laws governing mental life upon real things" and "replace the laws of nature by psychological ones." Freud continued, "It is easy to perceive the motives which lead men to practice magic: they are human wishes. . . . The basic reason why what [a person] sets about by magical means comes to pass is, after all, simply that he wills it. To begin with, therefore, the emphasis is only upon his wish" ([1913] 1955l, 91, 83).

In a close parallel to the young child's important use of magical thinking, there is scientific evidence to suggest that some access to magical thinking is healthy in later development. People with high levels of dopamine (a neurotransmitter in the brain that is linked to many important moods and motivations and that tags experiences as meaningful) are more likely to find significance in coincidences and to pick out idiosyncratic meanings and patterns—evidence of what we classically term "magical thinking" (Philips 2002). To support her belief in the importance of magical thinking in adulthood, Helen Philips refers to Peter Brugger's data showing a strong correlation between a lack of magical ideation and anhedonia, the inability to experience pleasure. She describes Brugger's finding that dopamine floods the brains of people with schizophrenia, who see significance in everything, but merely trickles in depressives, who struggle to find meaning in life. She points out Brugger's argument that the ability to see patterns and make loose associations enhances creativity and serves an adaptive function: "If you're on the grassland, it's always better to assume that a tiger is there" (2002, 20). Thus, well into a person's adulthood, the belief that thoughts can somehow control events can be beneficial. Here, this magical belief becomes the antidote to the feeling of helplessness that so often accompanies depression.

Magical thinking occurs when people find themselves in a dangerous or undesirable situation with no effective way of coping and no power to act. In many circumstances, it can be adaptive and provide comfort and a sense of mastery. Although the young girl in "The Calling" is clearly in the sway of powerful and threatening magical thoughts, she is able to use her mother to help her reestablish a clear sense of reality. Her adult self writes later, *She sat me down and gently explained that a 'calling' just means a strong wish to do something, that it definitely would not come over the phone, and, most important, that the call came to girls who wanted to be nuns.* Thus, the girl initially uses her imagination to try to make sense of her world. Then, being summoned back to reality by her mother's gentle clarification, she can restore her sense of the predictability of her world. Developing this flexible capacity during childhood will set the stage for her successful adaptation to the psychological demands of subsequent developmental tasks.

4 NEW FURNITURE

A girl's conscience is forged in a family drama.

I was eight years old when my parents decided to buy a new couch. My family didn't buy furniture very often. My parents owned a small business and worked long, hard hours. We lived in a modest apartment near their store and owned a house in what we called "the country," an hour out of town. The house was furnished with cast-offs, but it was cozy, and it fulfilled my immigrant father's dream of having a garden with a majestic view of mountains in the distance.

The couch in our house was old and ugly, but I loved its welcoming softness and its musky smell. Still, the day came when my parents decided to buy a new sofa for the apartment. My mother said that the couch in the city would be moved to "the country."

Shopping for a new couch was excruciatingly boring. I had envisioned everything from the grandeur of plush velvet to the funkiness of a folding futon. Despite my eager opinions, however, no one ever asked me what kind of sofa I thought we should get. After dragging my sister and me all over the city, my parents bought a new couch that looked remarkably like the old one. More formal than the cozy one we had, it was far less comfortable to me. We sadly discovered that the sofa's cushions, upholstered in the light blue plush velvet that my mother chose, did not fit properly. They stuck out ridiculously from the arms of the couch. I remember my mother gazing at the couch with a furrow across her brow, deciding to let well enough alone rather than insisting that the cushions be redone. "Who knows?" she sighed. "If they fix them, it might look worse." Her resignation infuriated me and laid the groundwork for my future adolescent rebellion.

After the imperfect new sofa was installed in our apartment, my father leased a small truck to bring the old one to the country. The truck was rusted and had no seatbelts. There was a connecting door between the cab and the back of the truck. My sister and I thought it was the most fascinating vehicle we had ever seen. There was something about the act of moving a piece of furniture for the sake of home improvement—the vague promise that things were on the upswing—that excited us. Back and forth we climbed between the cab and the truck, cramming ourselves through the access door as though we were squeezing ourselves through a portal to a better world.

Our hilarity agitated and displeased my father. He sternly informed us that the only way to enter the back of the truck was to unlock it from the inside. It was essential that we not lock the padlock. This device was to hang loosely from the latch at all times. In our mad scrambling between front and back, it had not occurred to me to fasten the lock, but my father's interdiction had the fatal effect of drawing my attention to what was forbidden.

It's not that I didn't fear my father's wrath. On the contrary, I had reason to be vigilant. My father's demeanor—warm, twinkling eyes, playful sense of humor, pleasure in the moment—did not prevent him from titanic fits of rage. I knew how a single act of defiance could wreck an entire weekend, but I just couldn't help myself. I was Eve, and the lock was the apple, summoning me to discover how it worked. Was it really possible to seal off the portal? An aching curiosity filled me, obliterating the part of my thinking that was rule bound and should have warned me away from the danger of disregarding my father's prohibition.

It happened within moments of pulling into the driveway of our house. I touched the lock. It felt cool and malleable in my hands. It twisted and turned. I liked the heft, the movement, the sense of suspended mobility. Tantalized, I watched the gleaming metal dance in my hands. Then my fingers fumbled. With a *click*, the lock clasped itself shut with a dreadful finality. My heart thumped, and the wind whooshed between my ears. I grew hot.

When my father saw what I had done, he pursed his lips with disgust and climbed out of the truck. Watching his retreating back, I felt panicked as I shouted desperately, "I can fix it!" The look of reproach on his face melted me as he said, "It's LOCKED, and I don't have a KEY. You can't undo it. I can't take out the couch, so we won't have the couch." The door to the truck slammed, and my father walked off. My sister said, "Told you so . . . ," and then trailed off as she stepped down from the truck. My mother turned her face to me, and I saw what she was thinking: "What is wrong with you? How could you do this to us, to me?" I didn't know what was wrong with me. I was drowning in shame and guilt.

The horror I experienced transcended the locked door and the inaccessible couch. I wanted to be told what would happen next, what they would do. The dread lay in the knowledge that I had transgressed. I had broken the rules. No one would talk to me. My father ignored me. My mother turned her back and went into the house. My sister disappeared.

I had to undo the damage. Alone in the truck, I yanked at the lock. It was bolted, firmly and cruelly. I turned it over in my hands, squinting through the tears that were starting to blur my vision. I peered through the keyhole. An idea presented itself to me. I climbed out of the truck and found a small twig. It felt light in my hand. I began to push the tip of the stick into the keyhole. Too thick. I found another more slender twig and tried again.

A small miracle occurred. The lock's pins realigned themselves, and the padlock sprang open with a tiny hiss. My heart thumped. Joy and relief coursed through my veins, but the sense of redemption that I sought was not to be. When I showed my father what I had accomplished, his grave and stern expression revealed a truth that has lived inside me ever since: undoing the effects of one's crime does not remove the black mark imprinted on the conscience.

Analysts Reflect on Superego Development

In the story "New Furniture," the events that unfold in the truck can be considered in light of the development of the young child's conscience and emergent sense of right and wrong. As psychoanalytically trained psychotherapists, we draw on many different theories of the mind and of behavior to help us understand our patients. Some of these ideas originated with Freud, whose descriptions of the mind and insights into human behavior continue to possess great relevance. Since Freud's day, however, psychodynamic thinking has evolved. Numerous new schools of thought have emerged that have revolutionized how our field approaches issues related to development, gender, and sexual identity. Nonetheless, as clinicians working today, we are the grateful heirs of the Freudian tradition and all that has come afterward.

Although few today would call themselves classical Freudians, many practitioners—we include ourselves in this category—continue to view aspects of psychological life through a Freudian perspective. Freud was a remarkably broad and creative thinker who to a very large extent shaped the way European and American theorists and scholars think about relationships within nuclear families. Freud did not say everything that there is to be said about family relationships, but he described in great detail some significant dynamics still relevant today. Any parent who has ever heard her three-year-old daughter flirtatiously declare, "When I grow up, I am going to marry Daddy," intuitively grasps the truth of Freud's insight that children are innately sexual beings.

In the discussion here, we interpret a dramatic family incident involving a young girl's defiance and remorse from a Freudian perspective. This discussion sheds light on the development of her conscience and her sense of right and wrong.

Freud referred to a person's internalized sense of morality—his or her conscience— as the "superego." He described the superego as one of three components that constitute the self. The character Jiminy Cricket in the popular children's movie *Pinocchio* accurately depicts the child's struggle with the admonitions, strictures, and judgments emanating from "the voice over one's shoulder." Freud distinguished the superego from the two other structures of the mind—the ego and the id. The ego represents the thinking mind, with both conscious and unconscious elements. The id is like the mythological Pan—it is the part of each of us that demands to have what we want when we want it. The id is filled with passionate wishes and urges that press for immediate satisfaction.

In Freud's view, the work of the ego is to bridge the gap between everything we think and feel inside ourselves and all of the demands and contingencies of reality—that is, the external world. The ego's second job is to resolve conflicts between the superego and the id— our conscience and our desires. In order to maintain a core sense of balance and self-cohesion, the ego attempts to rein in or delay gratification of the id's wishes and impulses. For example, a married person might flirt at a party with a member of the opposite sex, but when his or her ego successfully balances desire (the id) with the demands of the conscience (the superego), then the flirtation will not ignite into an act of infidelity. This ability to delay gratification, to withstand unruly and dangerous impulses, and to adhere to more acceptable modes of behavior emerges slowly throughout childhood and adolescence as the superego develops.

Freud thought that the superego developed within the cauldron of sexual rivalry played out in the family. He believed that on some level all small children desire to drive their same-sex parent out of the family constellation in order to possess the parent of the opposite sex. He called this desire the "Oedipus complex"—after Oedipus, the figure in Greek mythology who unknowingly killed his father and married his mother. Freud believed that children must resolve their Oedipal desires in order to form satisfying, healthy relationships with members of the opposite sex later in life.

In the Freudian view, Oedipal wishes conflict with other powerful feelings—most notably the child's love for his same-sex parent. For example, in an intact heterosexual family, according to Freud, a boy desires to overpower and destroy his primary rival, his father, in order to keep his mother for himself. This impulse, however, exists side by side with the boy's strong love for his father. Freud thought the boy resolves this conflict by becoming like his same-sex parent, ultimately identifying with the feared yet loved rival. The boy's naysaying superego is forged in his largely unconscious effort to resolve his conflicting feelings of love and hate for his father. But there is a price to pay because the development of the superego introduces feelings of guilt associated with unconscious libidinal (sexual) and aggressive wishes.

In contrast, Freud's early theory of female development unfolded along a significantly different pathway. The young girl faces a dilemma: to gain her father's love, she must relinquish her mother as her primary love object. However, the young girl also inevitably aligns herself with her mother through a powerful identification. According to this early view, the girl blames her mother for not giving her a penis and turns instead to her father, transforming her penis envy into the wish for a baby.

This archaic conceptualization of the formation of the girl's superego suggests that the girl never fully resolves the Oedipal complex and thus never develops as strong a superego as her male counterpart. However, this view of female development has been refuted in more contemporary psychoanalytic theory (Mayer 1985, 1995; Richards 1996; Dahl 2002). We now consider that female development unfolds along a different, equally mature trajectory, which is consolidated around the value, pleasure, and pride in her own gender and body. For boys and girls, these two developmental pathways lead to the same endpoint: the superego.

In the story of the young girl and the tempting padlock, we see the imprint of the Oedipal family drama. To the girl, the "new furniture" reminds her of her exclusion from her parents' marriage; her mother and father together decide to buy a new couch, but from the young girl's point of view this exciting event carries with it the sting of exclusion: *"Despite my eager opinions, however, no one ever asked me what kind of sofa I thought we should get."* She wants to be counted as an equal partner, but her parents' indifference to her opinion serves as an uncomfortable reminder that the adults have the ultimate authority.

These psychological conditions set the stage for the further development of the girl's superego. The story's primary conflict can be expressed like this: In a highly charged moment, a girl cannot resist the impulse to do what her father has told her not to do. The girl's rebellion occurs on an unconscious level, so that what happens when she plays with the lock seems to her as if it happens of its own accord: *"It twisted and turned. I liked the heft, the movement, the sense of suspended mobility. Tantalized, I watched the gleaming metal dance in my hands."* When she realizes the consequences of her actions, she is flooded with feelings of intense guilt, shame, and self-recrimination. The girl's strong reaction has to do with her relationship to her father, a volatile but beloved parent whose anger is feared and whose approval is persistently sought. The girl is consciously excited by playing with the lock but unconsciously activated by the family drama—her anger at being excluded from the decision-making process, her eager anticipation that life for the family is getting better, her hunger to please her father, the tremendous unacknowledged thrill of defying him, and her repugnance at her mother's resignation.

With so much at stake, her superego's admonition to maintain self-control is easily overpowered, and her Eve-like curiosity overrides her good sense. As therapists, we look at this girl's intense curiosity as a libidinal surge—an unconscious surge of sexual energy—that rises up and demands instant gratification. The id, in this case, overpowers the young girl's superego, so she plays with the lock, with an inevitable yet disastrous result.

In Freudian terms, the severity and harshness of a young child's internal punisher—conscience—develops over time as she or he struggles to break free of the allure of the id and to regulate her actions and impulses. As this happens, school-age children tend to express very rigid, unforgiving ideas of what is right and wrong. As they are learning to say no to themselves, they pour their aggression into their superegos, which causes them to be very severe in their judgment of others. They see the world in terms of external rules and regulations that must be obeyed; in their limited understanding and experience, there is little room in their understanding for nuance.

Growing children attach a great deal of importance to the rules that provide scaffolding to help control their behavior. They face increased demands that they learn to tolerate frustration without undue rage or aggression (i.e., temper tantrums). At home and at school, they are expected to replace action and impulse with language and thought and are increasingly expected to conform to social demands. Just picture, for example, a typical early school environment where children must learn to share, take turns, use self-restraint, and be kind. These capacities unfold in a developmental matrix that weaves together a mix of powerful and competing phenomena, including children's desire for approval, their increased capacity for self-regulation, their nascent sense of right and wrong, their desire for mastery of themselves and others, and their emerging conscience and capacity for shame and guilt.

The pressures on children as they seek to resolve their Oedipal struggles are considerable. Trying to mediate between their hunger to do what is forbidden and their equally powerful wish for parental approval, the superego can become overly rigid. In "New Furniture," the lock itself can be understood as a metaphor for the superego's insistence on the highest standards of behavior. The girl feels drawn to the lock, as all children are drawn to pushing the limit of what is acceptable and to doing what is alluringly forbidden. In spite of her age-appropriate capacity for self-control, she cannot resist temptation. The lock also symbolizes the rigidity with which the superego supervises and criticizes the ego. Such rigidity can give rise to powerful feelings of shame: *"When I showed my father what I had accomplished, his grave and stern expression revealed a truth that has lived inside me ever since."*

The harshness of the superego notwithstanding, children also need the freedom to discover the consequences of defying authority. Their capacity for independent exploration and for the development of autonomy rests on experimentation and testing. Judgment, reasoning, and an internal moral and ethical compass grow out of this kind of experimentation, but so does shame. Although painful, shame can serve many important functions for a child growing up in a good enough family environment. For example, in a moment of ordinary frustration, a mother scolds her two-year-old son, saying, "Don't be a bad boy." He turns to her sweetly and replies, "I not a bad boy. I just a boy who does bad things." In this moment, his reply highlights a significant developmental achievement wherein the shame he may have felt in light of being reprimanded was transformed into a dawning awareness of the impact of his actions on himself and others.

Contemporary theorists believe that girls and boys develop a conscience in somewhat different ways. For both sexes, however, the superego includes two parts—the ego ideal and the punitive voice of the conscience. The ego ideal represents the individual's loftiest goals and ambitions. These goals serve to guide people in their pursuit of higher aspirations. David Milrod (2002) writes that the ego ideal follows a developmental trajectory beginning with the child's dawning awareness of separateness and vulnerability, which leads to an early form of identification known as "imitation." This behavior can be readily observed, as Milrod notes, in the young child, who in imaginary play imitates the parents' dress, behavior, and voice. When imitating can no longer satisfy, children proceed to a stage Milrod calls "identification," during which they aspire to a "wished for self-image" (135).

The latter phase is the precursor to the ego ideal. The ego ideal is counterbalanced by the punitive, inhibitory voice, which we often refer to as the "conscience." Its earliest form originates in what Anna Freud ([1936] 1954) called "identification with the aggressor." We all have seen this process in motion: a child, scolded by a parent, turns and scolds her beloved teddy bear. As Anna Freud noted, over the course of development this harsh sense of right and wrong is softened and becomes a more flexible and less rigid conscience.

The basis of the superego's force in guiding behavior ultimately resides in the child's experiences of parental expectations, social pressures, and societal norms. The child's gradual internalization of these values is based largely, on the one hand, on his love for the parents and wish for their approval and, on the other, his fear of punishment, blame, or rejection. The internalization of parental rules and behavioral guidelines becomes the bedrock of the child's conscience and lays down the groundwork for the development and maturation of his inner moral compass, capacity for self-control, and delay of gratification as well as for the reining in of destructive or dangerous impulses.

What cannot be overemphasized is the drama of the child's inner struggle as she seeks to control her impulses and behave in a way that is in accordance first with the demands of her parents and later with her own idea of right and wrong. We see this drama unfold in the story of the girl and the lock. Her defiance of her father and her struggle to repair the damage she has done mark her—as such things mark all children—in a profound and lasting way. *"Undoing the effects of one's crime does not remove the black mark imprinted on the conscience."*

5 WOODBRIDGE

A young woman's dreams reveal her true feelings about her fiancé's former girlfriend.

It's a beautiful summer day. My fiancé, John, and I are driving through his hometown, a suburb of Manhattan. I periodically glance over at John, happily admiring his smile and deep blue eyes. I have just completed graduate school, and I am getting married. John suddenly stops the car and exclaims, "Hey, we're near Michelle's house. Why don't we see if she's home?" I pause. What can be wrong with meeting his first love? I'd heard so much about her, and, after all, it's been ten years since they broke up. I tell myself to be open-minded. This is the '80s. Other women are neither our enemies nor our competitors. I have nothing to be jealous about. I jauntily reply, "It'll be great to meet her."

We arrive at a house on a large wooded lot with views arising on all sides. At the end of the drive, I notice a kidney-shaped pool and a woman lounging nearby. John yells out a greeting, and she rises to meet us. I am face to face with a small, beautiful woman who has long blond hair and is wearing a string bikini. Michelle had been a dancer with a major ballet company before injuring one of her legs, and her body retains a glowing toned perfection.

Michelle's face lights up as she warmly kisses John hello. We walk down the hill to the house, with me lagging a few steps behind. Michelle is delighted that we stopped by. It doesn't take long before the two of them are happily reminiscing, absorbed in their memories. Despite their awkward but well-meaning attempts to include me, I begin to feel invisible. Michelle invites us in for lemonade. Although I wish we had never come, I say again, a little faintly, "Sounds great."

My fiancé particularly loves music and has a passion for fine woodworking. In his twenties, he became a luthier and built a series of acoustic guitars. These qualities are in the front of my mind as I look around a living room filled with many beautiful art objects. I enviously note that Michelle has given it just the right blend of grace and understated elegance. John and Michelle continue talking intently. There's a grand piano in the living room. John asks Michelle if she still plays. She announces that since her divorce she has been composing a piano concerto. After some brief encouragement, she sits down—string bikini and all—and plays a breathtaking piece of music. Her fingers effortlessly dance over the keys. The music is romantic, rapturous even. She smiles and asks if I play. "Oh, just the kazoo when I was a kid," I say breezily, feeling slightly sick.

In the kitchen, while she pours our lemonade, John comments on the cabinets made of rough-hewn wood with a gray, weathered facade. Michelle talks about a vacation in North Carolina, where she found an old wooden bridge about to be demolished. She bought the wood, shipped it home, and built the cabinets herself. "Isn't that remarkable," I say.

I tell myself this can't really be happening. John's former girlfriend. In a string bikini. Playing her own concerto. Building exquisite cabinets from an old bridge. I can't wait to get out of here. By the time we finally leave, my earlier, lighthearted mood has been dispelled, and I am quiet and subdued.

That night I sleep fitfully. Waking, I recall two vivid dreams. The first took place in what appeared to be an Old West saloon. I walk in and find a woman with long blond hair who looks like Michelle, only she has a wooden leg. A fight breaks out over a game of pool. It isn't clear whether I or someone else draws a gun and shoots her.

In the next dream, John tells me he is eager to move to a town called Woodbridge. I am upset that he wants to move there. I tell him I hate that town! I become increasingly irate as he insists that Woodbridge is a great place to live. I am not convinced.

Although neither I nor John ever saw Michelle again, the images of the dreams drifted back to me many times in the weeks leading up to our wedding. Now, many years later, the memory still retains a particular vivid quality. Despite how hard I might try to forget, the sound of her concerto still echoes in my mind.

Analysts Reflect on Dream Theory

Dreams have long intrigued artists, philosophers, scientists, neuro-scientists, and psychotherapists with their fascinating link between the mind and the body. For Freud, dreams were the "royal road to . . . the unconscious" ([1900] 1953d, 608). This view fit well with Freud's early ideas about the mind and about psychoanalysis, which he saw as a process of excavating unconscious wishes and fantasies. As psychotherapists today, we, too, believe that dreams illuminate our patients' conflicts and unconscious wishes. We see dreams as one way to gain access to our patients' inner world. Although the material of dreams is not always the most direct route, it offers an important and rich view of the internal landscape of the mind. Yet Freud later warned that exclusive concentration on a patient's dreams might lead to a neglect of other important events in the patient's life ([1911] 1955d, 93).

Freud was trained as a neurologist, and it was in this role that he first became interested in dreams. He viewed the content of dreams as a form of communication related to what he called "wish fulfillment." Buried within each dream lay a wish. "Dream work" is the phrase Freud used to describe the way the mind creates dreams. To explain how this work is done, he used such terms as *condensation, displacement,* and *secondary revision,* which we discuss later in this chapter.

The "Woodbridge" dreams illustrate how psychoanalytically oriented psychotherapists understand how dreams work in the unconscious. We think of dreams as incorporating images from the "day residue," which are memory traces left by actual events of the day that are reworked by the mind to create dreams. In the "Woodbridge" story, the young woman sees *"at the end of the drive . . . a kidney-shaped pool and a woman lounging nearby."* In her subsequent dream, *"A fight breaks out over a game of pool."*

In the other dream, she remembers her fiancé's admiration for the wooden cabinets: *"Michelle talks about a vacation in North Carolina, where she found an old wooden bridge about to be demolished."* This is the wood Michelle used to make her cabinets. In the dream, the dreamer is baffled *"that [John] wants to move [to Woodbridge]. I tell him I hate that town!"* Through the process of condensation, the wooden bridge and cabinets are transformed into a place that "bridges" different images and condenses them into one place—Woodbridge, a passionately disliked town. The narrator's mind has taken material from the day and transformed it into images that represent her conscious and unconscious envy and fantasies of revenge. This process allows her to express and perhaps resolve what would otherwise be forbidden sexual and aggressive urges.

The vignette allows us to examine how dreams operate in the unconscious. What the dreamer recalls when she wakes is known as the dream's "manifest content"—that is, the apparent rather than the latent meaning. The dreamer walks into a saloon only to *"find a woman with long blond hair who looks like Michelle, only she has a wooden leg."* The "wooden leg" represents both an exaggeration of Michelle's dancing injury and her talent as a woodworker, and it ties the dream image to the real experience.

Dreams often hide real feelings. When we are dreaming, our mind covers up unacceptable thoughts by focusing on minor details and producing apparently innocent images—a process Freud called "secondary revision." The dream disguises Michelle, somewhat thinly. For example, the dreamer might have created a decoy figure to shoot instead of the blond woman who resembles the real Michelle. The decoy would have served as an extra layer of protection against the dreamer's acknowledging her murderous wishes. Secondary revision helps the mind create a dream that tells a more or less complete but obfuscated story. In this vignette, the process of revision enables the dreamer to hide from herself her own unacceptable impulses yet still achieve a meaningful narrative.

In psychoanalytic terms, dream work protects the ego from threatening ideas and wishes. In other words, dreams disguise what we do not want to know about our own feelings. They make the unbearable bearable. Because what is frightening is disguised, the dreamer need not blame herself—she can sleep peacefully, untouched by feelings of guilt, shame, or overstimulated longing. The young woman does not know consciously that she wishes to "shoot" her fiancé's former girlfriend. She is protected from acknowledging her murderous wishes. The highly stylized image of the Old West saloon—temporally distant from the dreamer's life in the 1980s—sets the dream in a time when shootings might have been more commonplace and acceptable, thus neutralizing the forbidden aggression and distancing the dreamer from her own wishes.

From a contemporary post-Freudian perspective, dream images can be examined "for what they reveal metaphorically and thematically, not [only] for what they conceal" (Fosshage 1997, 444). In other words, psychotherapists today view dreams as useful tools that elucidate our patient's hidden conflicts and guide our understanding of their real-world anxieties. In "Woodbridge," the dream speaks to the dreamer's real-world concerns about her fiancé's loyalty, and it may also speak to experiences from her past. Meeting Michelle may well have reactivated the young woman's childhood feelings of jealousy and rivalry. In this way, dreams are useful to the dreamer both in protecting her sleep and in leading the way, through analysis, to deeper understanding and conflict resolution.

Heinz Kohut (1977), the founder of self-psychology, offered yet another approach to dream interpretation. He believed that attention to the person's sense of self is the central tenet of a self-psychological treatment. He described what he called the "self-state dream," which attempts to restore the dreamer's feeling of psychological cohesion in the face of otherwise frightening assaults on the self. In his view, the dream can be understood as an attempt by the dreamer to work through her feelings of inadequacy. A self-psychologist might interpret the Woodbridge dreams in light of the dreamer's fear that she does not measure up, which then triggers her aggression toward both her fiancé and Michelle. This approach leads us also to look at dreams as making concrete and visible what are otherwise hidden aspects of experience.

In an expansion of Kohut's theory, James Fosshage argues that the main function of dreams is to "organize" experience. He calls this purpose the "developmental function" of dreams. He writes, "Dream mentation [thinking] develops, regulates, and restores psychological organization, in keeping with [the person's] developmental strivings and the need to preserve self-cohesion" (1997, 443).

In the "Woodbridge" story, the dreamer restores her psychological equilibrium through the barely disguised gratification of the wish to defeat her rival. As Robert Stolorow and George Atwood (1992), two other self-psychologists, explain, dreams express "personal purposes" that go beyond wish fulfillment. In this example, the personal purpose is adaptive and "curative." This function would have been fulfilled if the dream had led the dreamer to an awareness of her unresolved insecurities in her relationship. In therapy, this awareness might lead her, for instance, to explore her disavowed feelings of apprehension with regard to her upcoming wedding.

Although different schools of thought offer varying approaches to dream theory and interpretation, the clinical work of psychotherapy is to penetrate and understand the deeper meaning of the dream. This understanding is accomplished in treatment when the therapist invites the patient to share thoughts and associations about the dream's curious images. The therapist might consider significant emotions the dreamer may have felt or ask about the central images of the dreams, such as the wooden leg in our storyteller's dream. For example, if the therapist knew that the patient had lived near a town called Woodbridge, she would likely be interested in the dreamer's associations to that town. The dreamer might also be asked to consider the meaning of any unusual details, such as the wooden leg or the kidney-shaped pool.

There are many ways to approach dream interpretation, but dreams never fail to captivate our imagination and enrich our clinical work. Surprise, delight, and even, at times, horror are elicited when we discover the multiple meanings folded into our dreams. We all share a simultaneous pull toward and a desire to escape from our own private Woodbridge.

6 WEARING MY TUTU TO ANALYSIS

A young woman "accidently" shows off her party dress to her psychoanalyst.

I learned my father was to receive a "Contractor of the Year" award at six on a Friday evening, one month hence. My analytic session was scheduled for five that same day at an office a mere mile from the conference hall. After enjoying my father's good news, my thoughts turned to my analytic hour. How could I have my full session, change into my fancy clothes, and fight my way through traffic to get to the dinner on time?

As an analysand (a person undergoing psychoanalysis), I had recounted many recollections of my childhood adoration of my father. I recalled fantasies of playing Sleeping Beauty rescued by the Prince or poor Cinderella rushing home from the ball with one glass slipper missing; all my little girl yearnings for Prince Charming were concentrated on my beloved father. I'd reveled in dressing up in my special party dress that flared out when I twirled. In sessions, I would play back the cherished memory of my ballet recital at age six. I recalled prancing down the stairs in my frilly pink tutu. My father, seated in his usual brown leather chair, watched me as I proudly pirouetted across the floor, a smile playing across his lips. "My, don't you look beautiful," he said.

As the date for the awards dinner approached, I obsessed about my dilemma: I did not want to come to analysis in my formal dress, yet I feared I would not have time to go home and change. The image of me lying on the couch in my pink taffeta dress, with its bell-shaped skirt of tulle, was unthinkable—or, possibly, too exciting and dangerous to consider. Could it be that I wished to see the glow of admiration in my analyst's eyes that I had seen in my father's? I struggled with what to do. I could neither allow myself to cancel the session nor arrive in full party splendor. Finally, after much agonizing during our sessions, I came to a solution that seemed perfect to me, although I kept it a secret from my analyst. I would transport my dress in the car. After the session, I would tiptoe into my analyst's bathroom, transform into a princess, and sneak off to the "ball."

The Friday of the awards dinner arrived. When my session ended, I surreptitiously whisked out to my car, collected my outfit, and crept back into the bathroom, hoping my analyst would not hear my return. The plan went perfectly. Relieved and satisfied, now in my party attire, with my street clothes in hand, I scurried back to my car, only to find, to my horror, the door locked, and no keys in my hand. My heart sank, and my pulse raced as I glimpsed my keys dangling from the ignition. There I was, stranded, with the sinking recognition that I had no choice but to return to my analyst's office to call a locksmith.

Sheepishly, undoubtedly red-faced, click-clacking in my heels, I knocked on my analyst's door and heard the familiar "Come in." There sat my classically trained analyst, expectantly waiting in his brown leather chair. Never one to shy away from warmth and ready humor, he looked up at me and said with a wry smile, "My, what a pretty party dress."

Analysts Reflect on Transference and Enactment

Transference—the idea that we transfer onto figures in our "real" lives the feelings and expectations we attribute to figures from our past—is a core psychoanalytic concept much explored in the literature. Transference occurs in all relationships all the time, not just in those taking place in clinical settings. This happens because we all experience others through the lens of our earliest relationships (Bird 1972).

In psychodynamic treatment, such preordained scripts provide an important avenue for examining our relationships and our selves. The therapeutic situation, by its very nature, brings forth new versions of old feelings, conflicts, and expectations. As Freud wrote in 1910, "Psychoanalysis does not create [transference], but merely reveals it to consciousness and gains control of it in order to guide psychical processes towards the desired goal" ([1910] 1953a, 51). Otto Fenichel gave one of the clearest definitions of this early view of transference: "In the transference the patient misunderstands the present in terms of the past; and then instead of remembering the past, he strives, without recognizing the nature of his action, to relive the past this time more satisfactorily than he did in his childhood. He 'transfers' the past attitude to the present" (1945, 29).

In classical terms, as a result of a patient's transference, her symptoms are thus unwittingly transformed into a neurosis—maladaptive patterns of behavior and thought that are influenced by conflict and defense. Psychodynamic treatment is based on the belief that these neurotic conflicts are inevitably transferred onto the therapist, where they can be experienced, discussed, and worked through during the course of treatment. As Freud ([1914] 1955j) said, the patient does not just remember, he repeats.

In "Wearing my Tutu to Analysis," the analysand's childhood yearnings for her father's admiration and love were reawakened in the course of her analysis. As she anticipated the pleasure of dressing up for the party, the childlike fantasy of dazzling her analyst came dangerously close to the surface, giving rise to an obsessional defense and behavioral disorganization. The patient is trapped between the demands of an adult dilemma (how to get to the party on time), on the one hand, and her childlike longings to win the love of her analyst/father and the need to protect herself from knowing her little girl wish to win her analyst's admiration, on the other. In the story, she writes, *"The image of me lying on the couch in my pink taffeta dress, with its bell-shaped skirt of tulle, was unthinkable—or, possibly, too exciting and dangerous to consider."*

Since Freud first discussed transference in 1905, the concept has become central to psychoanalysis and other forms of psychodynamic psychotherapy. In fact, in his early writings Freud described transference as the psychoanalytic lynchpin of treatment. However, although the interpretation of the transference is important, the analyst must also attend to other significant aspects of the patient's outside life.

Transference was early on understood as a form of displacement (Fosshage 1994). The role of the therapist was that of "a blank screen" upon which the patient could project these early conflicts. Nonetheless, Freud, in describing transference as involving "new editions of the old conflicts" ([1917] 1955a, 454), anticipated that this process of modifying conflicts was a dynamic one. Regarding "Wearing My Tutu to Analysis," Freud would likely view the early longings for the father's adoration as displaced onto the current relationship with the analyst.

Today our view has been expanded to include the idea that transference is a fusion of what the child actually experienced and the adult's own set of fantasies and defenses. It is not the past that gets played out, but rather a person's unconscious fantasies about the past that must be reworked in the present. This idea is borne out of the understanding that each person possesses a unique fantasy life and psychic reality that are more than just the veridical unfolding of events. We look at these differences in our mental life as both psychologically and biologically determined. Children often respond differently to the same life circumstances based on the impact of nature and nurture. It can even seem at times as if siblings in the same family were raised by different parents, because the stories they tell often bear so little resemblance to each other.

Transference arises because it is impossible to be an accurate witness to our own lives. Our internal representations of important figures from the past are not exact replicas of our original relationships. We cast the shadow of our fantasied objects—the mythologically dashing father of the story—upon our real relationships. Over time, unconscious fantasies about the past become the organizing principles of our psyche. Treatment offers the opportunity for the patient's unconscious fantasies to come alive in the room and be understood.

In "Wearing My Tutu to Analysis," the patient's Oedipal wish to become her father's one and only love and to have his admiration all to herself unconsciously influences her interactions with her analyst. The Oedipal longings reawakened in the young woman are dangerously close to the little girl's universal wish to do away with all other rivals for her father's affection. The collision of the patient's forbidden wish to be seen in her party dress and the reality of returning to her analyst's office to ask for help leave her nearly undone: "*Relieved and satisfied, now in my party attire, with my street clothes in hand, I scurried back to my car, only to find, to my horror, the door locked and no keys in my hand. . . . There I was, stranded, with the sinking recognition that I had no choice but to return to my analyst's office to call a locksmith.*"

In another contemporary formulation, we now understand that therapy is a two-person interaction and that the nature of this interaction helps to shape the transference. George Frank describes what this shared experience means: "It is recognized that the neuroses that patients come to experience with the analyst (i.e., transference) are influenced by the nature of the interpersonal relationship that exists between the patient and analyst, and are not simply 'figments' of the patient's unconscious, though the patient's unconscious is certainly involved" (2000, 464).

The therapeutic relationship is played out in the treatment room between patient and clinician; it is also played out separately within the patient's mind and the therapist's mind. The therapist inevitably *enactments ??* [handwritten margin note]

responds to the patient's transference in real ways, leading to what contemporary thinkers call "enactments." This term means that some aspect of the patient's past is played out within the therapeutic relationship, creating a set piece that is not fully understood or verbalized (Jacobs 1986). Enactment represents what one writer has called the "reuniting of Freud's concepts of transference" with our contemporary idea of "acting out" (Katz 1998, 1129). Implicit in this idea is an understanding that transference can be enacted through actions as well as words, and it can be viewed as a way to let the therapist know what is happening when words are not available.

Enactments provide clinicians with valuable information about the patient and about their relationship with the patient. Judith Chused has suggested that the analyst inadvertently actualizes the patient's transference fantasies. She distinguishes enactment from acting out in that the former involves the analyst as a participant rather than as an observer: "Enactments occur when an attempt to actualize a transference fantasy elicits a countertransference response" (1991, 629). In "Wearing My Tutu to Analysis," we cannot know what is in the analyst's mind, but we can speculate from what he says that he intuits his patient's wish to be admired by him.

Stephen Mitchell (1988), one of the founders of the relational school of psychoanalysis, believes that treatment is not truly engaged until the analyst discovers himself within the patient's fantasy world. The same holds true for the patient. In "Wearing My Tutu to Analysis," the young woman can no more resist her wish to have her analyst admire her more feminine self than she can consciously embrace this desire. Thus, she "creates" a situation, or enactment, in which her elaborate scheme to avoid this eventuality actually leads to its occurrence. Modern psychoanalysis focuses on the interpretation of transference in the here and now of the analytic relationship, where the analyst's wry comment, *"My, what a pretty party dress,"* immediately conveys his appreciation of the transference wish. Although in the moment our analysand is likely red-faced with embarrassment, nonetheless we can picture her giving a tiny imaginary twirl.

PART TWO
Development

7 ODE TO A TISSUE

A mother observes how her infant daughter endows a bit of paper with magical properties.

It was just a sneeze, but to Rachel's infant ears it must have sounded as if her father had exploded. Lying in her father's arms, startled by the sudden loud noise, she began to wail. Standing nearby, I quickly handed my husband, John, a Kleenex and soothed Rachel with comforting words. With the tissue's appearance, her father was restored to his normal, nonsneezing, nonfrightening self. As babies do, Rachel quickly associated the thing itself—a tissue—to the emotional state with which she connected it.

Seeing Rachel's curiosity and response to the tissue, John and I initiated a game. He would pretend to sneeze, and I would hand him a tissue. Rachel's smiling delight turned to laughter as we continued the play.

From that day forward, ordinary tissues became baby Rachel's magical talisman, enabling her to soothe herself. They absorbed Rachel's fears whenever she approached a new or unknown situation. Although she was too small to help herself, I sensed her fright and intervened with a tissue. The tissue enabled her to move from fear to excitement to a contented calm. When I handed her a tissue, we both seemed to believe that I was giving her a little piece of me.

For the next two years, Rachel's love of tissues did not falter. Small pieces of tissue covered our floors, our cars, and me. She could instantly identify by touch whether a tissue was her beloved "Kleenex" or not. If handed a substandard brand, she'd crinkle her nose in disgust, saying, "No 'issue! No 'issue!"

Each new morning brought another chance for me to witness Rachel's pure joy over her rediscovery that the tissue was still there. Entering her sunlit room, glancing around at her beloved stuffed animals everywhere, I'd peer into the crib, see her broad smile, and smile back as she unfurled her chubby little fingers to reveal a small piece of " 'issue" curled up in her hand. Once again, all was good and safe in the world.

Analysts Reflect on Transitional Objects and Phenomena

The story of Rachel and her tissues demonstrates how babies use and create transitional objects to calm and comfort themselves. A transitional object is defined as an actual object, usually a soft toy or cloth, that stands in for a baby's caregiver, providing comfort and a sense of continuity when the adult is temporarily not available. D. W. Winnicott, the originator of the concept, believed that "transitional phenomena are healthy and universal" (1953, 95).

Transitional objects, such as Rachel's tissues in our story, are familiar aspects of infant and toddler development. Between the ages of four and eight months, during times of discomfort or transition, such as going to sleep, many babies establish a self-soothing routine in which they rub a soft bit of cloth. This routine sometimes includes sucking their thumbs and babbling or wiggling. Winnicott (1953) used the term *transitional phenomena* to describe the intermediate area of human experience between inner reality and the outside world, which includes the transitional object. Holding, sucking, or caressing a corner of a blanket or diaper (or, in Rachel's case, a soft tissue) becomes associated with the mother or other beloved person and provides a feeling of security. The story author writes, *"From that day forward, ordinary tissues became baby Rachel's magical talisman, enabling her to soothe herself. They absorbed Rachel's fears whenever she approached a new or unknown situation."* The feel and even the scent of the object help to regulate states of distress.

In the long run, what matters is not the actual object but the particular use that the baby makes of the object. Over time, transitional objects become vitally important. Indeed, there will be times when even the parents' presence will not suffice, and only the transitional object will provide solace (Barkin 1978). Many parents have discovered, during those frantic midnight searches for the missing "blankie," that the transitional object is more essential than the beloved person for whom it initially served as a stand-in.

In "Ode to a Tissue," the author is present at the creation of the transitional object and sees the moment when the mother-provided tissue becomes linked with comfort in her daughter's mind. That link between the baby's feelings of distress and her capacity to soothe herself soon takes on a life of its own, and for several years Rachel's beloved " 'issues" are never far from her reach and never fail to comfort her.

In his original formulation, Winnicott (1953) emphasized that the transitional object, unlike the usual psychoanalytic notion of an "object"—i.e., the internal representation of a significant person—is not internalized. Its significance eventually just fades. Others have disagreed with Winnicott over the fate of the transitional object. Child analyst Marian Tolpin posits that the transitional object eventually loses meaning because it is internalized: "It go[es] inside as mental structure; and precisely because of this the treasured possession is neither missed, mourned, repressed, nor forgotten. It is no longer needed" (1971, 321). In our view, the transitional object may lose its original meaning, but the child relies on it less and less over time. As such, it does undergo a transformation over the course of the child's development.

Winnicott theorized that the transitional object is a precursor to the infant's capacity to hold in mind the image of "mother" when she is not present. He derived his theory of transitional objects in the 1950s, when mothers were considered to provide the most important parental functions. Development was thought to unfold primarily within the mother–baby matrix. Good enough parents were always referred to as "good enough mothers." Winnicott believed that the infant requires a real-life "good enough mother" in order for the transitional object to become fused with the experience of soothing in the baby's mind. In Rachel's story, this connection between parent and object is made visible. The author can see that Rachel *was too small to help herself. I sensed her fright and intervened with a tissue. The tissue enabled her to move from fear to excitement to a contented calm.*

In Winnicott's view, the magical properties of the transitional object depend on the child's ability to maintain a warm and loving bond with the real mother. This process is illustrated in the story: *"When I handed her a tissue, we both seemed to believe that I was giving her a little piece of me."* In situations where the beloved parent is away too long and the baby's frustration exceeds what he or she can handle, the transitional object can lose its magical function. In a similar way, Winnicott emphasized that an infant deprived of good enough adaptive mothering cannot create a transitional object.

The idea that infants create transitional objects only when they enjoy a meaningful relationship with a primary caregiver is supported by research. Sally Provence and Rose Lipton (1962) conducted observational studies of institutionalized babies in the early 1960s and found that babies lacking strong relationships with primary caregivers did not create transitional objects, even when soft blankets and toys were available to them. Interestingly, those babies who were favored by the staff, who tended to receive more direct one-on-

one interaction, did show interest in special objects. In non-Western cultures where babies maintain bodily contact with their mothers for two or more years, children seem to have a diminished need for the creation of a transitional object (Hong 1978).

Winnicott described a healthy developmental progression that runs from babies' devotion to their transitional objects to their emergent ability to play (1953) to their development of the capacity to be alone ([1958] 1965a) and to their possession of the ability to participate fully in the life of their culture (1967). As with all aspects of maturation, successfully negotiating one stage of development prepares a child to master upcoming developmental challenges (A. Freud 1963). In "Ode to a Tissue," as Rachel acquires language and representational play, her much-loved and magical " 'issues" gradually lose their importance and become a fondly remembered relic of an earlier developmental era.

8 MOMMY BROKE IT!

After seeing his baby sister's umbilical cord fall off, a little boy is terrified that his mother might "break" his penis.

My twenty-seven-month-old son Sean scampered upstairs, chattering excitedly about his "job" supervising his ten-day-old sister's bath. Once in the bathroom, he happily gave orders, pointing to the various creams and powders I would need. He was the boss of baby Emma's bath, a role that perfectly suited his budding need to be in charge. He ordered me to gather the necessary potions as he intently peered at the small bundle in my arms.

"Don't be scared. *I* will help you," he told Emma, imitating as best he could the crooning way grown-ups talk to newborns. Sean loved splashing in his own bath, and he was happy to share this ritual with "his" new baby. As I unwrapped Emma, he smiled at her and held her hand, entranced when she reflexively grabbed his fingers, though a scowl crossed his face when she soon started to wail. Emma quieted, however, when I lowered her into the warm water. Sean quickly became absorbed in wetting the washcloth, applying baby soap, and gently wiping her tiny body. When it was time to wash her few strands of hair, Sean used the lather to make elaborate soap designs. The baby was happy, and Sean was happy, too.

I scooped baby Emma out of the water, wrapping her loosely in a towel and patting her. Laying her across my lap, I wiped around her umbilical cord with a cotton swab dipped in alcohol. The small, dried stump chose that unfortunate moment to detach itself from Emma's belly. I loosened it then gently pulled it away. A beautiful new belly button!

Only then did I look at my son. His face was transfixed with horror as he gazed at the now separated umbilical cord that was carefully—yet undeniably—held in my hand. Sean jumped back, grabbed the front of his pants, and gave a strangled yell for his father. Then he streaked out of the bathroom and down the hall.

As quickly as I could, I swaddled Emma and followed Sean downstairs. By the time we entered the kitchen, Sean had his arms tightly wrapped around his father's neck and was tearfully telling him, "Mommy broke it! *Her broke it right off*, and now it's gone. *Her breaks things.*" I quickly explained to his perplexed father why Sean was so distressed. No matter how I explained what had happened to Emma's body, Sean would have none of it and none of me. Each time I reached to scoop him into my arms, he backed away from me and clung even more tightly to his father, where he remained for most of the evening.

During the next few weeks, we worked hard to reassure him. We explained that all babies shed their umbilical cords—that it was a natural part of baby Emma's getting bigger. We tried to explain to him about the difference between boys' and girls' bodies. Even so, bath time was scary for him. Again and again he asked if he had "a 'bilical cord to lose." Each time we told him that his body was safe, and so was Emma's. But it was several nights before he slept as peacefully as he had before and even longer before he was completely comfortable with his previously adored bath—especially when I was with him. Sean may not have known the term *castration anxiety*, but it was abundantly clear that he was no stranger to it.

61

Analysts Reflect on Castration Anxiety

Sean's world is filled with new and exciting experiences. Warmly connected to his parents, filled with a nascent sense of his own power, and possessing a growing trust in the integrity of his own body, he is able to greet the arrival of his sister with relative equanimity. All is well until he sees his sister's umbilical cord, looking much like a small boy's penis, break off in his mother's hand. Fantasy and reality collide in one excruciating moment. *"Sean had his arms tightly wrapped around his father's neck and was tearfully telling him,* 'Mommy broke it! *Her broke it right off,* and now it's gone. *Her breaks things.'"*

Castration anxiety, the term used to describe a boy's fear of the loss of his penis as punishment for forbidden wishes, is one of the central ideas in psychoanalytic theory. As psychoanalytically oriented psychotherapists, we encounter this fantasy again and again in our own unconscious and in that of our patients. Whether viewed literally or metaphorically, this fear of castration—of maiming, of the loss of our own power—seems to resonate in the minds of men and women alike.

Freud first proposed the idea of castration anxiety in his early writings about the Oedipus complex. At the time, Freud himself was the father of a growing family, and his observations likely came from watching his own children at play. He wrote that the Oedipus complex arises during the third year of life and subsides when children develop a superego—an internalized sense of right and wrong. In his original and classical understanding, castration anxiety is a component of the Oedipus complex that emerges in boys sometime between the ages of three and five. During this period, boys experience deep-seated and often unconscious anxiety about their bodies and their sexual intactness. Freud called this period the "phallic stage of sexual development." It corresponds to the years when children are increasingly aware of the world around them. For the first time, many little boys notice the relative size of their genitals as compared to their fathers'.

At an age when they see themselves as weaker and smaller than their fathers, young boys are also often "falling in love" with their mothers. A drama unfolds in heterosexual nuclear families wherein the boy hungers for the exclusive attention of his mother. Freud believed that this drama lays the groundwork for powerful, forbidden incestuous wishes. Wanting his mother all to himself brings the boy face to face with his most potent and dangerous rival, his well-loved father. The wish to replace his father in his mother's affection terrifies the little boy because in his fantasy and in line with his concrete way of thinking he anticipates a retaliatory attack on his penis—which he associates with size and power—by his father.

In classical theory, the positive resolution of the Oedipus complex occurs when the little boy is able to repress his incestuous wishes toward his mother. Repression, in Freudian terms, is an unconscious self-protective maneuver that enables all humans to push unacceptable thoughts and feelings out of awareness. Freud thought repression thus functions to allow the young boy to preserve his close relationship with both of his parents.

According to Freud and other early theorists, castration anxiety originates when a little boy first sees a female's genitalia. This event inevitably contradicts his egocentric belief that everyone possesses a penis, a highly valued part of himself that is tied to his sense of bodily integrity. Using the reasoning of a child, the little boy hypothesizes that the girl (who clearly lacks a penis) must have had it taken away from her, either as a punishment or in retribution for some dreadful thought or action. When he sees a girl's body, this encounter provides him with undeniable confirmation that castration does occur—a terrifying thought. As Sean's mother writes, "*Even so, bath time was scary for him. Again and again he asked if he had 'a 'bilical cord to lose.'*"

The ultimate anxiety for a little boy is that the same castration that he believes must have happened to girls may also happen to him. He knows he harbors bad and aggressive impulses that according to his child's view of the world "deserve" to be severely punished. Approaching three years old, Sean is entering the Oedipal age of development and is therefore primed to believe that the loss of his sister's umbilical cord proves that his own little penis is in danger: *"His face was transfixed with horror as he gazed at the now separated umbilical cord that was carefully—yet undeniably—held in my hand."* Such a startling "confirmation" of his unconscious fear led to terror and panic.

For little children, developmental issues of control, mastery, and pride converge with their concerns about bodily integrity. Castration anxiety emerges as little boys are asserting their own will and as they are starting to value their genitals as a source of pleasure, gratification, and primary symbolic identification with the powerful father. The pleasurable genital feelings that children experience occur at the same time that they are increasingly expected to control their own bodies, give up diapers, and learn to contain their aggressive impulses. Demands, the wish for parental approval, punishments (real and imagined), and guilty pleasures thus loom large in the mind of a small child.

The traditional Oedipal fantasy is associated with feelings of aggression and envy toward the father, which inevitably make the child feel vulnerable. For example, the young boy in the story first seeks to protect himself from feeling profound anxiety by embracing his role as big brother. The birth of Sean's sister has no doubt aroused conflicting emotions that include envy and rivalry, which he attempts to cope with by identifying himself as "Mommy's helper." Tucked into the idyllic scene of Sean and his mother caring for "their" new baby is Sean's unconscious fantasy of replacing his father in his mother's eyes.

Sean's terrified reaction demonstrates the convergence of several developmental strands. First, his egocentricity, typical of two-year-olds, renders him utterly unable to imagine that others do not think and feel as he does. Second, witnessing the loss of his sister's umbilical cord, which so closely resembles his own penis, challenges his belief that all bodies resemble his and at the same time raises the specter of attack. Third, Sean now understands that he must share his mother's attention with another, a rival who inevitably stirs feelings of jealousy. Finally, Sean, like all preschoolers, is preoccupied with concerns about bodily integrity and damage. These factors result in his extreme anxiety and a subsequent fear of his mother, whom he sees as the perpetrator of bodily harm.

Sean's terror illustrates the power of the little boy's fantasies. Castration anxiety and the entire Oedipal drama are freighted with tremendous emotion. Children's love and fear possess an epic quality that Freud recognized when he named the familial sexual drama after Oedipus, the king who tragically loved his mother and killed his father. The tragedy of the Oedipus complex is the inevitable impossibility of the fulfillment of the young child's fantasy. Thus, the hoped-for resolution of this conflict is that the little boy will identify with his father and simultaneously relinquish the fantasy of laying exclusive claim to his mother's affections. This process is a complicated and painful one.

Over the course of this developmental stage, the young child no longer starkly divides the world into good and bad. He increasingly can tolerate ambivalent feelings and repress dangerous fantasies without resorting to action. As the Oedipal child successfully navigates these demands, he slowly achieves the capacity to establish and maintain a balance of intimacy and autonomy without retreating from others or becoming excessively dependent on them. Unless the boy emerges from the Oedipal complex and successfully represses his castration anxiety, it is likely that his capacity to function successfully in future relationships will be compromised.

British psychoanalyst and theoretician Melanie Klein (1945) disagreed with Freud on the question of how children resolve their Oedipal wishes. She suggested that the successful resolution of the Oedipal conflict culminates in children's ability to view the significant people in their lives in an integrated and whole way. She calls this developmental capacity "the depressive position." The name is derived not from what we think of today as "depression," but rather from the child's newly acquired ability to grieve and mourn for lost loved ones. One element of this capacity is the ability to view the previously internalized parents in a nonidealized way. This developmental achievement contrasts with the paranoid-schizoid position that Klein conceptualized as an internal world characterized by splitting, in which the child experiences the significant people in his life as either all good or all bad. When a child successfully resolves the Oedipus complex, he understands that one can feel angry, disappointed, or frustrated at a loved one without causing harm or permanent damage. This resolution involves the ability to see others as human—not perfect, but still worthy of love.

Although Freud and his contemporaries saw castration anxiety as applying only to boys, current theory postulates an equivalent process in girls. For example, Elizabeth Mayer (1985) theorizes that girls also experience a form of castration anxiety, which she calls "female genital anxiety." She notes that this anxiety is characterized by an unconscious fear of an attack on the female genitalia. In this fantasy, the young girl may also express a fear of losing the vaginal opening or of not being able to have a baby. Mayer thinks that the girl's fears, like the young boy's castration anxiety, arise out of the normal egocentrism of childhood and the childlike belief that bodily differences are a result of attack. In addition, Mayer (1995) believes that just as young girls, like boys, fear castration, they also derive pleasure from their genitals. Current theory, in other words, provides a modern-day counterpart to the earlier deficit model in which girls are viewed in terms of what they are lacking—penises—rather than in terms of what they actually do possess.

In recognition of the varied constellations of modern families, contemporary theory also no longer assumes that children are raised in traditional nuclear families. Today's family takes many forms. No matter the shape of the family, however, we believe all children still experience Oedipal longings. In our view, in order to take their places in society as competent and loving adults, all children must find a way to resolve these powerful Oedipal dramas successfully.

9 BUMPS AND ALL

A young girl longs for puberty to transform her body.

When I was twelve, I worried that I might never grow breasts. There I was, all of eighty pounds, nothing but skin and bones, with knobby knees, bruised shins, a mouth full of braces—and not a curve in sight. I worried that I would remain forever a little girl with nothing on my chest but bumps—bumps that my well-endowed older sister unkindly referred to as "pimples in need of Band-Aids."

Although I had my older and younger sisters, the person I needed most was my mother. She had died two years earlier, leaving me with an aching pit in my belly and too many unanswered questions in my mind. I couldn't imagine what my mother would have said if I had complained about my flat chest. I just knew that she would have known exactly what to do. So there I was, in the midst of our once again bustling household, with a lingering feeling of loneliness. Without my mother, how could I possibly picture who I was to become?

Desperate to understand all the puzzling transformations—or lack thereof—in my friends and me, I read *Our Bodies, Ourselves* from cover to cover and sneaked peeks at my parents' old copy of

The Joy of Sex. I eavesdropped on my older sister's private phone conversations. Mostly, though, I watched.

Before gym, I would surreptitiously look around the locker room to see who had developed. How I envied those girls whose large breasts were barely contained in their T-shirts. Thank God for flat-as-a-board Mary Jane Kowalski, who, like me, turned her back when she changed into her gym uniform under her clothes, hoping no one was looking.

To make matters worse, two lockers down from Mary Jane and me was popular Linda Farrow with her 38D breasts. What did it feel like to have breasts like that, to be the fascination of all the boys in middle school? To actually need a bra! I couldn't stop comparing myself to her.

Hoping I would soon be similarly transformed, I decided what would help. I nervously scrounged up the courage to ask my father to take me to the store to get a bra. Without missing a beat, he responded, "Sure, honey, if that's what you need." Off we went to Sears, where I lagged two steps behind my dad, head down, hoping to be invisible. We strode through men's colognes and men's shoes, finally arriving at our destination: the world of women's finery. We walked up to the lingerie counter. A saleswoman appeared. Dark hair, red lips, short skirt, high heels, tightly buttoned shirt, and, of course, what do you know, large breasts.

"Can I help you?" she asked my father with a flirtatious smile.

"Yes," my father replied, unperturbed. "My daughter needs a bra."

She glanced down, as if just noticing I was there, and said with a little laugh, "Oh, no, I don't believe she does. It's much too soon." My heart sank. I wanted to disappear into the floor. I reached for my father's hand to pull him away, to go home and pretend this never happened. Instead, my father turned to the woman and met her eyes with a steady gaze. He firmly responded, "I'm sorry, but you must be mistaken. My daughter is here for a bra. Please help her find the one she needs." I felt of twinge of relief breaking through my embarrassment. If my father thought I needed a bra, then I must actually need one. Well, at least I wanted to believe he was right.

I cringed as I meekly followed the disapproving saleswoman into the fitting room. I reassured myself with the words of my best friend, Sandy: "It's just when you look down that they look so small. Straight ahead, to everyone else, they look big." Oh, how I hoped this was true.

Analysts Reflect on Early Adolescence

In the story "Bumps and All," the young girl is on the cusp of adolescence. In order for her to manage this transition successfully, she must navigate a difficult and contradictory course. Although she yearns for greater independence, she still needs to rely on the familiar, supportive relationship with her father. The push-and-pull situation exerts pressure on the parent–child relationship, which necessarily shakes up the previously comfortable bond. This dizzying oscillation in development is one of the primary characteristics of early adolescence.

Adolescence begins with puberty—a physical turning point marked by the onset of menses in girls and nocturnal emissions in boys. During this time of transition, girls and boys are buffeted by hormonal fluctuations. As their bodies change, so does their sense of who they are in the world. All of these changes result in the profound instability that characterizes this phase of life.

Peer relationships become paramount in the young teen's sense of belonging. As adolescents form new identifications, outside relationships and accomplishments assume greater importance. To some extent, the peer group takes on the role of family, providing emotional support, shared goals, a common culture, and so forth. Peter Blos (1967) refers to this adolescent shift from identifying with parents to identifying with the peer group as a "second individuation process of adolescence." The first occurs around the age of three, when children begin to see themselves as separate, a process supported by the attainment of object constancy—children's growing understanding that their caregivers will not disappear when they are out of sight. Just as the attainment of "object constancy" marks the individuation process for toddlers, individuation for adolescents represents "the shedding of family dependencies, [and] the loosening of infantile object ties [in order] to become a member of . . . the adult world" (Blos 1967, 163).

Phyllis Greenacre noted in 1958 that all children struggle to incorporate a "sense of identity [that] involves comparison and contrast—with some emphasis on basic likenesses, but with special attention called to obvious unlikenesses" (613). She believed that the concern with sameness and difference continues to matter across the developmental trajectory. A central and oft revisited theme of "Bumps and All" is the young girl's acute awareness of how she shapes up in relation to peers: *"Before gym, I would surreptitiously look around the locker room to see who had developed. How I envied those girls whose large breasts were barely contained in their T-shirts."* As we can see in this story—and, perhaps, remember from our own experiences as young teenagers—early adolescence is one of those times when self-appraisal of sameness and difference is centrally important.

The overarching attention to issues of similarity and difference is seen in the narrator's hyperfocus on physical development. Her preoccupation with the size of her breasts is characteristic of young teens, especially those whose physical development falls outside of their anticipated, fantasized, or idealized parameters. As the narrator poignantly remembers, *"To make matters worse, two lockers down from Mary Jane and me was popular Linda Farrow with her 38D breasts. What did it feel like to have breasts like that, to be the fascination of all the boys in middle school? To actually need a bra! I couldn't stop comparing myself to her."*

The narrator's narcissistic vulnerability becomes a catalyst for seeking and finding emotional support outside herself. In our therapy offices, we often see young adolescents with fewer internal and external resources, who then withdraw from peer relationships and develop entrenched negative self-images; at other times, we may see adolescents who lose their identity in the frenetic pursuit of belonging. Both responses impede the adolescents' successful "launch" into adulthood.

If the young teenager in "Bumps and All" were to come to us for a psychotherapy consultation, we would evaluate her developmental difficulties in light of her emotional strengths and parental support. We would consider the many intrapsychic meanings she attributes to her slow-to-bloom body. As is evident from the story, we would recognize that her mother's death has profoundly affected her sense of self just as she is beginning to transition into womanhood: *"the person I needed most was my mother. She had died two years earlier, leaving me with an aching pit in my belly and too many unanswered questions in my mind. I couldn't imagine what my mother would have said if I had complained about my flat chest. I just knew that she would have known exactly what to do."* We would consider that she is struggling with the concrete evidence of her own "lack of resources" (i.e., her immature breasts) at the same that she is also painfully experiencing that same "lack of resources" in the tragic loss of her mother. As therapists, we would understand her mother's death to have particular resonance at this developmental stage, which is characterized by an often ambivalent mother–daughter relationship and during which all children to some extent want their parents to disappear.

Growing up requires a girl to identify with her mother as a woman and at the same time to identify firmly with her own peer group. Both of these tasks become more difficult for the narrator in light of her mother's death. She can neither protect herself from her older sister's teasing nor console herself as her mother would have. As is evident in the story, however, she also displays considerable psychological resiliency. In his study of resiliency, Norman Garmezy (1987) finds that childhood stress can have a "sensitizing" effect on children, causing them to develop psychological symptoms. This is not always the case, however. Similar stressors can in some cases have a "steeling" effect, thereby helping children develop an enhanced capacity to resist the negative impact of adversity.

In our story, the young girl shows her resiliency when she turns to her father for the necessary support needed to reestablish some sense of mastery over her situation. Phyllis DiAmbrosio notes the importance of adults for providing an outside source of regulation. "Out of these experiences, a 'core sense of self with other' is formed." With this support, the adolescent draws on these experiences to develop an enhanced "capacity to self-right" (2006, 269).

Research reliably demonstrates that although fathers are important for optimal development and behavior of both boys and girls during their teenage years, they have a particularly significant impact on the future lives of daughters. A girl's good relationship with her biological father is associated with lower rates of depression, later physical development, delayed sexual activity, and better academic outcomes (Ellis and Garber 2000; Hetherington and Kelly 2003). As Jessica Benjamin (1991) points out, the girl's "identificatory love" for her father (her love of and identification with him) symbolically represents her tie to the world outside the home. Thus, her father's approval and support allow her to engage more confidently and securely with other people and to participate in the larger world. Fathers play a role in helping girls control anxiety and maintain a healthy dose of self-esteem. Theorists have suggested that this is so because a girl's strong relationship with her father allows her to draw on his healthy adult capacities at the same time that she is differentiating from her mother. Her unsteady adolescent ego is strengthened by her experience of him as strong, confident, and assertive.

None of this happens overnight. In our story, the narrator embraces an immature ego ideal focused on the concrete, physical characteristics of development, such as the *"popular Linda Farrow."* This concrete, all-or-nothing thinking reveals that she is not yet ready to stand on her own. To move forward, she needs her father's support.

His mature judgment and reasoning bolster her immature psychological capacities. She turns to him for tangible help and emotional connection. She has a clear expectation that her father will provide her with what she needs, and as the story demonstrates, she is right to think so. Her request to go on a shopping trip with him to obtain a bra, in spite of the fact that her young body has just begun to bud, illustrates in psychoanalytic terms her attempt to strengthen her internal equilibrium by using her father as an auxiliary ego who can mediate between her and the larger world, which is represented in this case by the disapproving sales clerk. Her father's empathy allows the girl to soften her momentary shame and to rework her idea that everyone judges her as harshly as she judges herself. For example, she consoles herself with the notion that *"if my father thought I needed a bra, then I must actually need one. Well, at least I wanted to believe he was right."* Such parental scaffolding provides the narrator with the support that takes her beyond her narcissistic vulnerability.

The developmental process described in "Bumps and All" highlights the pain and the exhilaration that are characteristic of the early teenage years. We watch as during this psychic "launching" the narrator oscillates between fantasy and reality, resiliency and negative self-image, independence and dependence. She makes use of her father to help her interpret reality, gain needed resources, and find respite in the face of overwhelming internal and external demands for conformity and peer acceptance. Despite the significant stressors she has already experienced, the flexibility and movement between the security of her relationship with her father and her engagement with her peers and the larger world provide her with the means to continue a successful journey through adolescence. In the end, both her father and her best friend, Sandy, teach the same lesson: they love and accept her just as she is, "bumps" and all.

IO FIRST PARTY

A teenage girl experiences the excitement and danger of sexual experimentation.

I was thirteen years old, feeling sassy, and on my way to my first party with a boy. It wasn't a "date-date," but there I was in my red sleeveless sundress and little black heels, a white sweater thrown over my shoulders, with Frankie from across the street shuffling along beside me. As we moved down the block, several mothers leaned out of their apartment windows, smiling and waving at us. Frankie nearly died of embarrassment, but I took it as a kind of benediction. I was pleased with myself, with my growing breasts and tanned, bare legs. I was up for something thrilling, but I couldn't quite imagine what that might be.

The party was at a large Victorian house, surrounded by an ornate wrought-iron fence. Paper lanterns dotted the lawn. The mere two blocks we had walked felt like miles away from my familiar

We thank Shelley Singer for granting us permission to use her story, which she wrote for a New Directions workshop.

one-bedroom apartment. I was nervous and excited as we headed down to the basement, where all the kids had congregated. I scanned the room, hoping to find a familiar face and wondering if I looked okay. This was where the popular crowd hung out, and I wanted to be one of them. I tried to look nonchalant in spite of the sweat gathering at the small of my back.

Party dresses shushed and tight pants chafed as we settled into a circle on the linoleum floor to play Spin-the-Bottle, while the top forty provided the beat in the background. *Okay, this I can handle.* I even enjoyed the quick, off-target kiss one of the boys planted on my untried lips. I was feeling happy to be here, accepted into this group. Here, I had found a place where I could invent myself.

We all gathered around for a game called "Seven Minutes in Heaven." We girls wrote our names on little pieces of paper and threw them into a basket, glancing sidelong at each other, giggling nervously. One by one the boys reached in, plucked out a name, and read it out loud. The chosen girl would invariably flush while stumbling to her feet. As the others waited their turn, each pair would disappear into the next room, and for seven long minutes they were on their own. Johnny, the dreamiest dreamboat and most popular boy by far, was the one who drew my name. I followed him into the storage room. My heart pounded in my chest as he pushed me up against the wall and kissed me wetly with the grace of a sloppy, overeager dog. Yet, still, I was delighted. *I am being kissed. So this is what it feels like. Nice.*

Suddenly it stopped feeling nice. His two palms smashed hard into my little breasts and started making circles, as if he were cleaning smudges off a window. It hurt. I didn't like this anymore. I was scared, and I began to feel something I didn't quite know how to name. I wanted to flee, embarrassed. I was exactly where I'd always wanted to be, but it wasn't what I'd imagined, and now I just wanted to get away. I started to cry and ran out of the room, forgetting that I would be facing my restless and excited friends, all waiting for their seven minutes in heaven. "Virgin! Virgin!" they taunted, with

Johnny, laughing, leading the chant. I stumbled through the crowd wondering, *What is a virgin, anyway?* I had no idea, but I knew that was it: I'd never be invited to another of their parties again.

I raced upstairs and out of the house as fast as I could, mortified and crestfallen. Their taunting jeers echoed in my head as I trudged those two long blocks back home.

Analysts Reflect on Emergent Adolescent Sexuality

"Sex," Mary Day Winn stated long ago, "is the tabasco sauce which an adolescent national palate sprinkles on every course in the menu." Sexual curiosity and exploration pervade the experience of all adolescents. In "First Party," the young girl's tentative sexual awakening and her struggle to understand and gain entry into the fast-moving world of her peers contains a mix of emotions that are timeless and universal. Although the story evocatively re-creates a specific time and place, variations of this theme are archetypal within many cultures and eras. Change the music, the decade, or the place, and the central tale nevertheless remains readily recognizable.

Like many teens, the girl in the story experiences two intense yet competing desires. On the one hand, she feels compelled to know herself, to look inward, to understand the confusing yet exhilarating changes in her body, but on the other hand she longs to be out in the world, integrated into and accepted by her peer group. Such longing for peers enhances her capacity to turn away from the regressive siren call that pulls her back to her childhood dependency (Adatto 1966).

These competing developmental imperatives are both intensely physical and intensely relational. In the presence of insistent physiological and hormonal changes, sexual feelings sometimes swamp adolescents, driving them to create or to submit to sexually infused relationships that are psychologically limiting and unsatisfying. This is true for boys as well as for girls, and surviving such experiences becomes a rite of passage. In our society, erotically tinged danger and delight are integral to the formation of adolescent identity. Such experiences become the catalyst by which separation from the parents is achieved and the portal to mastery in the mysterious and enticing world of adult relationships is found.

The developmental shift from the primacy of the love for one's parent to the centrality of peer approval and acceptance parallels earlier developmental achievements. The young adolescent's response to the physical and interpersonal changes taking place during this phase of life is invariably shaped by the quality of his or her development during the earlier Oedipal and latency stages. These earlier developmental stages occur between the ages of four and eleven, when children first achieve a sense of identity and self-cohesion (Ritvo 1971). With sturdy, resilient egos, children are better equipped to withstand the subsequent "Sturm und Drang" of adolescence.

The psychic discomfort of loosening their emotional ties to their parents drives teens to forge idealized relationships with their peers. The young adolescent may also likewise develop highly idealized parent substitutes during this time. Such adults can play a vital role in the adolescent's life. The early teen thus begins to "fall out of love" with the childhood order, in which good enough parents are perceived as all powerful and benevolent. Instead, she now turns toward current, often eroticized relationships. The resultant overheated longing so typical of this developmental stage is readily apparent in our author's intense yearning to be "like" (and thus accepted by) her popular peers. As the girl in the story describes, *"I scanned the room, hoping to find a familiar face and wondering if I looked okay. This was where the popular crowd hung out, and I wanted to be one of them. I tried to look nonchalant in spite of the sweat gathering at the small of my back."*

As anyone who remembers his or her teenage years will attest, adolescence is not a simple, painless, or linear journey. As the teen cavalierly "tries on" new relationships and varied identities, he or she generally oscillates between periods of developmental progression and periods of regression. The result: a series of incomprehensible gy-rations during which episodes of emotional disregulation, impaired moral and ethical judgment, and behavioral impulsivity alternate with times of well-regulated and organized behavior and mood as well as of a capacity for empathy and delayed gratification.

These profound disruptions are psychological, physiological, and social in origin. Just as the young teen in our story longs to find a sense of belonging in the "popular crowd," launching herself figu-ratively and literally from the safe, familiar streets of her childhood, she is fiercely buffeted by the ebbs and flows of hormones.

It is important to realize that the relationship between hormones and behavior is not a simple linear one. We now understand that sexual identity produces different experiences for boys and girls. Be-havior originates in the brain, and it also changes brain structure. The same is true for hormones: they have an impact on behavior and are in turn altered by behavior. Relationships and family culture have an impact on these complex systems as well. For example, despite the clear relationship between testosterone and risky behavior (includ-ing risky sexual behavior), researchers have found that the environ-ment is uniformly a significantly more powerful behavioral predictor than is testosterone in middle-class families. Alan Booth, a Penn State University longitudinal family researcher, measured the testosterone levels in both male and female adolescents in four hundred stable, middle-class families. According to his findings, when the relation-ship between teenagers and their parents is poor, hormonal varia-tions significantly affect behavioral outcomes, such as engaging in risky behavior and depression. This negative correlation disappears when teens enjoy good relationships with their parents (Booth cited in Strauch 2003, 142). Thus, according to this study, attachment trumps biology in determining adolescent behavior.

Sexual orientation is a key aspect of sexual identity, which be-comes more firmly established during adolescence. As psychothera-pists, we believe there are many factors at work in establishing an adolescent's sense of herself as a sexual being. These factors include the feedback that teenagers receive from their social environment, the sexual signals they emit, their fantasies, and their unique physiological and psychological arousal patterns. Sexual orientation can be quite fluid during adolescence. Bisexuality is common in early adolescence, especially among girls, as is same-sex sexual experimentation. Such early explorations, however, have only a limited impact on the adolescent's definition of himself or herself as heterosexual, homosexual, or bisexual (Levy-Warren 1996).

According to Freud's theory of sexuality and many other more modern theories, all humans possess some bisexual potential, both biological and psychological. Psychoanalysts view this potential as rooted in children's earliest attachments to their parents. Because early attachments are never fully renounced (Beebe and Lachmann 2002), a child's later sexual orientation is posited always to contain elements of his or her powerful attachment to the same-sex parent. Irwin Hirsch believes the bisexual aspect of our attachment to our same-sex parents causes much unconscious fear because "inherent bisexuality implies that everyone is capable of sexual desire for both genders . . . [and] a fair measure of homosexual anxiety is virtually universal among heterosexual men. It is the primary basis for a prevailing homophobia" (1997, 472).

As analysts, we often see the simultaneous playing out and renunciation of bisexual impulses in adolescents' language and behavior. Teenage boys, we note, are drawn to intensely physical roughhousing with each other that has a clear, if sub rosa, sexual component. Teenage girls, in contrast, typically tend to share their bisexual attraction far more openly, with many public and private displays of affection. Echoes of this bisexual ambivalence can be seen in the intensely idealized—and often eroticized—same-sex adolescent crushes that are so characteristic of early to middle adolescence.

Much of adolescents' confusion and anxiety about sexuality results from their newly established sense of self as a sexual being. This newness gives rise to a heightened self-awareness that requires continuous validation and reassurance. Through this lens, we can understand the narrator's delight in her own body and the pressure she feels to establish herself socially and relationally. In this story, for example, readers see the twin upsurges of narcissistically invested body awareness—"*I was pleased with myself, with my growing breasts and tanned, bare legs*"—and peer orientation/identification in her wish to "*invent*" herself into one of the "*popular crowd.*" As is often characteristic of this age, body awareness and relationships (fantasized and real) occupy much of her energy.

Successful progression though adolescence depends on the simultaneous capacity to feel safe with others without either seeking merger or sabotaging intimacy and the development of the concomitant ability to tolerate separateness. It is only then, late in this process, that adolescents become capable of true emotional closeness and rewarding, reciprocal sexual relationships. As Louise Kaplan notes, "If they are to arrive at psychological adulthood, all adolescents must face the loneliness and heartbreak of bidding 'farewell to childhood.' . . . All adolescents must reconcile their newly awakened genital desires with the moral authority of society" (1984, 110). It is only at this juncture of self and society that the adolescent becomes truly adult.

II CUSTODIAL CARE

A high school student's "mistake" highlights her ambivalence about leaving home.

Who knows how a teenager chooses a college? Maybe it was that my friend Noreen's older sister went to Boston College or that I thought Boston would be a cool place to live. I remember seeing pictures of cute guys as I flipped through the pages of the school's recruitment material. Whatever the reason, after going through what felt like hundreds of brochures and well-worn college guides, I was certain I had found the perfect college for me. Exhausted by the abundance of choices, my mind finally settled on what seemed to be a clear, if somewhat random first choice. I suddenly wasn't willing to consider anything else for my future education. With my mind made up, I breathed a sigh of relief—everything would fall into place, and I wouldn't have to worry anymore. Satisfied, I tossed away my stacks of brochures with abandon.

That's how I found myself on a rainy Sunday afternoon in October boarding a Greyhound bus for a weekend in Boston, bound for an interview at Boston College. I had scheduled my appointment for ten on Monday. I felt nervous and excited. Earlier that morning I had stood in front of the mirror, trying on various combinations in pursuit of the perfect look. Now here I was, dressed in what I imagined to be collegiate attire, with a dash of the school colors thrown in. I boarded the trolley in downtown Boston and headed out to Chestnut Hill, home of Baldwin the Eagle.

As I approached the campus entrance, I was enthralled by the beautiful Gothic architecture. This is just what I imagined my college would look like. My mind lingered on an image of myself amid the bustle of students hurrying between classes, surrounded by an animated group of new friends. . . . But the image dissolved suddenly as I became aware that the campus was eerily quiet. I looked around, but I couldn't find anyone to tell me how to find my way. I eventually stumbled across a campus directory with the familiar "You Are Here" icon marking my path to admissions.

I entered the building a little before ten o'clock and followed the signs to the Admissions Office. I was disconcerted when I saw the noticeably dim lights and empty reception desk. As I anxiously crept through the office, a man peered out from one of the rooms and distractedly said, "We're closed today." "But wait," I protested, "I have a ten o'clock interview!" "You must be mistaken," he replied, looking puzzled. "The school is closed for Columbus Day." I nervously explained that I had expressly made the appointment for Columbus Day because I was off from school that day. He walked over to the receptionist's desk, asked for my name, and flipped through the appointment book. "Well . . . I see your name here last month, on September 16," he offered.

Through my tears, the words tumbled out of me. I said that Boston College was my first choice, and I was desperate to be accepted. "I even took the bus yesterday so I wouldn't be late!" I pleaded. With a look of both hesitancy and empathy, he responded, "Well, I came in to clean up the office, but I guess I can interview you." With profuse thanks, I followed him as he ushered me into a cluttered office with a clunky, oversize wooden desk. I sank into a chair, relieved to be sitting across from this kind man. Thirty years later I cannot recall the questions he asked or the answers I gave. All I do remember is the feeling of relief that he was there on his day off and was compassionate enough to interview me.

As acceptance day approached, I ran home each day to check the mail. Finally, a slim envelope from Boston College arrived at my door. Anxious anticipation washed over me because it seemed that I was holding my fate in my hand. Perched on the end of my bed, I nervously ripped open the envelope. There in front of my eyes were the words "We regret to inform you . . ." As tears welled up in my eyes, the rest of the letter was a blur. My mind could barely absorb those words.

I ran to tell my parents the devastating news. In despair and disbelief, I heard myself repeatedly asking, "How could this have happened? I thought it went so well." My father, always the optimist, finally suggested that I call the school because they might have made a mistake. After all, he pointed out, my grades and board scores were excellent, and I had told them my interview had gone as well as could be expected.

The next morning I mustered up my courage and dialed the school's Admissions Office. The crisp voice at the other end of the line said, "Boston College Admissions, may I help you?" Swallowing nervously, I gave her my name. I explained that I had received a rejection letter and hoped someone could tell me why I hadn't been accepted. "It's my first choice," I said in a quavering voice. "I *thought* I'd get in." The receptionist politely put me on hold. After a few long minutes, she returned and said, "Well, it says here that you never showed up for your interview." My heart sank. I quickly explained that I *had* indeed come for my interview—I was there on Columbus Day. I told her that I had met with a man cleaning his office. "He's the one," I said, "who interviewed me." She asked if I knew his name. I realized with a start that I had been so nervous, I had never even thought to get his name. I replied hesitantly, "He didn't tell me his last name, but I think his first name was, maybe,

Jerry?" I added helpfully, "He was kind of short . . . he was really nice. . . . " There was an awkward silence on the other end of the phone. I tacked on, "You can speak to him about my interview. I'm sure he can explain." Another silence. When she next spoke, I again heard those ominous words "I regret to inform you" echo in my mind. She gently explained to me that Jerry, who was indeed a very kind man, was a long-term employee of the Admissions Office custodial staff—not a faculty member, as I'd thought. "Perhaps," she asked, "He was the one who 'interviewed' you?"

It took me a few moments to grasp the meaning of what she had just told me. I was crushed. Now it all made sense. Years later, looking back, I smile a little at the picture of myself, sitting across from Jerry, with all my earnest hopes unquestioningly placed in the palms of his sympathetic hands. How could I have possibly known the unintended consequences of his genuine wish to help me? I didn't even know the right questions to ask. As things turned out, I loved my college experience. Even so, whenever I think about it, I am still a little hurt that Jerry didn't accept me.

Analysts Reflect on the Transition to Adulthood

The teenage girl at the center of this story, poised between late adolescence and young adulthood, is making her first solo foray into the larger world. The story captures her uncertain attempts to navigate between the safety of home and the confusing world of adulthood. Such an attempt is difficult, especially because the stress of preparing for college gives rise to insistent internal pressures that pull her toward regression.

Late adolescence is a way station that marks the shift between two different developmental stages. Although adolescence has traditionally been defined as the period between ages eleven and nineteen, recent advances in brain science have expanded the upper limit of this developmental phase. Current research shows that the brains of young adults in their midtwenties display the same characteristics that are associated with adolescence. During this time period, significant neurological change and maturation continue. As a result, we understand that adolescence is less clearly biologically delineated into stages than was once thought.

Late adolescents possess varying capacities for judgment, self-regulation, and future orientation. Young people in their late teens and early twenties are ideally characterized by a steadily unfolding ability to live more fully in the present while simultaneously planning for the future—a capacity that is less developed in the earlier stages of adolescence. Late adolescents are better able to acknowledge the limitations imposed by reality. They know they are unlikely to become a famous actor or the star player of the winning Super Bowl team and thus pursue more reality-based plans. Accepting such reality allows for significant change and growth.

In "Custodial Care," the internal and external demands of late adolescence impede the young narrator's autonomous judgment. Her schedule mix-up and her subsequent failure to recognize that something is amiss highlight her age-appropriate difficulty in navigating a novel, anxiety-inducing situation. She ultimately seeks the comfort of her parents' guidance to reestablish a forward-moving trajectory: *"I ran to tell my parents the devastating news. In despair and disbelief, I heard myself repeatedly asking, 'How could this have happened? I thought it went so well.' My father, always the optimist, finally suggested that I call the school because they might have made a mistake."*

Such movement between variable levels of judgment and maturity—when demands for greater autonomy collide with feelings of increased vulnerability—characterizes late adolescence. This understanding of adolescence sheds light on the frequently stormy family relationships during the final years of high school, when parents and teens are anxiously preparing for the upcoming leave taking. Late adolescence also gives the teen another chance to change and refine his or her earlier ways of being, enabling him or her to develop a fuller sense of self in relationship to others. Kurt Eissler pointed out many years ago: "Adolescence appears to afford the individual a second chance; it is a kind of lease permitting revision of the solutions found during latency which have been formed in direct reaction to the Oedipal conflict" (1958, 250).

Identity and belonging are central as adolescents envision moving away from home and launching themselves into adulthood. Mourning mixes with delight, terror with exhilaration, and to the degree that this mix cannot be acknowledged, it may cause the activation (or, more likely, the reactivation) of a variety of defenses and symptoms. As our narrator explains, under the stress of multiple choices and overwhelming decisions that need to be made, her mind goes blank and ceases to function: *"Exhausted by the abundance of choices, my mind finally settled on what seemed to be a clear, if somewhat random first choice. I suddenly wasn't willing to consider anything else for my future education. With my mind made up, I breathed a sigh of relief—everything would fall into place, and I wouldn't have to worry anymore. Satisfied, I tossed away my stacks of brochures with abandon."* Unable to process her mixed emotions, she impulsively and defensively cuts short her deliberations, failing to sift carefully through the range of options that lie before her.

When late adolescents prepare to leave home, ongoing traditions and a sense of belonging to a larger group become important components of identity. This sense of belonging ideally helps to alleviate the separation anxiety that most people experience during major transitions. In the story, the narrator's hunger for belonging, mixed with her separation anxiety, is clearly articulated: *"I felt nervous and excited. Earlier that morning I had stood in front of the mirror, trying on various combinations in pursuit of the perfect look. Now here I was, dressed in what I imagined to be collegiate attire, with a dash of the school colors thrown in."*

The quest for a sense of personal and group identity is familiar to everyone. According to Marsha Levy-Warren, "Feeling rooted in the sociocultural world provides each adolescent with an anchor during the years of transition from childhood to adulthood" (1996,

132). When adolescents leave for college, they may try to diminish their separation anxiety by joining clubs, sororities, or fraternities. The passion with which they immerse themselves in campus life and identify with their college teams, themes, and cultures highlights their strong urge to establish an identity and to create their own sense of place. Young adults' identification with their peer group provides them with an anchor around which to bind their anxiety during this literal and figurative move away from their familiar childhood identities. Some adolescents may alternatively seek to oppose the cultural norms by forging an outside-the-mainstream counteridentification that can take a variety of subsequent forms.

By late adolescence, most teens have begun to solidify some sense of themselves as sexual beings. The later teen years are characterized by the consolidation of the vast changes that occurred throughout childhood. This gathering together of different strands of identity leads to a calmer, more inwardly focused, and stable sense of self. Less vulnerable to the ebb and flow of momentary experience, the silhouette of the emerging adult takes shape (Ritvo 1971; Dahl 2004). This stability enables older teens to establish fully reciprocal relationships. For the first time, they are able simultaneously to be physically and emotionally close to someone and to respect similarities and differences. Such a capacity for intimacy is known in the psychoanalytic world as the achievement of "full genitality"—that is, the idea that pleasure and satisfaction can be fully integrated in the context of a meaningful relationship (Chasseguet-Smirgel 1988).

Themes of separation are constantly revisited in the teen years. Such strivings toward separation assume varied forms as a result of underlying shifts in developmental needs and pressures (Blos 1967). For younger adolescents who are just beginning to experience themselves as sexual beings, dangerous Oedipal feelings provide the impetus for moving away from their previously all-encompassing and now overheated relationships with parents and toward the comfort of their peer group. Phyllis Tyson notes that "the passage through adolescence" is "a monumental challenge" because of the reactivation of early Oedipal conflicts within the context of a sexually mature body (2003, 1125).

In contrast, in late adolescence successful resolution of the revisited Oedipal complex is achieved when there is a sense of one's self as capable of functioning within a committed relationship. The newly acquired capacity for intimacy involves both a celebration and a kind of mourning because intimacy requires acknowledging the limits that reality imposes—that saying "yes" to one relationship means giving up the pursuit of others. The earlier heated struggle to disengage from the control of the internalized parents gives way to a greater capacity for self-awareness and "a consolidation of new internalizations at a higher developmental level" (Behrends and Blatt 1985, 33).

As Freud ([1915] 1955f) observed, a resolution of each subsequent stage is built on the integration of all preceding developmental achievements and allows valued traits to be integrated into an adult sense of self. In "Custodial Care," the author is still searching for direction while envisioning the autonomous self that she longs to become: *"My mind lingered on an image of myself amid the bustle of students hurrying between classes, surrounded by an animated group of new friends. . . . But the image dissolved suddenly as I became aware that the campus was eerily quiet. I looked around, but I couldn't find anyone to tell me how to find my way. I eventually stumbled across a campus directory with the familiar 'You Are Here' icon."*

According to developmental psychologist Erik Erikson (1956), the capacity for engagement with others is due to a newly emerged capacity for "self-delineation." In order to achieve mature, intimate, and committed relationships with family and friends, there must be an integration of the adolescents' emerging sense of self with the valued traits they have observed in important others. It is only when these relationships are integrated that they develop the values and principles by which they will live. As Levy-Warren writes, "How one wishes to be, who one wishes to be, to what one aspires, what one believes in—all of these constitute the mature ego ideal" (1996, 105). For the narrator in "Custodial Care," this process unfolds during her college search but is expressed immaturely in her longing to attain magically a more fully formed sense of self: *"With my mind made up, I breathed a sigh of relief—everything would fall into place, and I wouldn't have to worry anymore."*

When late adolescents come to our offices for treatment, they often are in distress—or causing someone else distress—because of their difficulty in moving forward. This disruption is rooted in the collision of their intrapsychic need to separate from parents and the deeper and more enduring need to internalize their parents. It is only when both of these two opposing needs are satisfied that fully mature relationships can take hold. Deanna Holtzman and Nancy Kulish (2003) maintain that these struggles inevitably revolve around an intertwining of sexuality and aggression, with the resultant fear that the aggression will be punished by withdrawal of the mother's love.

The developmental period that spans late adolescence and young adulthood is characterized by a powerful reconfiguration of identity that begins with the processes of separation and individuation as well as the reactivation of childhood Oedipal conflicts and that ends with the hatching of an independent adult. David Brockman describes this time period as "the most exciting of all phases of development. . . . The monumental developmental tasks of integration, synthesis, and cohesion of multiple areas of personality result in a 'strikingly observable settling down' into a chosen career, searching for and finding a suitable partner with whom to achieve physical and emotional intimacy, mastery of the drives, fitting in with a social group identity, and the consequent establishment of clearly defined sexual and gender identities" (2003, 257).

The resolution of the Oedipal conflict and the formation of a stable identity allows the late adolescent to achieve a committed relationship, to dedicate himself or herself to a career, or to pursue a creative passion. What begins as a tentative "moving away" from the family of origin after high school is, when resolved, a "movement toward" a secure adult identity and a rich life with others and within oneself.

12 NESTLED

A woman ponders the meaning of motherhood.

I am on my hands and knees on the pavement outside of the entrance to the hospital. My husband has gone to fetch a wheelchair. The world is perfectly still around me, and I can feel the baby coming. I breathe in and out, and in that moment there is nothing but me and my baby, pushing her way through the light of day.

Suddenly there is bustle all around me, and I am being lifted onto a stretcher and wheeled into the delivery room, where within moments Caitlin slides out of my womb. She gazes at the room with wide, calm eyes and a benign expression that tells me she is ready for anything.

Caitlin was born shortly before New Year's Eve. The hospital was crowded, and the nursing staff moved the two of us into a small room way in the back. From the tiny window above my bed, I could just see the New Year's fireworks blazing across the rooftops. For much of the time that we were in the hospital, Caitlin nestled close to me. There was something vital about another heartbeat keeping rhythm and time with my own. While she slept, I drank her in. I studied her miniature features, her clear dark eyes and perfect mouth, and I fell permanently under her spell.

Sleeping with her at my side felt sweet and natural, so I continued to bring her into our bed once we were home. I was exhausted, and it was easier for me to have Caitlin right there when she needed to nurse. So Caitlin's crib went untouched, never to be slept in. In truth, sleeping with Caitlin was profoundly comforting not just to her, but to me. The way she snuggled in, emanating warmth and love, satisfied something in me that always felt a little unsettled in the dark.

As Caitlin grew older, she slept more fitfully and kicked in her sleep, awakening us nightly. We got rid of the crib and bought a bed for her. The bed, however, held no attraction for her. Each night Caitlin would call for me to come and get her, and, half-asleep, I would stumble down the hallway and take her back to our room. Once ensconced in our bed, she would burrow under the covers with a contented sigh and fall instantly asleep. To me, it was a matter of her feeling secure. I knew because I had felt that way myself.

However, I did wonder whether I was indulging something in Caitlin that was better dealt with head-on. I began to question my choices as a parent. Hadn't I read all the expert advice about teaching your child to fall asleep in her own bed and sleep there through the night? Of course I had, being one of those experts myself, yet I wasn't ready to draw what now felt a line in the sand. It was as if the mother part of my brain was not communicating with the therapist part of my brain. I didn't know what to do. All I had to go on was my gut sense that this was what she needed. I told myself that she would stop sleeping in our bed when she was ready. Should I have worried more?

Development gradually worked its wonders and solved the dilemma in its own time. Caitlin no longer called me in the night to come and get her. Sometimes, when she had a bad dream, I would still hear her soft footsteps pattering down the hall as she would run into our room as fast as she could, seeking the warm cocoon of our bed. The sound of her padded feet was completely recognizable and made me smile. But still I worried, wondering whether I was inadvertently reinforcing Caitlin's nighttime habit.

The answer came unbidden to me one morning. There had been a fierce storm the night before. When the alarm rang, I pulled the covers up, hoping to capture the last whiff of sleep before it fell away. The day ahead promised to be busy and full, and I wanted to sleep just a little longer. Just then I felt Caitlin shift under the covers beside me. In a moment, she popped her head up with a dazzling smile. "Ahhh," she crooned, "warm and cozy." Then she wriggled her body around, creating a little nest for herself, and promptly plopped back to sleep. I knew finally that although she left her own bed out of ordinary nighttime fears, she was drawn, as I was, to the warmth that enveloped us both. It was all the reassurance I needed to know my intuition had not led me astray.

Analysts Reflect on Motherhood as a Developmental Phase

Mothers feature prominently in the collective unconscious and conscious mind: in the consulting room, in literature and drama, in tragedy and in humor. Take this familiar joke: A man walks into his psychiatrist's office and breathlessly announces, "I had a major breakthrough last night! I realized I've been thinking of you just like my mother! I was so excited to tell you that as soon as I woke up this morning, I got ready, grabbed a Coke and a donut for breakfast, and rushed here to tell you!" The psychiatrist peers at him over her glasses, frowning deeply, and then replies, "You call that breakfast?" The story resonates with a universal experience of being mothered: that peculiar blend of fierce love, pride, and hovering anxiety motivated by the maternal instinct to protect and preserve the offspring—an anxiety that unfortunately can also run the risk of rendering an otherwise adequate mother tone-deaf to the nuances of a child's experience, so focused is she on the care and keeping of her young.

In Western thought and literature, mothers are understood to be children's first and most passionate love object. But what of the mother's experience? In our contemporary middle-class culture, children are at the epicenter—we are preoccupied with providing the most enriched developmental experience, leaving little to chance. The 1950s image of June Cleaver, providing unobtrusive sustenance and comfort, has given way to the "soccer mom" or "helicopter parent," whose primary identity is organized around her child's accomplishments and activities.

A deeper view of the experience of motherhood can be gained by considering the psychological and developmental meaning of becoming a mother and raising a child. In the early days of Freudian theory, psychoanalysts viewed having a baby as a replacement for the woman's "deficient" anatomy. In this nineteenth- and early-twentieth-century view, fantasies of pregnancy and birth were understood as unconscious compensation for lacking a penis or as a displacement for the woman's wish to have a baby with her father. Freud wrote, "It is a common usage to speak of a baby as a 'gift.' The more frequent expression is that the woman has 'given' the man a baby; but in the usage of the unconscious equal attention is justly paid to the other aspect of the relation, namely, to the woman having 'received' the baby as a gift from the man" ([1918] 1955b, 82).

Later in the twentieth century, psychotherapists began to gain a deeper understanding of female development and psychology. Psychoanalyst Helene Deutsch, writing in midcentury, shifted the emphasis away from the idea that having a baby is reparative. Deutsch viewed women to be essentially "receptive," which she saw as a primary feminine quality that forms the basis of motherhood. Eva Lester and Malkah Notman, referring to Deutsch, state that motherhood was believed to be "the fulfillment of the woman's most powerful and guiding wish" (1986, 357). This line of thinking can be seen as a profound shift in psychodynamic thought: for the first time, a woman theorist had defined women's emotional and psychological development in its own right rather than looking at it through a male-focused lens. In Deutsch's view, women's emotional development progressed along a distinctly different path than that of men, a view that many but not all contemporary theorists shared.

For many women, pregnancy and early motherhood provide an experience of fulfillment and pleasure that can seem both novel and deeply familiar. Samuel Ritvo writes that "as Freud said, nothing brings greater pleasure and satisfaction than the fulfillment of an old wish or dream. Many women find [motherhood] the most moving, enriching and profound experience of their lives" (1976, 136).

The earliest expression of the desire to nurture can be seen in the play of toddlers and young children. It is an early theme in the symbolic play of boys and girls—for example, feeding and comforting a baby doll. Themes of nurturance are then reworked throughout development in both unconscious (i.e., fantasy of being given a baby by the father) and conscious (i.e., caring for a younger sibling, being a mother's helper) ways. These themes can be thought of as the arc of a developmental trajectory that has at its base instinctive nurturing fantasies and at its culmination the fulfillment of a desire for generativity. Many women, for a variety of reasons, do not have children, but they nonetheless find equally significant pathways toward fulfillment and satisfaction.

The mother's attachment to her new infant is made up of several intertwining psychological strands: the fulfillment of her early desires and idealizations, her narcissistic wishes, her conflicted feelings about separation and individuation, her reworking of important childhood relationships, and her childhood identification with her own mother. In "Nestled," the writer presents interwoven experiences that lay the groundwork for the relationship between mother and infant: *While she slept, I drank her in. I studied her miniature features, her clear dark eyes and flawless mouth, and I fell permanently under her spell.*

These early moments between the mother and infant capture the "falling in love" quality that can accompany birth and that set the stage for what D. W. Winnicott referred to as "primary maternal preoccupation." Winnicott beautifully described this state: "Towards the end of the pregnancy and for a few weeks after the birth of a child the mother is preoccupied with (or better, 'given over to') the care of her baby, which at first seems like a part of herself; moreover she is very much identified with the baby and knows quite well what the baby is feeling like. For this she uses her own experiences as a baby. In this way the mother is herself in a dependent state, and vulnerable" ([1958] 1965b, 85).

This maternal preoccupation has tremendous benefit for the infant, who is completely dependent on the parent to feed, protect, and care for her. The baby's earliest experiences of parental responsiveness thus form the basis of later secure attachment.

As the writer in the story illustrates, this period is as important to the mother as to the baby. For the mother, bonding with her infant establishes a new phase in her own development, one that may result in a clash between her early and unresolved conflicts and the present-day demands and expectations on her. Inner turmoil may increase the mother's stress at a time when she is feeling vulnerable and under the sway of her own idealized expectations of motherhood. The confluence of emotional, biological, and hormonal strains with life demands and fatigue can set the stage for emotional tension, postpartum depression, conflicts with partners, and a diminished sense of maternal adequacy.

We now understand that the bond between mother and child possesses profound biological and neurological components, which are facilitated by the surge of hormones that initiate labor, produce lactation, and powerfully impact the mother's body and psyche during those early months. In the early days and weeks after the birth of the infant, a new mother finds herself in a protective, secure shell that envelops her and her baby. As the writer of the story describes, *"The world is perfectly still around me, and I can feel the baby coming. I breathe in and out, and in that moment there is nothing but me and my baby, pushing her way through to the light of day."*

The interconnected functions of biology, neurology, and psychology work in synchrony to establish the mother and newborn as a uniquely focused and tightly bound unit. Psychotherapists describe this relationship as one in which the dependent newborn requires that her mother "hold her in mind" at all times, anticipating her needs with a minimum of frustration and delay. In fact, it has been established that new mothers are biologically primed to accomplish this. The same hormone, oxytocin, that is responsible for onset of labor and delivery also serves to heighten maternal attachment and caretaking (Bartlett 2005).

For most mothers—and, of course, for fathers, too—children provide a source of significant narcissistic gratification. Mothers are filled with many powerful wishes and fantasies of what their children will become, who they will resemble, what needs they will fulfill, what accomplishments they will achieve, but they are also filled with inevitable fears and dreads. As psychotherapists, we understand these fantasies and fears to be projections—aspects of oneself or one's internal world that are projected onto one's child. There is an aspect of the maternal tie that is powerful, instinctive, and driven by feelings of possessive merger.

The mother's struggle to balance, on the one hand, her wish to gratify her own fantasies through her child and, on the other, her capacity to accept her child's individuality sets the stage for a lifelong dance between mother and child. This conflict is revisited and reworked throughout the course of the mother–child relationship.

The mother's relationship with her infant can also be freighted with images from the mother's prior experience of being mothered and contains her future hopes for a relationship that may be similar or different from what she experienced previously. As Selma Fraiberg, Edna Adelson, and Vivian Shapiro point out, "In every nursery there are ghosts. They are the visitors from the unremembered past of the parents, the uninvited guests at the christening. Under favorable circumstances, these unfriendly and unbidden spirits are banished from the nursery and return to their subterranean dwelling place. The baby makes his own imperative claim upon parental love and, in strict analogy with the fairy-tales, the bonds of love protect the child and his parents against the intruders, the malevolent ghosts" (1975, 387).

Fraiberg and her colleagues describe the mother who has experienced trauma in her own childhood. They suggest that if the mother is able to gain access to her own early disappointments or childhood trauma, she will be able to avoid repeating those traumatic object relationships with her child. Doing so, however, is not easy. The mother's repression and disavowal of her feelings about her childhood trauma put her at great risk for repeating it in the relationship with her own child.

In the late 1950s, Therese Benedek suggested that parenthood provides an opportunity for the mother to rework early traumatic aspects of her own infancy and childhood through her connection with her child. Parenthood can thereby serve to unstick developmental fixations and regressions and to allow a new maturational unfolding for the mother. Benedek believed motherhood can best be understood as its own developmental period—one that represents for the mother the possibility of resolving earlier conflicts and achieving greater personality integration: "The study of the psychodynamic processes of the female reproductive function reveals that the drive organization, which motivates motherhood and the activities of mothering, maintains dynamic communication between mother and child and leads to changes not only in the infant but in the mother as well. Thus there are reciprocal ego developments. In the infant, through the introjection of good mother = good self, the infant develops confidence. In the mother, through introjection of good-thriving-infant = good-mother-self, the mother achieves a new integration in her personality" (1959, 393). The notion that the mother–child relationship promotes the development of both members of the dyad represents a significant advance in psychoanalytic thinking about women.

Elizabeth Loewald reminds us how the developmental changes about which Benedek spoke actually take place. She writes that "the good mothering of her child returns to the mother, both through identification with him and through the sense of her own reliability in meeting needs, to deepen her confidence in her own goodness." Loewald suggests that for new mothers the baby is a kind of "transitional object" and that the "baby has actually, as yet, developed few clear characteristics which are *his*, as distinct from projections of someone else's. He *is* in part an 'illusory experience'—of very great value" (1982, 400, 397, emphasis in original). The mother's early experience of the baby is thus as a highly treasured "object" with whom she can experience aspects of love and hate, sameness and separateness, holding on and letting go, all within the context of the mother–child bond.

As the baby matures, if the relationship between mother and infant is a good enough one, the "transitional" object relationship will be gradually transformed into a "real" relationship with a "real" baby. This real baby is a person in his own right who brings to the relationship the forcefulness of his own personality as well as all his other capacities. When the developmental process between mother and infant goes awry—because of difficulties on the part of either mother or infant—the mother may struggle to remain empathically attuned and responsive to her child. A young mother overwhelmed with fatigue and stress, for example, may mistakenly experience her newborn's distress as a sign of rejection or hate.

In describing the complex emotional field that envelops mother and child, Winnicott (1969) called attention to the mother's capacity to endure her own conflicted feelings toward her baby as the infant becomes an increasingly real, authentic, and separate "other." In the earliest moments of an infant's development, it can be said that mother and baby are wrapped together in a cocoon of sorts—what Margaret Mahler (1972) refers to as the "symbiotic phase" of development. As the author of the story writes, *"Caitlin nestled close to me. There was something vital about another heartbeat keeping rhythm and time with my own."* Thus, the mother's primary focus is trained on attuning and responding to the subtle shifts in the baby's state, intuitively seeking to achieve a general state of calm, consistent well-being, or what Winnicott referred to as "going-on-being."

As the baby "wakes up" to the world, growing increasingly alert, active, curious, and competent, the physical bonds of attachment must stretch to meet his increasing need for movement. Mahler (1972) emphasizes the importance of this period for the child's emerging awareness of himself in the world. She points out that, for the toddler, the readiness to separate from the mother and increasingly to explore the world on his own coincides with a period of tremendous cognitive growth. Such a process leaves the child in a psychological bind of sorts. On one hand, he seeks to pull away, but as he does, he experiences an intensification of his need for the reassurance of a close-by, steadying maternal presence. In the face of the child's push-and-pull, the mother is faced with her own dilemma. As Mahler notes, "The toddler's renewed active wooing and demand for his mother's constant participation seems to her contradictory. . . . During this subphase [rapprochement] some mothers cannot accept the child's demandingness; others are troubled by the fact that the child is becoming increasingly independent and separate" (1972, 494).

Although focused on the child's developmental progression toward a more autonomous sense of self, Mahler brings to the foreground the mother's experience of her child's growing independence. As both mother and baby emerge from the "cocoon" of early infancy, where the mother's primary maternal function was to provide regulation, soothing, and comfort, the mother must now learn to adapt to the young child's push-and-pull toward autonomy, his shifting back and forth between, on the one hand, movement toward self-reliance and, on the other, a more regressive pull. Mahler points out that for some mothers the regressive pull can seem overly demanding or babyish, whereas for others who may experience a need to hold on to the baby a bit longer, the strivings for autonomy can feel distressing.

This dynamic endures throughout development: it is a dance of separation where both partners, depending on internal shifts and readiness for separation, move closer to or farther from each other, sometimes in tune with one another, at other times completely out of step. As Winnicott's "good enough" mothering suggests, perfect attunement between mother and child is neither possible nor ideal. Rather, the relationship is in an ongoing process of realignment, re-attunement, and repair. Indeed, Winnicott (1971) pointed out that some frustration—what he referred to as "an optimal level of frustration"—allows for the infant's development to unfold. Without such frustration, he queried, where is the impetus for change? A degree of frustration motivates the infant to strive toward growth and change, propelling him toward increasing motility—grasping, reaching, crawling, and walking—and toward language acquisition, from babbling to speech.

What, though, becomes of the mother's frustration when her own needs go unmet? For her, the development process is a continuous striving for balance between maintaining her own internal equilibrium and simultaneously remaining attuned to her infant's needs. At times, both her needs and her infant's needs line up in ways that are in harmony; at other times, they can be disruptive to one or the other of the pair. As the mother of our story muses, *"The way she snuggled in, emanating warmth and love, satisfied something in me that always felt a little unsettled in the dark."* Although her child's need for physical closeness and comfort at night awakened her own early longings, she ultimately was able to bring into focus her daughter's experience and rely on her own steady maternal function.

PART THREE
Technique

13 GRAHAM CRACKERS

A little boy crumbles his snack and opens a door to treatment.

Joey was my first child therapy patient, and his history was emptier, sadder, and more deprived than any seven-year-old's should ever be. Unfortunately, his was a familiar story at the clinic where I trained—families torn apart by poverty, violence, and substance abuse. Joey's father had abandoned him, and his mother was in jail. When there was no family left to care for Joey and his two younger sisters, they were removed to temporary shelter. Their social worker found them a spot with Mrs. Moore, who was an experienced and competent foster parent. Following his placement there, Joey was withdrawn and sullen. He rarely played or spoke to anyone. He would cling to Mrs. Moore silently but fiercely.

When I met with Mrs. Moore, she dutifully—but dubiously—promised to truck all three children to the clinic every week. She was a tired, skeptical, and overburdened woman who regarded me—and the whole clinic, filled as it was with young, earnest, well-intentioned graduate students—through half-lidded eyes. "These foster kids, you know . . . ," she complained wearily, "Joey won't even talk to me. He just sits and sulks." She rolled her eyes and sighed.

I found myself doubting whether she would actually bring the children to their first session. However, on the appointed day, there they all were in the waiting room. Mrs. Moore was squeezed into a too low, too small waiting-room chair, with three young children draped around her, seemingly unaware of where their own bodies ended and hers began. Two other young therapists and I introduced ourselves to the children and invited them to accompany us for juice and graham crackers, as was the custom in our clinic.

Joey, clutching tightly to his food, walked silently a pace or two behind me to the consulting room. The clinic space was scarce, and the room we were assigned was oddly shaped and scantily furnished, but toys of all kinds lined the shelves, and an easel was propped open beside the window. Joey slid silently into a chair at the table, and I sat across from him and smiled. He carefully spread out a napkin and his graham crackers. Despite my awkward novice attempts to strike up a conversation, he said nothing and avoided my gaze. I could hear the clock ticking loudly and felt myself growing hot and anxious as I searched my mind for something to say.

I eventually stopped trying to find a topic that would get his attention, and I just settled in to watch him quietly. He became engrossed in breaking the crackers into tiny crumbs and piling them in his napkin. Minutes ticked by as he crumbled and crumbled. "Aren't you going to eat those?" I asked brightly. He didn't answer. He just kept crumbling and piling. I thought, How can I ever overcome the seemingly insurmountable distance between us?

I felt helpless, mesmerized by the ticking minutes and the tiny crumbs. I watched until he finally crumbled the very last tiny bit of his very last cracker. Now there was a heap of crumbs on the napkin in front of him. His red T-shirt was covered in crumbs, and bits of cracker clung to his hair, chin, and fingers. Together we gazed at the pile. When he glanced my way, I remarked, "Huh . . . that's pretty big." With wide eyes and a huge smile, he shouted, "Now see, I have a HUNDRED!" With equal delight, I shouted, "Yes, you have a whole MOUNTAIN!" The laughter erupted from both of us, and right then and there I knew our work together had launched.

Analysts Reflect on Beginning the Treatment

One of the most exciting aspects of our work as psychotherapists is the element of surprise. With new and old patients alike, there is a powerful sense of expectancy that comes from not knowing what is about to unfold. A long-term patient may startle us with a new insight, a new mood, or even an out-of-character pair of shoes. In a session with one of our patients, the analyst's thoughts wandered to her patient's hair, which she had worn in the same style for many years. The analyst pictured her with a softer, more feminine hairstyle. In retrospect, she may have sensed something shifting, loosening in the patient. A few weeks later the patient appeared with her hair pulled away from her face and tied in an attractive knot. The analyst was surprised both by this dramatic shift and by the way she had unconsciously signaled it to the patient weeks earlier.

As with Joey, the content of a first meeting with a patient may contain some kernel of insight that later proves to be important. Psychoanalyst Ted Jacobs describes such a first session:

A colleague of some renown, who, though large in reputation, was extremely small of stature, received a telephone call from a man who wanted a consultation. The appointment was made, and at the arranged time the new patient arrived. About to enter the waiting room to greet him, the analyst suddenly stopped at the threshold and, momentarily, stood transfixed. There in front of him was a Paul Bunyan of a figure, fully six feet, eight inches in height, weighing perhaps 260 pounds, and wearing cowboy boots and a ten-gallon hat. For several more seconds the analyst looked at him in silence. Then, with a shrug of his shoulders and a resigned gesture, he motioned toward his office. "Come on in, anyway," he said. (1986, 289)

Jacobs points out that transference begins within the first moments of the encounter and is thereupon present and active throughout the entire course of therapy. We would assert, however, that the transference actually begins prior to the first meeting or at the initial contact with the patient. Even after a brief conversation, therapist and patient have already begun to form an image of each other, which they bring to the subsequent session.

This is true with Joey. The therapist comes to the initial meeting with some knowledge about the patient that may influence her initial assessment. She knows the child's sad history and even wonders whether the therapy will actually take place. She worries whether she can make meaningful contact: *Two other young therapists and I introduced ourselves to the children and invited them to accompany us for juice and graham crackers, as was the custom in our clinic.* Her goal in this first meeting is to convey something important to Joey: here is a place where you can feel safe and where you can count on getting something that you need. However, as in this story, a huge distance must often be traversed in order to arrive at such an understanding.

What takes place in the initial session often sets the stage for the nature of the transference and countertransference that will unfold later. Phyllis Meadow has written about what she hopes to convey in the initial session: "I hope to let [the patient] know my willingness to work with him, that I intend to consider his views and to cooperate with his requests. In the initial stage of treatment the analyst's cooperative attitude may be a new experience for the patient, and as the sessions continue communication of this cooperative attitude may be limited by the patient's intolerance for cooperation" (1990, 4).

At the beginning of treatment, the patient often demonstrates those dynamics—both conscious and unconscious—that will become an important part of the treatment, although we may not yet understand them. These dynamics may be conveyed verbally, embedded in the material, or acted out in the session. For example, a mother once made a first appointment to evaluate her young child. She was eager to come in as soon as possible, but more than halfway through the planned time she and the child had still not appeared. Ten minutes before the end of the session, the door to the waiting room burst open, and a harried-looking woman rushed in with her little boy. Looking at the therapist, she mouthed, "Just a minute!" She dragged her son into the bathroom and soon reemerged with a very dirty-looking boy wearing nothing but sneakers! This time his mother mouthed to the therapist, "Accident!" as she sat on the floor beside him. She quickly pulled off his shoes and unceremoniously dumped a bucket's worth of sand onto the middle of the carpet. She then pulled clean clothes from her Mary Poppins–like bag and proceeded to dress him and tidy him up. "Well," the therapist thought, "I guess I've seen just about all there is for me to see, and with five minutes of the session left to spare!"

In a process that parallels what happens for the therapist, the patient arrives at the first meeting with a mix of emotions and expectations. Many patients talk about the difficulty they have experienced finding a therapist. They may have tried to interview the therapist over the phone, asking questions such as "What is your style?" "How do you like to work?" and "Have you treated many people with my type of problem before?" Therapists listen for the underlying meaning hidden within such questions: "Can you help me?" and "Will I be able to trust you?"

On one occasion, when a therapist greeted a potential patient at the door, the patient took one look and said, "Sorry, I really don't think this will work. But I guess I'm here; I'll come in anyway." During the course of the hour, the therapist learned that she was the latest in a long line of therapists that the patient had deemed unsuitable. In this case, the patient did not return. In another of our practices, a patient arrived at the initial meeting, looked the therapist up and down, and remarked, "Oh . . . no . . . I don't think this will work." But from this unlikely beginning, that patient subsequently embarked on a successful treatment (Malawista and Malawista 1999, 24).

Whether treatment is eventually successful or not, the therapist's job is to provide a secure and predictable frame for the patient as he embarks on a journey of self-discovery. Just as surprise can produce delight, however, it can also overwhelm, engulf, or render one helpless. The patient must come to rely on the therapist to create a safe and predictable "holding environment" that can withstand whatever happens next. In the case of the little boy standing stark naked, the therapist hoped to convey a sense of ease and unflappability so that the chaos of the moment did not overwhelm them both. As Meadow writes, "I want to enter the session relaxed, that is, free enough of distractions so that I can be interested in what the patient wants to talk about. However, I don't want to be overly interested— I don't want to lean forward in my seat or hang on the person's every word" (1990, 10).

The physical space that we as therapists create in our offices is important. Our workspaces need to address internal/emotional factors—Does the environment encourage reflection?—and external factors, such as light and sound, privacy and safety. These factors are especially important for patients who are highly sensitive to subtle changes.

For child and adult patients alike, the therapeutic space and other nonverbal signals have a significant impact on the beginning of the treatment. It is equally important that the room feel safe and inviting. For a child, a play therapy room that contains fragile and easily breakable objects may subtly derail the beginning of the treatment, unwittingly conveying to the child, "Be careful where you go and what you do when you come here." This sense of restraint may invoke unconsciously the child's restrictive and harsh superego defense mechanisms. But even when the therapy room is equipped with toys to facilitate and encourage imaginative play, it is important not to overwhelm or overstimulate the child.

Instead of evoking the predictable and at times punitive responses of the adults in a child's life—such as parents and teachers who attempt to teach self-control—the therapist tries to respond to the child with interest, curiosity, and respect. By allowing Joey to play with his food, for example, the therapist sets the stage for a moment of genuine contact. She notes, *"Now there was a heap of crumbs on the napkin in front of him. His red T-shirt was covered in crumbs, and bits of cracker clung to his hair, chin, and fingers. Together we gazed at the pile. When he glanced my way, I remarked, 'Huh . . . that's pretty big.' With wide eyes and a huge smile, he shouted, 'Now see, I have a HUNDRED!'"* In this moment, the therapist glimpses what is to become a meaningful theme in the course of Joey's therapy. Turning the crackers into a "mountain," Joey displays something of his resilience in the face of deprivation. He also shows that he can establish a potentially meaningful connection with his therapist, whom he sees as a possible source of good and plentiful supplies—internal resources that he most definitely needs.

As Meadow rightly points out, the initial session brings into the foreground the rearousal of the patient's early unmet needs and longings. However, the therapist's emotions are also in play. Meadow describes this two-person dance thus: "From the first contacts with the patient, [the therapist] is also responding to feelings the patient arouses within her. The response is a silent response. She will use most of her feelings later in the treatment. . . . [T]here is not much room for interpretation so far and there is not much value in exposing my own personality, thoughts, or feelings" (1990, 9).

In "Graham Crackers," the therapist's attention to her own initial responses to the patient will eventually suggest important themes that will emerge in the treatment: *"I could hear the clock ticking loudly and felt myself growing hot and anxious as I searched my mind for something to say. . . . [H]ow can I ever overcome the insurmountable distance between us? I felt helpless, mesmerized by the ticking minutes and the tiny crumbs."* In this early, nonverbal exchange, the therapist's experience of sitting with her young patient gives her access to this child's neediness and loneliness. This access comes to the therapist through her awareness of her own yearnings for connection and her excruciating feelings of aloneness in the presence of this silent, enigmatic young boy. Her wishes to understand her patient and to have a positive impact on his young life are already mingled with her doubts and feelings of sadness in the face of her patient's history of disruption and loss. Thus, in this opening phase of treatment, we see the outlines of the transference and countertransference that will likely unfold over the course of the weeks and months to come.

The beginning of treatment establishes a therapeutic frame or structure within which the work between therapist and patient can unfold. Fees are established, session hours are agreed upon, and vacation policies are discussed. This "regulating effect" essentially defines the *analytic frame*, a term that applies equally well to psychoanalysis and psychotherapy. A frame, of course, marks a boundary. Therapy sessions are thereby safely contained within predictable boundaries that are unvarying and unlike any other experience in the patient's life. Only within such clearly delineated parameters can the work of psychotherapy unfold. The frame conveys to the patient the idea that it is safe to examine one's internal world and that fantasies, conflicts, intense emotions, and traumatic memories will be acknowledged within that frame. Patients express their feelings, and therapists listen, try to understand, offer interpretations, and, to the degree possible, refrain from acting in a manner that disrupts this process. This model of a therapeutic frame is, of course, an ideal that we strive for and within which any deviations are important to identify and address (see chapter 19 for discussion of boundary violations).

For a child patient who is likely not involved in establishing fees or schedules, the essential analytic frame has to do with the continuity and predictability of the sessions. The therapeutic frame contains the steady and accepting presence of the child therapist. Each session, for example, has a clearly marked beginning and end. Implicit and explicit agreements exist between therapist and patient concerning confidentiality, safety, mutual respect, and autonomy. In "Graham Crackers," the offering of juice and crackers, the walk down the hall, the entering into the clinic room, all convey to Joey, "Here is where we will do our work together, with patience, empathy, and consistency. And here is where our work each week comes to a safe and predictable end."

Freud ([1913] 1955g) emphasized that the work of therapy unfolds within the context of a two-person relationship and that the beginning of the treatment must be devoted to developing a "rapport" with the patient rather than to trying to create change. In "Graham Crackers," the therapist works to understand her young patient, to establish contact, to discover the meanings that lie hidden within his silent actions. The patient, in his intensity and focus, signals unconsciously to the therapist, "This is important to me; something important is happening here." Through her comment on the big pile of crumbs, the therapist mirrors that awareness, implying, "I see you've created something important here, something we'll come to understand together over time." Thus, from day one the therapeutic dyad develops a shared language, within which these important communications can be deciphered.

Evelyn Liegner (1977) points out that although many of Freud's early ideas regarding the beginning of a treatment remain the same, the conventions of modern-day psychotherapy and psychoanalysis have changed. She contrasts a list of "rules" that reflect classical analytic technique with a list of "rules" that are more reflective of contemporary psychodynamic thought. She shows how certain fundamental ways of thinking about treatment have remained unchanged, whereas others have markedly shifted. Liegner highlights a significant trend in modern psychotherapy that emphasizes the partnership between the therapist and the patient. Within this pairing, the therapist invites the patient to create a relationship that is very different from those in their outside lives. For Joey, therapy is an environment in which he is permitted to use his food as a vehicle to display a highly meaningful aspect of his internal world.

The early sessions of psychotherapy let the patient know that the rules of treatment are not the rules of home or workplace. They provide essential data, hint at what is to come, and establish a rhythm between patient and therapist that will become deeper and more complex over time. With the frame firmly established, therapist and patient soon begin to recognize themes that recur and to note their variations. This is the beginning of a shared language that has already begun to develop as a little boy walks down a hallway clutching his graham crackers.

14 IN MY EYES

A silent boy finds safety in his treatment and thus finds his voice.

When I was in graduate school, I was pleased to get the chance to work in a therapeutic nursery. There, young students like me could treat children with a variety of developmental disorders. As students, we had the luxury of time. We worked with child patients over many months and years, having ample time to learn from the school's senior faculty. We also had the opportunity to observe children in their classrooms. It was a rich experience and unlike anything else in my training. I was as hungry for knowledge as my patient, Petie, was for my attention.

Petie was a sweet, tow-headed four-year-old who had been referred to the therapeutic nursery for significant developmental delays. Petie spoke readily at home but would not utter a word outside of the house. Teachers and staff wondered whether the cause was a developmental glitch, selective mutism, a traumatic response, a means of control, or perhaps acute social anxiety. Knowing he was to be assigned to me for therapy, I listened carefully when Petie was discussed in our clinical conference. I wondered how I could possibly make contact with this doe-eyed, silent little boy.

I first met Petie in his classroom. He was playing by himself, assembling large blocks in a fairly random manner and scooting them across the floor like cars without wheels. I watched him for a while then sat down on the floor and picked up a block of my own. I, too, shot blocks across the floor, then almost under my breath I murmured, "Zoom, zoom." Petie stopped his play momentarily. He glanced at me and smiled slightly. Then he ducked his head down and resumed what he was doing. The second time I saw Petie, he was again in his classroom. That was the one place where I knew he felt comfortable. On my third visit, I brought Petie to the play therapy room, after explaining to him that we were going to get to know each other and see each other three times a week. I told him that I had a room with lots of toys for him to use. He came with me willingly, putting his small, warm fist into my outreached palm.

When I met Petie's mother at the clinic, she told me that Petie freely prattled away at home but had never spoken to anyone else. She was somewhat suspicious of therapy and asked several questions about how it worked. I tried to explain the open-ended, exploratory method of play therapy to her. Finally, I told her that I would be observing her son and learning about him and his feelings while we played. She shrugged her permission but hinted that I was probably wasting my time because Petie would not talk to me. Nevertheless, I hoped that he would.

So Petie and I played. At first, I'd sit near him on the floor and mirror his actions. His play was repetitive and stilted—just a lot of back and forth with toys. We mostly sat in silence unless I could think of words or sounds to accompany his actions.

I'd come for him three days a week. Petie always seemed happy to see me. Playing together, Petie and I seemed to exist in a silent but pleasant bubble. The lack of words started to feel irrelevant; the play became fun. Petie began to seem more connected to me. The shift was subtle, like the glance he'd give me when we started a new game, as if inviting me to join. In our play, I would try to mirror his movements, to give words to the expressions I thought I saw flitting across his face.

Things changed more when we moved to a new therapy space. The room was long and narrow, and it was outfitted with a large file cabinet with oversize drawers and a huge blue ball. The ball seemed to thrill Petie. In fact, it was the first time I ever heard the sound of his voice: a warm, delighted guffaw came straight from his belly and burst into our bubble world.

A ritual soon emerged. As Petie and I approached the playroom, he would yell out, "Ball!" Once the door closed behind us, he'd pounce on the ball with glee. He'd roll on top of it again and again until he was at the far end of the room. I sat facing him at the other end of the room, and then we'd roll the ball back and forth between us. I'd shout, "Here it comes, Petie!" and he'd reply, "Ball!" and then eventually, "Ball! Comes!" and still later, "Ball! Comes! Petie!" He'd throw back his head and laugh, and I realized that we were having our first conversation.

After a while, Petie discovered the bottom drawer of the file cabinet. It became his magic disappearing box. He'd place a toy or a book or even his hat in the drawer. Then, with a bang, he'd roll the drawer shut, and the hunt would begin. I'd furrow my brow and ask, "Petie, where did it go?" This query would lead to highly excited play. Petie would shake his head with silent laughter, sometimes shouting out "No!" as I searched in all the wrong places. Finally, I'd peek inside the drawer, and Petie would yell "Ha!" as I'd dig out the buried treasure.

One day Petie wore his winter jacket to our session. He carefully laid it inside the drawer. The next day he again hid his jacket, this time adding his hat and mittens. For several sessions, Petie solemnly laid down pieces of himself as if laying claim to this space. One time he wanted to take off his shirt and place that in the drawer, too, but I intervened, and the shirt stayed on. He repeated this ritual again and again, adding new elements, so that it took up much of the first half of the session. This act was no longer a ritual in preparation for the play; it had become the play itself. So absorbed was he in laying out each article of clothing, smoothing it down, then smoothing it over once more, that he didn't seem aware of the other toys anymore. I felt something building, but I didn't know what.

The day before I was to leave for two weeks, I learned something about the intensity that this ritual had taken on. On his way to the therapy room, Petie clutched the calendar I had made for him a few weeks earlier—my effort to show him concretely that I'd be away, but that I'd come back. Ever so slowly Petie laid his jacket, hat, and gloves in the drawer, patting them and smoothing them down tenderly. He gazed into the drawer for several long minutes while I watched. Then he carefully took off his shoes and climbed into the drawer himself. I held my breath, torn. I worried about his safety—What if the cabinet collapsed with his weight? What if his fingers got caught?—but my instinct told me not to intervene. I felt mesmerized by the intensity of his actions. I could sense his yearning to be in that small, safe space—I saw it as an expression of his desire to be held, to be protected and swaddled. It was as though he had built himself a nest. In this way, on the eve of my vacation he found a way to show me that I was integral in creating the sense of containment he was seeking.

Over time, Petie's play continued to expand, as did his language, his emotional range, and his relationship with me. In the classroom, he grew more confident, and his teachers were delighted, too, when they were allowed access into his world. He still lagged behind his peers in many aspects of his development, but he had been transformed from a silent, inaccessible child into an exuberant little boy who was eager to engage in the world around him.

His teachers and I worked with Petie for several years. Petie was eventually ready to leave the therapeutic nursery and move on to elementary school. Sadly, it was time to end our play therapy. I worked hard with Petie, using every way I could think of to convey to him that our good-bye day was coming. We made books and calendars, but I still didn't know if he grasped the meaning of our impending termination.

On the day of our last session, Petie and I sat together on the floor. I was still unsure whether he really understood that our therapy was ending. We leafed through the pages of our good-bye book, with pictures we had drawn to tell the story of our time together. There were pictures of the blocks and cars and of the big blue ball. We looked at pictures of the two of us in the therapy room and even of the file cabinet.

Then Petie suddenly set the book aside and sat facing me, kneeling on the floor so that our knees touched, and he stared at me. I was caught off-guard. I'd grown accustomed to the rhythm of our play, and this was different. I wasn't sure what to say, so I waited. Petie stared at me and then leaned forward, closer and closer, until our faces were only inches apart. He peered at me intently. The closeness felt strange and uncomfortable. I thought, "Is he going to kiss me?" But he didn't. He just kept staring a moment longer. Then he spoke, his voice filled with awe. "I see Petie!" he declared. Startled, I said, "What?" He laughed out loud now and repeated, "I SEE PETIE!" Abruptly I understood. He had gazed into my eyes and seen his reflection in my pupils. I finally relaxed and smiled back at him. "Yes," I said, "You can see Petie."

In that moment, I understood that this was Petie's parting gift to me and to himself. Through our play, I'd learned to "see" Petie, and now he could finally "see" himself reflected in my eyes.

Analysts Reflect on the Holding Environment

The concept of the holding environment refers to both a developmental phenomenon and a therapeutic phenomenon. In the early months of an infant's life, the primary caregiver regulates the infant's capacity to tolerate stimulation by holding him. In her arms, the baby experiences safety and physical and emotional contact.

D. W. Winnicott wrote that the holding environment "has as its main function the reduction to a minimum of impingements to which the infant must react" (1960, 590). He meant that the holding environment limits the amount of stimulation, especially unpleasant stimulation, to which the infant must respond.

Winnicott (1963) saw the mother–baby connection as a metaphor describing the clinical relationship and the holding environment as the affective (emotional) background for the treatment. In his view, the therapist becomes a reliable and constant figure, like the good enough mother holding her infant. Recapitulating the infant's earliest experience of the parent, the therapist is experienced as a nonjudgmental, emotionally available figure on whom the patient can rely. As Winnicott described this process, "The analyst is *holding* the patient, and this often takes the form of conveying in words at the appropriate moment something that shows that the analyst knows and understands the deepest anxiety that is being experienced, or that is waiting to be experienced" ([1963] 1965c, 240). This process can be likened to a mother's remaining calm and grounded while she holds her distraught child. In a similar way, the therapist shows herself able to withstand the patient's intense feelings in whatever shape they take—whether anger, envy, aggression, or love. Winnicott (1960) believed that some patients, especially in situations of extreme deprivation, are unable to benefit from interpretations. Instead, such patients need metaphoric "holding" until their sense of stability is sufficiently reestablished.

Many clinicians see the holding environment as the atmosphere that facilitates the clinical work. Arnold Modell (1976) describes it as the silent but empathic backdrop to the work that goes on in the treatment. Such a safe place is particularly important to narcissistically fragile adults, who are constitutionally vulnerable or who missed essential, predictable nurturance when they were infants; for such patients, the holding environment enables them to contain the frightening omnipotent fantasies that are their defense against abandonment. Such containment must occur before the patient is able to make use of an interpretation. The treatment, then, becomes "a second chance for developmental growth" (Ginot 2001, 421) from what can be described as an arrested development. Theorists have adopted a variety of terms to describe concepts that are similar to that of Winnicott's holding environment. For example, Heinz Kohut (1971a) talked about mirroring, the idealizing transference, and the self-object environment—all references to the holding environment. Edward Bibring's (1937) idea of the therapeutic alliance and Wilfred Bion's (1962) concept of the container and containment also refer to the holding environment.

Our understanding of the holding environment includes therapeutic settings that provide intensive treatment opportunities for severely impaired children, adolescents, and adults. One example is the therapeutic nursery attended by Petie. This small, supportive, child-centric milieu promotes imaginative play, early socialization, emotional development, and skill enhancement. It is based on the model of separation–individuation developed by Margaret Mahler, Fred Pine, and Anni Bergman (1975). Their theory focuses on the importance of establishing separateness, individuality, and self-cohesion during the first three years of a child's life. This intensive therapeutic model has been widely utilized to move at-risk children such as Petie back toward a healthy developmental trajectory. Such a setting promotes attachment and enhances the child's ability to express his or her needs through play. In other words, the therapeutic nursery effectively creates a holding environment.

In early analytic writings, Freud and others didn't feel it was necessary to focus on these containing aspects of the therapeutic relationship. However, Freud's follower and friend Sándor Ferenczi (1949) wrote about the necessity of creating an atmosphere of nonjudgmental acceptance with regressed patients. Forty years ago, looking at this subject, Modell wrote, "Where there is ego distortion, the analytic setting as a holding environment is central to the therapeutic action" (1976, 305). Today we assume that therapists and analysts of all theoretical orientations are sensitive to these issues. It seems unlikely that any patient will participate in a treatment that isn't in some way supportive, but such concerns have recently become more central to our discussions of treatment efficacy. Yet it is important to remember that what feels safe to one person may differ greatly from what feels safe to another. For example, a patient fearful of close contact may actually feel greater support from a more neutral therapist.

It is important to keep in mind that the holding environment is a *metaphor* for or an approximation of the mother–infant relationship. The infant is born in a complete state of dependency; in contrast, the patient is not completely dependent, nor should he be encouraged to move in this direction. Many analysts, including Anna Freud, have questioned the validity of viewing the therapeutic relationship as a parental one because no patient actually returns to infancy during treatment, and no therapist can truly be the patient's parent.

In whatever form the holding environment takes, it facilitates the process of treatment when words are not yet available. In our story, the therapist describes worrying how she will successfully engage her mute patient in the therapeutic process. She muses, *"I wondered how I could possibly make contact with this doe-eyed, silent little boy."* The therapeutic relationship creates a safe haven for play, which then engages the patient's imagination and fantasy life. As we see in the story, Petie's play expands when he begins to feel safe. In time, his playing becomes a meaningful communication between himself and his therapist. In this way, play and creativity in treatment promote the patient's symbolic thinking and the use of language.

When Petie takes his therapist's hand, we see a first step toward closeness. She writes, *"He came with me willingly, putting his small, warm fist into my outreached palm."* This was an early positive indicator of Petie's potential to form a close connection with his therapist. Their play highlights the reparative function of a good enough therapeutic relationship. Such a connection is an essential ingredient for the beginning of a therapeutic environment on which the therapy must be built. Early on, the holding environment facilitates Petie's parallel play—an early developmental stage in which children play with shared toys in parallel with one another rather than in relationship. The author describes how she *"then sat down on the floor and picked up a block of my own. I, too, shot blocks across the floor, then almost under my breath I murmured, 'Zoom, zoom.' Petie stopped his play momentarily. He glanced at me and smiled slightly. Then he ducked his head down and resumed what he was doing."* As Petie came to feel safe with his therapist, he began to explore the play room. The early sense of protection and safety was evident in the therapist's description of their world: *"Playing together, Petie and I seemed to exist in a silent but pleasant bubble."*

For young children, the ability to play becomes the medium for the therapy. Thus, interpretation occurs primarily in the displacement of the play. Such displacement of strong emotions makes them more bearable and thus more available to therapeutic understanding. We see that Petie's game of rolling the ball back and forth gave him a sense of control, affirmed his competence, and provided him an avenue through which to connect with his therapist. *"He'd roll on top of it again and again until he was at the far end of the room. I sat facing him at the other end of the room, and then we'd roll the ball back and forth between us."* It was during these encounters, when Petie felt in control, that he notably first used his voice with his therapist. She writes, *"In fact, it was the first time I ever heard the sound of his voice: a warm, delighted guffaw came straight from his belly and burst into our bubble world."* For adults and children, the holding environment makes the treatment possible, and some may view it as the therapy itself. Joyce Slochower writes that with severely disturbed patients, the holding environment becomes "the crucial curative element which must at least temporarily replace interpretive work" (1991, 709).

Petie's therapist provided an atmosphere that allowed room for autonomy and growth. As his comfort increased, Petie began to play with the file cabinet, repeatedly reenacting disappearances and reunions. *"After a while, Petie discovered the bottom drawer of the file cabinet. It became his magic disappearing box. He'd place a toy*

*or a book or even his hat in the drawer. Then, with a bang, he'd roll
the drawer shut, and the hunt would begin. I'd furrow my brow and
ask, 'Petie, where did it go?' This query would lead to highly excited
play."* It appeared that for the first time he had control over the com-
ings and goings of what was important to him.

Some have argued that the concept of the holding environment is
too gratifying to the patient because the focus is on supplying an environment that suits the patient's needs to the degree that is possible.
There is certainly gratification in any therapeutic relationship, but a
holding environment doesn't necessarily function as a warm backdrop to the treatment. Indeed, patients with destructive aggression
need to experience that aggression repeatedly and see that it does
not destroy them, their therapist, or the treatment. In such a case,
the therapist has the difficult task of tolerating the patient's anger
without retaliation, like the parent who "holds" the child through a
difficult tantrum.

All patients must be able to access experiences and emotions that
are threatening and risky. In adult therapy, this process includes accessing scary thoughts, fantasies, or dream material. With a child patient, what is feared is enacted in the play and at times may lead us
to question how much mess, danger, and excitement both therapist
and patient can tolerate. For example, in our story the therapist wonders whether it is too dangerous for Petie to risk climbing into the
cabinet. She writes, *"I worried about his safety—What if the cabinet
collapsed with his weight? What if his fingers got caught?"* Just as the
parent needs to stop providing certain functions and protections to
allow the child to advance and grow, the therapist also at times needs
to contain her fears and allow the patient to regulate himself. Yet at
other times a good holding environment may require setting just such
a limit. For example, Petie's therapist stops him from taking off his
shirt when the play threatens to become overstimulating.

For Petie, the cabinet becomes a concrete representation of the
holding container—a metaphor, perhaps, for being contained inside
of the therapist's body. Petie first climbs into the file drawer right

before a therapy vacation. He wishes to hide, but, more important, he needs to be found. The cabinet becomes an enclosure, a refuge where he can feel safe and cocooned. Such a wish can hold true for patients of any age. The therapist explains: *"I could sense his yearning to be in that small, safe space—I saw it as an expression of his desire to be held, to be protected and swaddled. It was as though he had built himself a nest."* This space can be likened to Roger Willoughby's (2001) concept of the claustrum, an enclosed boundaried space that can also represent the womb. Without words, Petie finds safety in this space. Feeling bounded, with a clearer distinction between inside and outside, he begins to use words to link thoughts and feelings.

At every stage, the holding environment is one that leads to growth and the possibility of healthy separation. As with the mother, a good enough therapist or analyst facilitates autonomy, separation, and "the individual's discovery of self" (Winnicott 1969, 711). Modell similarly notes that "holding facilitates growth to the point where the separateness from the analyst can be accepted" (1988, 228–29). The narrator writes that Petie *"had been transformed from a silent, inaccessible child into an exuberant little boy who was eager to engage in the world around him. . . . Petie was ready to leave the therapeutic nursery and move on to elementary school. Sadly, it was time to end our play therapy."*

The therapist describes Petie peering intently in her eyes in their last session together. In that moment, she understood that this was his "parting gift" to her. It was his way of showing—albeit outside of his awareness—that therapy had allowed him to experience himself as whole and complete in relation to his therapist. In saying good-bye, he found a way to express his gratitude in a way that he felt was safe. Over the course of their work together, his therapist came to see him as cohesive, separate, and intact, which allowed him to "see" himself reflected in her eyes.

15 HOW TO SAVE A LIFE

A woman reveals a secret, and her therapist's interpretation opens up new possibilities in her treatment.

When I was a young graduate student, my first patient, Christina, was my trial by fire. At six feet tall, she towered over me. Her eyeliner was dramatic, her lipstick fire-engine red, and her gaze fierce, hungry, withering. As a fresh-faced, earnest, and naive therapist, I accepted the referral eagerly and was determined to make it work. Only later did I learn that Christina was a legend around the clinic, having cycled through many novice graduate students. It was not without warning that I took on Christina. When her previous student therapist lifted one eyebrow and said, "Oh, just wait . . . ," I smiled faintly and nodded but had no idea what was to come.

Christina's former therapist had been transferred to another unit. Every once in a while, Christina would run into her in the hallways. Such meetings not surprisingly created havoc during the early months of our work together. Indeed, well into our first year I heard the constant refrain: "Oh, I wish you were Joanna! She would know exactly how I feel!" In most sessions, Christina spoke without pausing for a breath because the sound of my voice reminded her that I was not the therapist she had lost. In my head, I knew she was protecting herself against getting close to me, another in a long line of disappearing therapists, but I was frustrated to be constantly cast in the role of inadequate substitute.

As a twenty-eight-year-old college student, Christina was hanging on by a thread. She had trouble concentrating on her work and felt anxious much of the time. She had pleaded and wheedled her way through two years of school with a whirlwind of incompletes, dropped courses, and late papers. She was dogged in her pursuit of her education, however, which provided an important window to an immense resilience and perseverance that were not evident in her relationships. With the important people in her life, Christina enacted an unvarying pattern: intense engagement followed by rejection, followed by disillusionment, followed by rupture.

During the first two or three years that we worked together, Christina spent many sessions telling me her story, one of abuse and neglect by a self-absorbed mother and an alcoholic, abandoning father. Sessions focused on the past were interspersed with ones centered on current crises in love and in work. Christina complained a great deal about her boyfriends. "Why can't I have that starry-eyed passion?" she pouted. "Why can't they ever make love to me for more than thirty minutes? Why is everything always so boring?" The underlying message was always the same: there is nothing on this earth, short of complete devotion, that will ever fill me up.

Christina had a unique name for her day-to-day experience: "boredism." I pictured this state as an uneasy blend of disconnected parts: her profound loneliness, her retaliatory rage, and the schism between her and the rest of the world. I had no satisfying answers to her persistent questions. When I'd inevitably weary of trying to engage Christina in a more meaningful dialogue, my thoughts would wander to details of her history that she rarely talked about but that were described in clinic reports.

Christina spoke often about a sister who struggled with depression and anorexia. However, she rarely spoke of her younger, developmentally delayed brother. His name was Patrick. Though she wasn't sure, she thought he may have been autistic. He couldn't communicate well, and he could not take care of himself. He also couldn't swim, and from the clinic reports I learned that he had drowned at a public pool. Christina later told me that she was the one with him in the water when he drowned.

It took Christina several years to talk about Patrick. She approached the topic gradually, almost imperceptibly, inching toward it, as if not wanting to attract too much attention. I understood that talking to me about Patrick meant she was beginning to trust me. It was at this point that the sessions finally took on a different tone. She was sad and reflective, and I found that I connected with her in a different way. I thought she, too, must have felt it because she started to worry about becoming too attached to me. She knew that as a student I would eventually leave. She started to ask me questions for which there was no answer: "If you had a baby, and you had to choose between me and the baby, who would you choose?"

As we began to explore these questions more deeply, I learned that Christina had a persistent fear that I would judge her as harshly as she judged herself. She harbored a fear that she was nothing short of a murderess who deserved to be punished, condemned to a life of torment and unhappiness. Since her brother's death, she had made an unconscious pact with herself to experience neither love nor happiness nor satisfaction.

One day Christina arrived at her session late and in a rage. Her boyfriend had reneged on their dinner plans. She could think and talk of nothing but feeling humiliated and heartbroken. She was so angry that she'd gotten on the wrong train, noticed her error, gotten off, and then eventually boarded a different train, only to discover that she'd made another mistake. I told her that I was struck by how her upset about her boyfriend seemed to eclipse anything else that might need her attention. She was momentarily silenced, then she told me, "It was like that on the day my brother died. I had a crush on a guy, and I was thinking only of him when I should have been thinking of Patrick." Into the silence spilled memories from that day: the temperature of the water, the heat of the sun on her skin, and the feel of Patrick's hand as she grasped it. She was standing in the water thinking about her boyfriend when she heard the sounds of children playing in the deep end. She suddenly remembered Patrick pulling away from her. "I called my mother for help because I couldn't hold on to him," Christina said slowly. "I looked over to where my mother was supposed to be, but she wasn't—oh." She was quiet again and then said slowly, "My mother had gone to talk to a man she liked. They were sitting at the deep end together. Her legs were in the water, kicking. His hand was on her shoulder. Patrick must have seen her. I think he was trying to get to her. But she didn't see him, and she didn't hear me. She was just throwing her head back and laughing. I think she was flirting. She didn't notice what was happening. I never thought of that before."

In the stunned silence, Christina looked transfixed. She sat utterly still for several minutes. It was only then that I realized how Christina's profound guilt and self-recrimination had served another purpose all this time. During the next few sessions, I gradually pointed out that by blaming herself, she also protected herself from the awareness of an even more painful reality—that of her mother's neglect, of her mother's inability to protect her children, not only at the pool, but throughout their lives.

From this moment, Christina's therapy shifted. She wasn't magically cured. She still questioned me relentlessly and complained about her boyfriends. Nonetheless, something happened that day that began to alter the trajectory of her treatment. Over the next two years, her life slowly stabilized. When it was my turn to leave the clinic, we decided that for the time being she had completed her therapy. She believed—and I concurred—that she could now hold inside of her the good work we had done. The endless cycle of new graduate student therapists came to a close. The understanding that passed between us that day bound us together for that instant and, perhaps in a sense, forever.

Analysts Reflect on Interpretation and Insight

In "How to Save a Life," we witness a particular moment that has a profound effect on a traumatized young woman during the course of her long-term treatment. Christina has been through the revolving door of a clinic that has done its best to help her. Despite rotating therapists, Christina has found something meaningful in her therapy. Her attachments are strong, and they keep her returning to treatment. As the writer tells us, *"Only later did I learn that Christina was a legend around the clinic, having cycled through many novice graduate students."* At the same time, she keeps important parts of herself tucked away, less accessible to both the therapist and herself. The writer suggests that when she is able to address the hidden aspects of Christina's experience, the interaction changes and feels more authentic. The awareness of that subtle shift in the air when Christina speaks about her brother serves as a signal to the therapist that she needs to listen carefully: *"She approached the topic gradually, almost imperceptibly, inching toward it, as if not wanting to attract too much attention. I understood that talking to me about Patrick meant she was beginning to trust me. It was at this point that the sessions finally took on a different tone."*

When therapists speak about change in therapy, they often use the term *therapeutic action*. What therapeutic action is and how it leads to meaningful change is hotly debated within psychoanalytic literature. Freud's own ideas about the curative nature of analytic treatment changed repeatedly throughout his career. In his 1912 paper "Recommendations to Physicians Practicing Psychoanalysis" ([1912] 1955i), he attributed change to the power of the psychoanalyst's interpretations. He suggested that the analyst's capacity to comprehend and interpret comes from his unconscious attunement with the patient's unconscious. Insight is "transmitted" to him during clinical hours spent listening to the patient's free associations as well as to his random thoughts and fantasies. Freud believed that the role of interpretation was to translate the patient's inner world into conscious thoughts. Interpretation was supposed to lead to transformation.

Contemporary psychotherapists now consider that therapeutic growth is not primarily a result of carefully formulated interpretations. Neat "truths" delivered by the therapist can often paradoxically rouse the patient's resistance. Even if the therapist thinks she is "right," she rarely sees sustained change occurring when she imposes a view from the outside that the patient has not come to on his own in some way. Nonetheless, for many years in classical psychoanalysis, the standard approach to treatment involved some version of making the unknown known through the interpretation of unconscious fantasy, dreams, and wishes. Warren Poland (2002) points out that in this early analytic style the insight required for the patient to improve emerged when the analyst understood the patient and interpreted his conflicts. Thus, the analyst was the silent listener and the authoritarian figure, the "knowing one" whose job was to free the patient from the grips of the unconscious conflict that held him in its throes. This belief was not monolithic, however. For example, Hans Loewald (1960) questioned whether the therapist ever really had access to knowledge and emotional awareness that the patient did not possess. He thought that the impetus for change resided within the patient—that the therapist's job was to be attuned to the patient's developmental shifts, always with an eye toward reinforcing the patient's potential for future growth.

D. W. Winnicott, like Loewald, disagreed strongly with the notion that the interpretation is something to be discovered by the therapist and given fully formed to the patient. Winnicott viewed the exchange between therapist and patient as a collaborative process. Change, he believed, comes when the therapist identifies "with the patient . . . imagin[ing] what it is like to be that person at that moment—and then the more unexpected consequence of 'believing in' what he needs," as his biographer Adam Phillips puts it (1988, 140).

In counterpoint to the prevailing technique of the time, Winnicott felt that the silent analyst ran the risk of portraying himself as all knowing and all powerful. This stance left the patient both dependent on the analyst's authority and simultaneously resistant to it. Interpretations handed down "from above" only intensified the patient's resistance and symptoms. The only interpretations Winnicott viewed as meaningful were those that emerged directly from the patient when he gained a greater capacity for self-reflection and insight. Winnicott made clear to his patients his own fallibility and his willingness to listen. He believed that as with the good enough mother, the analyst's role was to facilitate the patient's growth and self-discovery rather than to force new knowledge onto him. He thought of the treatment as a transitional space within which patient and therapist could play. By "play," he referred not to the opposite of "work"—in his view, play *is* the child's work—but rather to the opposite of "coercion" (Phillips 1988, 142). According to Joseph Sandler and Anne-Marie Sandler, "A major analytic goal is to get the patient to become friends with the previously unacceptable parts of himself. . . . To do this means that the analyst has to provide, through his interpretations and the way he gives them, an atmosphere of tolerance of the infantile, the perverse and the ridiculous" (1983, 369).

Poland has suggested that the purpose of interpretation is to help the patient "search for whatever hidden meanings can throw new light on present emotions and experiences" (2002, 825). The therapist's open, curious, and respectful attitude invites the patient to consider different ways of thinking and working through long-standing problems. Interpretation enables the patient to generate new solutions and encounter old relationships in a new way. The belief in the effectiveness of interpretations is based on the idea that the inner world is emotionally meaningful and can be accessed through the dynamic interaction between therapist and patient. In contemporary terms, it is this mutual quest for understanding that is referred to as "therapeutic action."

This relational approach to interpretation does not render the therapist silent. She may notice patterns of behavior or intuit meaning before the patient does, and these insights can and should be shared with the patient. However, the contemporary idea suggests that these interpretations arise out of a shared emotional experience. Such is certainly the case in Christina's therapy. *"I told her that I was struck by how her upset over her boyfriend seemed to eclipse anything else that might need her attention. She was momentarily silenced. . . . Into the silence spilled memories from that day."*

Emotionally attuned interpretations are the only ones that truly come alive. Poland (2002) emphasizes that such interpretations are in fact "trial interpretations," open for revision and discussion, and can be set aside if the patient does not find them useful. Betty Joseph's view is that interpretations need to convey a sense that the therapeutic process is evolving and alive: "If one sees transference and interpretations as basically living, experiencing and shifting—as movement—then our interpretations have to express this" (1985, 449). As in Christina's story, the most powerful moments in treatment possess an intrinsic drama. Wilma Bucci (2010) notes that the language of these exchanges have a different quality than the language used during more prosaic interludes.

In the view of many therapists working today, interpretation and insight are useful in bringing to light aspects of the patient's internal world, particularly in areas of conflict. However, such insights are not necessarily sufficient to bring about therapeutic change. Fred Pine writes, "[Although] empathic understanding will be valuable to a person who grew up not heard, or not mattering, or used by another for the other's purposes, it is less clear that empathic understanding (beyond its place as ordinary human decency) is specifically change-relevant for developmental failures" (1992, 252). Such "developmental failures" include difficulties in affect regulation, poor capacity for self-soothing, and impairments in reality testing.

Poland's (2002) idea of the "interpretive attitude" within which the patient can "listen in" on his internal processes in the presence of an attentive therapist can be understood as the core of therapeutic action. The "interpretive attitude" promotes growth and allows the patient gradually to internalize a similar attitude of curiosity and openness toward his own inner world. Judith Chused points out that surprise also plays a role in creating therapeutic action. She suggests that when the patient is surprised in treatment by something unexpected, he comes to question his prior assumptions and gradually develops a new way of experiencing himself. Such surprise, she writes, "create[s] the emotional dissonance between expectation and experience needed for a shift in perceptual frame, so that what was once denied or ignored is now seen" (1996, 1051). In the story, the author writes, *"I gradually pointed out that by blaming herself, she also protected herself from the awareness of an even more painful reality. . . . From this moment, Christina's therapy shifted. She wasn't magically cured. . . . Nonetheless, something happened that day that began to alter the trajectory of her treatment."*

Whether to make a certain interpretation or to wait is a function of therapeutic technique and concerns both tact and timing. Joseph raises a related concern: "There is also the issue as to when and how it is useful to interpret the relation to the past, to reconstruct. I feel that it is important not to make these links if the linking disrupts what is going on in the session and leads to a kind of explanatory discussion or exercise, but rather to wait until the heat is no longer on and the patient has sufficient contact with himself and the situation to want to understand and to help to make links" (1985, 452).

A therapist will sometimes pursue a line of inquiry that takes the patient away from the immediacy of a powerful moment. Doing so allows either patient or therapist to seek refuge by moving away to more intellectual, safer, less affectively charged thoughts. However, it may also communicate something disruptive and unsettling to the patient about the therapist's ability to remain affectively attuned. As Christina's therapist in this story shows, it can be taxing for the therapist to stay attuned to a demanding patient who requires endless feeding and never seems full: *"When I'd inevitably weary of trying to engage Christina in a more meaningful dialogue, my thoughts would wander to details of her history that she rarely talked about but that were described in clinic reports."* Such restlessness and boredom may signal that the therapist needs to attend to the patient's unhappiness in a different way, perhaps by trying to hear the deeper meaning in an endless string of complaints.

In Christina's story, an important moment occurs when the patient experiences a sudden juxtaposition of her present-day experience with her boyfriend—*"One day Christina arrived at her session late and in a rage. Her boyfriend had reneged on their dinner plans. She could think and talk of nothing but feeling humiliated and heartbroken"*— and a past experience she had long since repressed—*" 'It was like that on the day my brother died. I had a crush on a guy, and I was thinking only of him when I should have been thinking of Patrick.' "*

The therapist's observation that Christina's distressed state momentarily overtook her capacity to think bridges the historic gap between then and now and allows Christina to access an aspect of her experience that had been previously outside of her awareness. It is as though by making a link between what she is feeling in that moment, in the safe presence of a therapist she has come to trust, and what she felt on the day of her brother's death, she sees a powerful truth that has long eluded her awareness: *" 'My mother had gone to talk to a man she liked. . . . Patrick must have seen her. I think he was trying to get to her. But she didn't see him, and she didn't hear me. She was just throwing her head back and laughing. I think she was flirting. She didn't notice what was happening. I never thought of that before.' "* The emotional aliveness of the moment is evident in the sensory nature of the memory—Christina recalls smells, sounds, and sensations such as the warmth of the sun and the feel of her brother's hand in hers.

With Christina's memory of her mother's failure to attend to her children now more fully in the room, Christina and her therapist are for the first time able to gain insight into her chronic feelings of guilt and badness and her unsatisfied and apparently insatiable yearning for love and attention. These feelings had long played out in her relationships with men, in her academic strivings, and importantly in the transference to her therapist and to the therapists who had come and gone previously.

The interplay between therapist and patient—which includes dialogue, reflection, nonverbal communications, and actions—is the currency we therapists have for expanding our patients' way of thinking about themselves and experiencing themselves in the world. Putting feelings into words is a transformative process when the words evoke an attuned response from the therapist. At such moments, a meaningful shared connection is established. A patient's musings—her recollection of sensations, dreams, and fragmented bits of experience—enable her to reflect in a different way and stimulate her curiosity. The patient wonders about her experience, gradually allowing her to symbolize through language an experience never fully owned or digested, which, in turn, emerges as a new self-narrative.

The new story opens up the treatment, making it possible for Christina to begin to stretch her repertoire of behaviors and expectations. She is not magically transformed, but she is changed by what she says in the treatment room and by her therapist's timely interpretation. *"In the stunned silence, Christina looked transfixed. She sat utterly still for several minutes. It was only then that I realized how Christina's profound guilt and self-recrimination had served another purpose all this time. During the next few sessions, I gradually pointed out that by blaming herself, she also protected herself from the awareness of an even more painful reality—that of her mother's neglect, of her mother's inability to protect her children, not only at the pool, but throughout their lives."*

16 FRIENDS OF THE HEART

A little boy and his therapist get ready to say good-bye.

"Oh, my God, not again," I think, my graduate student heart thumping away deep inside my chest. Here I am, stranded in the hallway, outside of the therapy room. I am definitely on the wrong side of the door. My young patient has succeeded in locking me out. Again.

I listen helplessly to the thwonking and banging coming from the other side of the door. I glance at my watch. Should I run to the main office to retrieve the master key? As soon as I race down the hallway, Lester might emerge. If he doesn't see me, he'll worry that I am gone for good: it is a feeling he knows all too well for his scant eight years. In my mind's eye, I see him scampering away down the hall, a hapless, mischievous boy looking for a way out. But if I wait much longer, our session will be over. My next patient will arrive, and Lester and I will have to take our leave from each other in this disappointing way. I lean my ear against the door.

Then I hear the tapping of heels coming down the hallway, and my supervisor rounds the corner. Each week she has listened to the unfolding of Lester's tale and provided me with ample strategies to handle this very situation. With her help over the course of his three-year treatment, Lester has learned to be in the room with me. He no longer hurls objects across the room. He has ceased dumping his toys haphazardly on the floor. Together he and I put words to his urgent impulse to re-create in the consulting room the storm that is his life. Together he and I came to understand how his destructiveness protected him from the inner turmoil and confusion that repeatedly threatened to overwhelm him. We gradually constructed meaning out of chaos. Wild play, unrestrained aggression, and devastating sadness transformed into meaningful therapeutic experience that is contained and understood.

Now, with just a month left before we terminate, here I am in the hallway once again, barred from entering and about to be embarrassed in front of my supervisor. I brace myself, plaster on a smile, and ready myself with the words, "Lester and I are working through saying good-bye." "Oh yeah?" I imagine her smirking. "I can see you've got it all under control."

As she approaches me, a quizzical look forms on her face. Just then the door swings open, and Lester says grandly, "You can come back in now." I step across the threshold and close the door. I stare agape at the room. It is spotless. Toys are stacked neatly on shelves. Blocks are lined up by size and stacked against the wall. Cars, also lined up by size, are parked along the shelf. The dollhouse looks brand new, every piece of furniture standing straight and in its place. Books, toys, paint, and paper—nothing is amiss. All is orderly and serene. A happy smile lighting his face, Lester says proudly, "See? I cleaned it for you." I suddenly understand the magnitude of what he is communicating to me.

On the day of our last session a few weeks later, Lester and I sit together on the floor of the play room, talking about our final good-bye. We look out the window and try to spot his apartment building amidst the vast cityscape. He feels certain he sees the window of his bedroom from my office. He tells me that he thinks if he squints from there, he might be able to see me moving about the play room. As we walk out the door, he puts his hand on my shoulder and looks straight into my eyes, saying, "We're friends of the heart, right?" I tell him that, indeed, we are. Then we say good-bye, each of us allowing the merest glint of a tear.

Analysts Reflect on Termination

Saying good-bye can be painful and something we prefer to avoid, but endings are as important as beginnings and happen just as often. In a good enough psychodynamic treatment, the time comes when patient and therapist must confront the sad reality of termination. For many patients, psychotherapy provides their first experience of putting painful feelings of separation, loss, and love into words.

Through the story of a lively little boy who uses the language of play to demonstrate the changes in his inner world, we see that endings, for all their sadness, contain much to be celebrated. In the story, we observe Lester's increased self-regulation, his newfound emotional resources, and his impressive capacity to mourn creatively the loss of his relationship with the therapist he has come to love. Finally, in his last session we witness his new ability to internalize her and to verbalize his feelings.

Reworking these analytic themes as part of termination demands that therapist and patient commit themselves to revisiting the oft repeated themes and dramas of the therapy and to finding a way to resolve them more satisfactorily than was done previously. It has been said that such revising and revisiting is the "end toward which the many moments of attachment, loss, and mourning that have filled the analysis have been heading. Every analysis is a multidirectional journey toward a termination" (Orgel 2000, 723). As part of the treatment, patient and therapist surrender themselves to an intimacy that they know from its inception will ideally end "under conditions of love and gratitude" (M. Bergmann 1997, 169). This is one of the unique aspects of therapy. Such foreordained closure rarely happens in "real life." In real life, people fight, break up, move, and die, but they do not willingly choose to end a loving relationship. Love and gratitude, however, are not the entire story. Patient and therapist must make room for the full range of feelings, including sadness, anger, and grief, evoked by the end of treatment.

Just as each therapy relationship is different, each termination is likewise different. From the time of the first phone contact between a new patient and therapist, both bring a complex set of hopes, wishes, and fears into the relationship they create together. As a result, every therapeutic dyad forms a unique dance, choreographed in a way that reflects the individuality of each participant. How the therapist and patient ultimately end the treatment—in both form and substance—reflects this same choreography.

Thinking of termination as a distinct phase of treatment helps therapists identify a number of themes to be expressed and worked through. In the course of termination, the patient typically revisits issues that appeared earlier in the treatment. Now, however, in the latest iteration of his struggles, he brings new insights and resources to bear. This process is beautifully illustrated in Lester's story. The therapist describes how, as the date for termination approaches, Lester once again locks her out of the playroom. This time, however, the familiar story of Lester's internal and external chaos and the therapist's feelings of exclusion and helplessness has a very different ending.

The therapist explains that over the course of therapy *"wild play, unrestrained aggression, and devastating sadness transformed into meaningful therapeutic experience that is contained and understood. Now, with just a month left before we terminate, here I am in the hallway once again, barred from entering."* When the therapist re-enters the room, however, she sees how these old patterns with Lester are profoundly reconfigured. In that moment, she becomes privy to the internal shifts that have transpired during Lester's "working through" of these previously primitive and overwhelming emotions.

She notes that in contrast to earlier times, *"books, toys, paint, and paper—nothing is amiss. All is orderly and serene. A happy smile lighting his face, Lester says proudly, 'See? I cleaned it for you.'"* Lester shows her in a child's literal way that he has transformed his internal chaos into a predictable, safe place into which he can now invite others.

When newly revisited themes are confronted, they can feel as tumultuous, intense, and painful as they did when first encountered. Now, however, there is a newfound liveliness in the "working through" process, and the elements of curiosity and surprise are present for both patient and therapist. "Working through" does not mean that the loss disappears as a presence in our unconscious minds. Instead, the ending is ideally a "surrender to the inevitable" (Orgel 2000, 732) and mourned accordingly. Acknowledging loss and allowing oneself to feel sad—to truly mourn—allows one to experience deeper, more meaningful relationships thereafter.

How termination is addressed determines whether this leave-taking process will be lively and productive or, alternately, drained of vitality. As Hans Loewald explains, the process of ending and the associated taking in (internalization) of the therapist determine "whether separation from a love object is experienced as deprivation and loss or as emancipation and mastery" (1962, 490). The process of internalization ideally enables the patient to take into himself aspects of the therapist's voice and presence and make them his own. If the therapist is able to maintain her ongoing attunement to the patient and use her countertransference productively, she will be able to understand the patient's experience of separation and loss and to facilitate its working through.

In the best situation, the therapist uses empathy and attunement to help the patient make sense of his personal journey during termination. If the therapist is too distant and intellectual during this time, the interaction and the termination will flounder. Lester's therapist clearly tolerates the destabilization and insecurity that come from not knowing. Her ability to bear the emotions triggered in the termination allows Lester to engage actively in a reciprocal process that transforms loss into mourning and mourning into an increased capacity to experience life. Sadness (unlike depression) occurs in response to love and genuine loss. In a deep and meaningful psychotherapy, therapist and patient must mourn the relationship they now share, allowing it to move into a new phase in which it will exist in a different way, through internalization and memory. It is only when the patient and the therapist can tolerate the deep sadness they feel about losing one another that they can become, in Lester's beautiful phrase, "friends of the heart."

Whether the termination is mutually agreed upon, forced, or unilateral, it will shape the emotional tone and subsequent memory of the leave taking. Unless real-life demands intrude, the impending realities of termination enter the treatment. Then the patient and therapist optimally work together to establish a mutually agreed-upon timeline for ending. It is important that the patient feel some ownership for this decision. As therapists, we generally consider that the patient has entered the termination phase when "the analytic process has shown this progressive development over time and . . . the patient himself begins to recognize these changes and movements" (Weiss and Fleming 1980, 44). Although this step might seem relatively straightforward, it is not. In fact, the more intensive the treatment, the more the "working-through" process creates a tempestuous reexperiencing of earlier dynamics. It is only at the later stage of treatment, however, that the patient is finally available to rework and to a greater or lesser degree master these issues.

Such "good enough" endings stand in contrast to premature terminations, which are initiated solely either by the therapist—based on relocation, illness, death, or an unresolved countertransference reaction (Klauber 1977)—or by the patient. Like therapists, patients terminate unexpectedly for a variety of reasons. Such reasons may include external realities or transference issues that are acted out rather than understood within the treatment relationship. Such premature and unresolved terminations are unfortunately common (Novick 1982) and often detrimental.

From the time that the ending date is established until the final good-bye is said, patient and therapist focus on the resolution of earlier therapeutic themes. In addition, they address the emotions associated with previous separations and losses, which are reawakened in the present. With children, dealing with such emotions may occur primarily in displacement, through fantasy and play, such as Lester's wish to see his therapist whenever he wants: "*We look out the window and try to spot his house amidst the vast cityscape. He feels certain he sees the window of his bedroom from my office. He tells me that he thinks if he squints there, he might be able to see me moving about the play room.*"

For termination to work as well as it does in Lester's treatment, the therapist needs to examine her conflicting emotions. If the therapist's own countertransference resistances to losing the patient go unexamined, she may encourage him to linger in therapy too long, or, conversely, she may end therapy prematurely (Viorst 1982). Early research considered termination primarily in light of an Oedipal drama, with the therapist standing in for a parent that the patient must renounce. Now, however, we recognize that the complex mixture of tender, painful, and nostalgic feelings the patient has are best understood as a form of genuine love. Such love includes profound gratitude—which may or may not be expressed at the time—and exhilaration and pride over what has been accomplished in treatment (Tessman 2003). Sheldon Bach's (2006) book on analytic love explores the complexities and importance of love in and out of the treatment room. He focuses on the "attentive presence" through which the analyst brings about a "meeting" with patients that invites trust. He writes that it is this trust—the love of patient for analyst and analyst for patient—that sustains the treatment.

Choosing a definitive date for leaving introduces stress into the therapeutic relationship. This stress heightens the power of the transferences and countertransferences and puts pressure on the patient to consolidate the gains he has made in treatment, thus heightening his functioning and self-awareness. This process helps the patient live well, love well, and play well following the completion of therapy. According to Jack Novick and Kerry Novick, such therapeutic achievements include the "capacity to be with another and oneself; the capacity to work together with another and alone in the presence of the other in a creative, mutually enhancing way; the capacity to be autonomous without having to separate and retain autonomy when separate; the capacity to say good-bye in a mutually enhancing way, acknowledging mourning and so internalizing the positive aspects of the relationship" (2006, 307). The process of saying good-bye changes both therapist and patient, whether child or adult. Such transformation is the gift of termination.

At its best, leave taking, in the midst of working through the loss, facilitates an awareness of new beginnings and new capacities in therapist and patient alike (Balint 1950). In "Friends of the Heart," the therapist describes saying good-bye to her young patient: *"As we walk out the door, he puts his hand on my shoulder and looks straight into my eyes, saying, 'We're friends of the heart, right?' I tell him that, indeed, we are. Then we say good-bye, each of us allowing the merest glint of a tear."*

PART FOUR
Treatment Challenges

17 JOINING THE PAIN

A psychotherapist struggles with the potent mix of emotions she feels in the presence of a self-injuring patient.

Before this patient comes through my door, I need to prepare myself. In the brief time between sessions, there is no trip to the restroom, no cup of tea to warm me, no quick phone call, no peek at my email. Instead, I arrange myself in my black leather Stressless recliner. Knowing how overwhelmed and alone this patient makes me feel, I settle in and let the chair's solid structure support me.

I do what I can to ready myself for the emotional barrage that I know is coming. Taking a sip of water, I make myself settle back in my chair. Breathe in . . . breathe out . . . I slowly recite a rhythmic meditation—deeply, fully breathe in the pain of the other; deeply, fully breathe out loving kindness. I sink into the quiet, and the tension gradually gives way. I rediscover a calm space in my center. As I settle, I once again tenuously find my capacity to listen and bear the pain that is about to inhabit my office. I open the door.

An obese, unwashed adolescent girl sits in my waiting room. Her dark thick hair is lank and needs to be washed. She wears jarringly mismatched clothes. Her appearance speaks for her—it screams out her feelings of not belonging and drives her family to distraction. The unwashed smell of her sometimes remains in my office after she leaves. I imagine it permeating my couch and my air. I cannot help but absorb it. Beneath my unease, I locate the stirrings of empathy. Part of me understands that her appearance is a powerful communication in the only language she knows, but I mostly just want her to take a bath.

She defiantly bares her tanned arms in a tight tank top, exposing an intricate web of cuts of different lengths, widths, and depths, some faint white, others recent. The pediatrician who treats her thinks she sometimes cuts herself hundreds of times a day. He tells me that there are thousands of scars on her body. He feels powerless to intervene. We all do, this team of professionals who are trying to save her from herself. Her cutting is so severe that it has resulted in anemia. Her self-loathing washes over everyone who tries to help her—parents, teachers, doctors, me—threatening to drown us all.

When she enters my office, my mind clears, and I am attentive. I cannot help but notice the beautiful olive hue of her skin, scarred though it is. What does it mean that I sometimes recoil and at other times deny? That I sometimes step back from her and at other times empathize with her suffering? That I sometimes feel hope but at other times feel utterly defeated? That sometimes I am able to see her, but sometimes I cannot—or, maybe, more truthfully—I will not? At different moments, I've done them all. In truth, I am constantly confused.

Her sense of shame and humiliation is palpable as she flops provocatively onto my couch. She throws herself on top of the soft down cushions, a toddler having a temper tantrum. As she hurls her body into my long-suffering couch, I fight the urge to respond to her aggression with retaliation. I struggle to bite back the disapproving words that arise in me. I want to take charge of her, to control her, to make her stop. Instead, I sit calmly in my Stressless chair, and I wait. She forces me—against my will—to see myself more starkly than do other patients, to face the dark and primitive responses that rise up in me so quickly. Rather than confront these feelings within me, I yearn to turn away. In such moments, I want to obliterate her need for me. I fight my impulse to "fire her," to say that she is too much to bear, and to leave her alone with the fires that lap at her feet. Sometimes with shame and sometimes without, I fantasize telling her that she repels me. With great effort, these words go unspoken as I struggle to find sufficient empathy to bear her suffering.

As this interaction plays out silently, her eyes angrily dare me to look away, to refuse to bear witness to the deafening cacophony of loss and terror and rage that she flagrantly wears on her body. I struggle to listen in the midst of this assault on my senses—to maintain my sense of connection with her. I know she needs me to stay centered so that she can experience me as someone who is able to withstand the barrage of pain. She frightens me, this is true. Nevertheless, I work to find a quiet place in my mind where I can make contact with her. I try to help her find words to tell me the meaning of the violence she has wrought on her body. Over time, she haltingly explains that as terrifying as it is to continue her slow, steady self-annihilation, it is equally terrifying to imagine stopping. She will tell me later what she fears most: if she quits cutting, she will be alone. Cutting has soothed her for years, warding off her overwhelming emptiness and terror. She is convinced that if she stops—if she gets healthy—she will lose everyone who matters. She says that the scar tissue is what binds all of us—her doctors, her family, her analyst—to her. She believes that if she heals, we will leave. I look at her. I do not look away. No matter how I prepare myself, though, I am always shocked by the stark scars from wounds she has so few words to explain.

Many years later she is still my patient. Echoes of these same issues still resonate in the treatment room. Although she often struggles with urges to hurt herself, she and I can increasingly put words to them, replacing action and impulse with understanding and representation. She occasionally succumbs to the primitive urge to cut herself, which is disorganizing for both of us. However, we now work together to recognize the nature of these pressures when they reemerge. She has learned to put words to her feelings of love, longing, and rage. I, too, can access a wider range of feelings toward her—these familiar internal landmarks now guide me through the analysis. With great relief, I find that my ability to experience surprise and delight has returned. Once again there is ample room for love and hate and all the places in between. The work goes on. Now we breathe more freely, in rhythm, when we are together.

Analysts Reflect on Countertransference

The experience of the analyst in the story "Joining the Pain" is more extreme than what psychotherapists typically encounter in their offices. Nevertheless, the therapist's powerful and confusing feelings are well known to anyone who works intensively with fragile or disorganized patients. In psychodynamic psychotherapy, how we register emotional responses toward ourselves and our patients—transference and countertransference—provides us with important sources of information that guide our clinical approach.

Transference (see chapter 6) is the psychological process by which the patient unconsciously transforms novel situations into familiar, predictable ones. Countertransference refers to the therapist's complementary emotional responses to the patient. Broadly stated, countertransference includes all the therapist's conscious and unconscious reactions to the patient and provides us with a valuable source of data. However, the information we obtain in this way exists only as a hypothesis until we verify it through the patient's clinical material (H. Smith 2006).

The urge to better understand her patient leads the therapist in "Joining the Pain" to plumb the depths of her emotional response, looking for clues to comprehend what initially seems incomprehensible—a young girl's cutting herself thousands of times. *"What does it mean that I sometimes recoil and at other times deny? That I sometimes step back from her and at other times empathize with her suffering? That I sometimes feel hope but at other times feel utterly defeated? That sometimes I am able to see her, but sometimes I cannot—or, maybe, more truthfully—I will not? At different moments, I've done them all. In truth, I am constantly confused."*

Countertransference has been an important topic in our field since Freud first proposed it as a way to conceptualize what he thought of as the analyst's "blind spots." As Freud saw it in his own time, the analyst was expected to "recognize this counter-transference in himself and overcome it" ([1910] 1953c, 145). In contrast, we now conceptualize countertransference more broadly. Our current models for understanding such ubiquitous countertransferences encompass the full gamut of responses. At one end of the spectrum are those responses that occur when the patient projects his own unacceptable feelings onto the therapist, a phenomenon known as "projective identification" (Klein 1946). At the other end are those responses located in and governed by the therapist's own psychological makeup. In the vast space between the two are those responses generated in the back and forth between therapist and patient. In our current understanding, the therapist no longer sees herself as a blank screen, someone who must rid herself of all countertransference reactions through self-analysis. Today we generally accept that countertransference is ever present and valuable so long as it is understood rather than played out.

Our understanding of therapeutic action has moved from a one-person psychological model in which the patient talks in the presence of a largely silent, "abstinent" analyst to a two-person model in which both analyst and patient jointly create the therapeutic space. As Betty Joseph ([1981] 1989) explains, treatment that does not focus on the analyst's participation in the moment-to-moment interactions may engage the patient primarily at a cognitive rather than an emotional level. In contrast, when the therapist draws upon an understanding of her countertransference reactions, interpretations are more emotionally alive.

W. W. Meissner (2000) expands on this idea by pointing out that as the therapeutic relationship deepens, the task of understanding the unconscious forces at play gradually transitions from the therapist's domain to the increasingly shared domain of the patient and therapist at work together. When this shift occurs, the work becomes markedly more reciprocal and productive. This process is described in the story when the therapist tells us that several years into the treatment the patient *"has learned to put words to her feelings of love, longing, and rage. I, too, can access a wider range of feelings toward her—these familiar internal landmarks now guide me through the analysis. With great relief, I find that my ability to experience surprise and delight has returned. Once again there is ample room for love and hate and all the places in between. The work goes on."*

Psychotherapy is most effective when the transference and countertransference are fully engaged and explored. Therapists must turn their attention in toward themselves as well as toward their patient. If these pressures are not adequately formulated or understood by the therapist, and they are instead acted out within the therapeutic relationship, they may damage or even destroy the treatment. *"I fight my impulse to 'fire her,' to say that she is too much to bear, and to leave her alone with the fires that lap at her feet. . . . With great effort, these words go unspoken as I struggle to find sufficient empathy to bear her suffering."* This danger is most apparent in the treatment of patients who are prone to more primitive, disregulated responses.

As we see in the story, intensive treatment with such patients often elicits powerful, confusing, and frightening countertransference responses in their therapists, whose reactions are often amplified, thereby providing us with a window into the ubiquitous presence of countertransference in all therapeutic relationships. Just as our patients use the therapy to contain powerful and often frightening feelings, therapists also need to titrate their own strong countertransferential reactions. Along with supervision, consultation, and ongoing self-analysis, we can also turn to theory as a means of anchoring ourselves. A theoretical framework offers an opportunity to understand what transpires in the treatment, especially when we are faced with novel or affectively overwhelming situations. As such, we can tolerate what might otherwise be intolerable.

When we treat patients with self-injurious behaviors, such as the young woman in "Joining the Pain," our heightened reactions are often painful and confusing. D. W. Winnicott (1949) described the intense feelings of "hate" that can be engendered in the therapist when working so closely with patients. Harold Blum points out that "analysts . . . seem to have more difficulty confronting and conceptualizing hate than they do love, both inside and outside the psychoanalytic process" (1997, 360). For example, the therapist in the story states, *As she hurls her body into my long-suffering couch, I fight the urge to respond to her aggression with retaliation. I struggle to bite back the disapproving words that arise in me. I want to take charge of her, to control her, to make her stop.*

In order to understand these internal and relational pressures as they are exerted in the transference–countertransference matrix, we can draw on a psychoanalytic understanding of sadomasochism. Sadomasochism has been a topic of ongoing interest and vexation since it was first introduced by Freud. In that phase of his development as a thinker, Freud viewed masochism as "sadism turned round on the subject's own self" ([1905] 1953g, 158) and thought that sadomasochism resulted from a linking of overheated libidinal and aggressive drives.

As his thinking moved in new directions, however, Freud came to conceptualize sadomasochism as an unresolved Oedipal phase issue. In a letter to Jung in 1909, he described how sadomasochism played out within the transference, stating, "In my practice, I am chiefly concerned with the problems of repressed sadism in my patients; I regard it the most frequent cause of the failure of therapy. Revenge against the doctor combined with self-punishment" (1974, 267). In a letter to Sándor Ferenczi in 1911, he similarly noted, "I hardly know a more deceptive and more complicated problem in our field than that of masochism" (2000, 281). Any therapist caught up in such a transference enactment will agree with Freud's lament, expressed later, that we are "specially inadequate" to deal successfully with masochistic patients ([1938] 1955h, 180).

Although we continue to face clinical difficulties in the treatment of sadomasochism, we now have a clearer understanding of the developmental dynamics that are involved. Classical analysts conceptualize sadomasochism as self-directed punishment for incestuous wishes. Despite the universality of aggressive and sexual drives, however, such an explanation does not adequately account for the fixed character pathology noted in sadomasochistic adults. One such understanding draws on attachment theory. This model suggests that when caregivers respond in highly unpredictable and inconsistent ways, children protect themselves from their feelings of helplessness and fear by developing what psychoanalysts call a "fixed omnipotent belief." Thus, a child may find it more bearable to assume that he "caused" a painful event to occur than to experience his utter helplessness in the face of ongoing abuse or neglect.

In contrast, a secure attachment is fostered when there is a clear and predictable cause-and-effect relationship between the baby's behaviors and emotions and the caregiver's loving response. When a young child cannot count on predictable and attuned responses—as is often the case when the caregiver is depressed, highly anxious, or inconsistent in other ways—he is filled with feelings of hopelessness and rage. Jack Novick and Kerry Novick explain that when "these [sadomasochistic] patients" were children, in the absence of other well-attuned caregivers, they "turned away from their inborn capacities to interact effectively with the real world and instead began to use the experience of helpless rage and pain magically to predict and control their chaotic experiences. The failure of reality-oriented competence to effect empathic attunement forced the child into an imaginary world where safety, attachment, and omnipotent control were magically associated with pain" (1991, 313).

Within this model, an already vulnerable child may confront the "reality" of feeling small and weak in relation to a powerful parent or when confronted by the real, physical differences between the sexes. Such vulnerability is then compounded by other failures to get what they want and need from their caregivers. Rather than encountering supportive situations from which to resolve this developmental conundrum, the sadomasochistic adult continues to rely on his childlike magical omnipotence by "murdering reality" when he refuses to acknowledge anatomical and generational differences.

Psychoanalysts believe that the therapist experiences the patient's infantile sadomasochistic urge to destroy the other's power in terms of countertransferential feelings of powerlessness, hopelessness, and incompetence. Knowing this response is likely to occur, the therapist needs to tolerate the activation of her own more or less dormant sadism (Wallerstein and Coen 1994). The analyst in "Joining the Pain" identifies these strong sadistic pulls when she acknowledges how the patient *forces me—against my will—to see myself more starkly than do other patients, to face the dark and primitive responses. . . . I yearn to turn away. I want to obliterate her need for me.* The therapeutic goal, then, is to contain and make meaning of the countertransference. Over time, doing so will enable the patient to understand his unique contribution to the sadomasochistic "knife dance."

The therapist likewise needs to appreciate the significant role of sadomasochism and the transference–countertransference matrix in her understanding of self-injury. Otherwise, it is unlikely that she will get to the heart of important questions such as: How can the patient do this? Why does self-injury happen? What is the patient trying to convey? And, finally, how is the therapist to grapple with this inchoate pain and help the patient articulate the unspeakable?

One such way to grapple might be Henry Kellerman's theory of symptom formation as a "process beginning with a thwarted wish as associated with repressed anger. The repressed anger is fused with the memory of the *who*—the person or object toward whom the anger was initially directed but toward whom it could not be expressed" (2008, 162). Kellerman views symptom formation as a "code" that can be potentially unlocked via "accessible symptoms"—that is, those symptoms that have not been present for an extended period or are not yet part of the patient's character structure. In essence, he believes that what produces symptoms is repressed anger rather than repressed infantile sexuality. The goal of treatment is to separate the anger from the memory of its perceived source. For example, in "Joining the Pain" the therapist looks for the anger underlying the patient's thwarted childhood wish for adequate parental containment and soothing. Thus, Kellerman provides a way to understand the etiology of how the patient's underlying feelings of anger and abandonment "locked in" her self-injurious behaviors.

The means by which this process of shared understanding happens is unique to each therapeutic relationship. Edward Tronick (2003) refers to this process as "mutual regulation." As the patient learns to express emotion toward his therapist in a more modulated way, the two ideally create an environment in which they are emotionally attuned. This ability to describe emotion and to experience it in a contained way promotes healing and self-soothing. Beatrice Beebe and Frank Lachmann explain the emerging attunement between patient and therapist, noting that during such moments of increased attunement "the way one is known by oneself is matched by the way one is known by the other" (2002, 32).

As in this story, such "knowing" is predicated on the therapist's availability and willingness to tolerate the patient's primitive and powerful emotions. The therapist must first digest the information, as a parent does with a young child's distress, and then make this new understanding available to the patient. In the story, the analyst writes, *I struggle to listen in the midst of this assault on my senses—to maintain my sense of connection with her.* Of course, any such "knowing" of one person by another is imperfect and incomplete, and it ideally goes through many transformations in the therapeutic space. It is within this lively space between the two participants that meaning is ultimately made (Lichtenberg 1999; Benjamin 2004; Renick 2004). As Hans Loewald eloquently pointed out forty years ago, "It is impossible to love the truth of psychic reality, to be moved by this love as Freud was in his lifework, and not to love and care for the object whose truth we want to discover. . . . Our object, being what it is, is the other in ourselves and ourself [*sic*] in the other. To discover truth about the patient is always discovering it with him and for him as well as for ourselves and about ourselves . . . as the truth of human beings is revealed in their interrelatedness (1970, 65).

As analysts, we come to recognize the meaning of our countertransference through an ongoing process of trial identifications with our patients. Over the course of treatment, we continually shift between engaging in the unfolding transference–countertransference enactments and then stepping back into a self-reflective stance. As Henry Smith observes, "The analyst's identifications *with* the patient and his or her projections *onto* or *into* the patient may be the fundamental way the analyst has of learning about the patient" (2006, 623, emphasis in original). In fact, Smith (forthcoming) also makes the point that we are in a continual process of enactment with our patients.

There remains a debate over how we can best understand the process of change as it plays out within the context of our clinical practices. In spite of theoretical differences, we increasingly struggle to draw on our own countertransference experience in the service of the patient's healing. Particularly when dealing with patients buffeted by intense emotions from early, less verbally mediated states, strong countertransference pulls can disconcert and disorganize us. Despite these forces, however, it is incumbent upon us to use the valuable information that becomes available in this way. As the therapist in "Joining the Pain" reports, *"She frightens me, this is true. Nevertheless, I work to find a quiet place in my mind where I can make contact with her. I try to help her find words to tell me the meaning of the violence she has wrought on her body."* Such information helps us grasp our patients' early experiences because these experiences are now being replayed in the current therapeutic relationship. It is only out of this process of shared meaning making within the transference and countertransference that we are able to understand the universal human potential for both love and the most murderous feelings of anger and hate—both our patient's and our own (Winnicott 1949). It is only from this extraordinarily painful and exhilarating process of coming to know ourselves and our patients more fully that we develop the necessary empathy to do this challenging work (Poland 1984).

18 THE TAXI

In light of a patient's rage, both patient and therapist question their assumptions about race.

His large hands clench into terrifying fists that pound once and then again into his thighs. I sit in my chair and watch, transfixed, as he glares at me in unblinking fury. A tangled knot in my stomach begins to form. I have never before seen this man in such a state of wordless rage. I watch as his blows land on the neat creases of his suit pants. I have no doubt that these blows are symbolically meant for me. I am almost positive he won't actually hurt me, but . . .

With a slow, guttural voice, he spits out, "I hope that someday I get to watch you get hit by a car. And, most of all, I want you to know that I am there, just watching. I want you to see me as you die. In the moment when the light fades from your eyes, I want you to recognize that although I could have helped, *I . . . do . . . nothing,* and that the last thing you ever know is that *I . . . just . . . let it happen*!" He sneers at me with utter contempt across the uncomfortably shrinking distance that separates his chair from mine. I have no clue why I am suddenly under assault by my usually self-contained patient. I compose my response as calmly as I can. "You want me to know what it's like to feel helpless, to be at your mercy, and to know that, in that moment, you won't have any. You also want me to know—right now—what that helplessness feels like."

As he continues to speak, the hardened mask of rage shifts, and I begin to see other complicated feelings emerge. He tells me how humiliating it feels to leave the large corporate law firm where he works and try to hail a taxi to take him to my office in the suburbs. Although he has been in treatment for less than a year, his need for me feels too vulnerable, too bitterly shaming, to be borne. He is a handsome, well-educated African American man who has spent a lifetime trying to perfect his need for no one, especially me, a middle-aged white woman sitting opposite him in a nicely appointed office.

Until this moment, we have barely nodded at the differences between us. Early in the treatment, I, to be fair, had dutifully raised questions about his reactions to the obvious fact of my whiteness. However, his primary focus had been on finding the similarities between us. I was complicit in this avoidance, reluctant to enter into the racial divide. Now race has become a gaping maw threatening to swallow us both.

I sit helplessly as Howard withdraws further and further into himself. The story painfully unfolds. How he stood outside his office today, the cold drizzle slowly drenching his suit, while taxi after taxi passed him by, preferring to stop up the block for the white fares waving their arms. He had always told himself that when he became a professional, this would not happen, and he would be safe. He bitterly realizes that this is not so. He tells me that these present indignities are layered on top of early, unbearable memories of powerlessness against countless childhood assaults, both psychological and physical. His wish to seek help from me, to be in a relationship with me, has now become an almost unbearable trigger for humiliation and rage. He is convinced that I will exploit his vulnerability and weakness. He'd be better off if I were dead.

As we sit together, Howard fills the minutes with previously unspoken memories. He describes struggling with a severe but undiagnosed learning disability in a predominantly white school. Taunted by his classmates, he fought back with his fists. He also learned not to trust through years of beatings at the hands of his mentally ill mother. He had no respite from the ongoing and often violent sexual abuse by his white babysitter. His beloved grandparents, who knew about his home life, did nothing to rescue him. He comes to therapy utterly convinced that it is infinitely better to be isolated than to risk yet another experience of abandonment or abuse.

Although he has reached some degree of professional success, he is always haunted by the specter of early disruptions and losses that make his achievements seem tenuous. He has been fired many times after erupting in rage in response to both real and perceived racial provocations. His usual belligerent stance of angrily railing against the world and all of its injustices leads him to be labeled "the workplace instigator." One time when his office was decorated with KKK symbols as a "joke" by his coworkers and supervisor, he was the one who ended up being escorted off the premises after he threatened the same violent retaliation he had just shown in my office. In his experience, there is no one willing to hear his story, and he is instead left—as he was as a child—to bear the memory alone. As he describes it, "The black man cries tears of white-hot humiliation."

Here I am with Howard, my patient, and I am scared. Everything I believe about myself is being challenged. What does it mean that I am suddenly aware of his fists, his size . . . his blackness? I tried to address the underlying meaning of the skin-deep differences between us, but until this moment it has never been alive in our shared space. In this moment, I suddenly understand in a new light the phrase Howard has often repeated: "If you speak it, you have to know it. And if you know it, it owns you." Now, for either of us to fail to "know it" will be catastrophic. In those stark and terrifying moments, I am given a window into the world of a black man who raises his arm to hail a cab that will not stop for him.

Analysts Reflect on Race and Racism

Racial, ethnic, gender, religious, and socioeconomic assumptions and prejudices are intrinsic to who we are and are integrated into our core sense of self. These "social categories of identity" (Dalal 2007, 148) are always present in the language we use, in our everyday experiences, and in our therapeutic encounters. Genetic science has proven that race, as a category, does not exist in nature. Its meaning is instead personal, fluid, and filled with unconscious fantasy, with no actual basis in biology. It is a concept used to describe individuals who share geographic origins and broad physical characteristics.

Within the idea of race, one sees that social reality and psychic reality are inextricably intertwined and interdependent. The psychoanalyst Farhad Dalal, who has written extensively about race and racism, points out that psychotherapists face a danger in seeing race as a purely psychological construct and not recognizing the fact that we are "living in a racist context" (2007, 139). As psychotherapists, we make a mistake when we view racial concerns as resistances that we need to get past in order to get to the "real material." It has been suggested, in fact, that "race as a psychological experience blurs the distinctions that we make between social reality and psychic reality" (Hamer 2002, 1221). Expanding this thought, Kimberlyn Leary (2000) describes race as occupying a transitional and complex space that resides somewhere between external reality and psychic reality.

Dalal argues that racism, like the concept of race, is basically a social construct, that it is "anything—a thought, feeling, or action—that uses the notion of race as an activating or organizing principle. Or, to put it another way, racism is the manufacture and use of the notion of race to serve consciously or unconsciously deleterious ends" (2007, 157). In common parlance, we tend to describe the members of racial, religious, or ethnic groups as homogenous. Yet, Dalal continues, "the attempts to define and distinguish race (physiology) from culture (behavior and beliefs) and from ethnicity (the internal sense of belonging) continually fail" (152). Yet our society is highly "racialized" (Leary 1997b). Human beings are biologically hardwired to notice differences and socialized to have clearly identified assumptions about racial categories. Henry Smith writes that "categorization of difference begins even earlier than language, with the first registrations of difference or otherness" (2007, 8).

Racism begins with the belief that one race or group of people is constitutionally superior or inferior, and this belief engenders feelings of hatred, contempt, disgust, and a divided world. In psychotherapy, subtle forms of racism exist and come to life in every encounter and in every treatment. Smith has written, "It is not so much a matter of when race and racism enter the consulting room, but whether and how we notice it" (2007, 4). In our story "The Taxi," the patient, Howard, would have immediately registered *"a middle-aged white woman sitting opposite him in a nicely appointed office."* Perhaps from the first phone call, our narrator similarly registered that her new patient was an African American man. Like any number of physical characteristics, race is often apparent but rarely acknowledged.

When a therapist and patient come face to face in the waiting room for the first time, they both are affected—sometimes outside of their awareness—by the other's skin color, age, dress, and gender as well as by all of the associations and experiences evoked in them by these outward appearances. Even when race is not directly addressed or acknowledged, it has a profound meaning for both participants. What we bring to bear in each new encounter is based on our individual constitution and history. When we meet a new person, we automatically categorize and locate the person in our internal world on the basis of our past experiences. Race, often instantly recognizable, is one overarching way we categorize people. We see how strong these automatic assumptions are when we encounter a reality that doesn't match the fantasized expectation. For example, in one of our practices a patient with a distinctively feminine name made several phone calls prior to the initial session, speaking in what the analyst thought was a high feminine voice. The therapist was startled when she opened her waiting-room door to discover a man instead of the woman she expected.

Leary (1997a) criticizes many theorists for thinking about race with the same either–or attitude that we have had historically concerning gender and sexual orientation. She encourages clinicians not to prejudge what race means in any treatment. Yet in our society, as in the psychoanalytic profession, speaking about race is complicated and risky. Silence about race reverberates in the psychoanalytic literature. Dorothy Holmes remarks, "Analysts are no less prone than is the general population to keeping racial and class issues repressed and unanalyzed" (2006, 221). As the writer of our story describes, *"I was complicit in this avoidance, reluctant to enter into the racial divide. Now race has become a gaping maw threatening to swallow us both."* Neil Altman writes that "we should expect to find racism in our countertransference and in our thoughts and feelings. . . . [R]eflection on our countertransference is an essential element if we wish to deal with race in our therapeutic work" (2000, 592).

In any therapeutic relationship, the topic of race is a difficult one to broach. Patients and therapists are often willing to collude in the denial of racial differences for fear that something will be said that is perceived as racist or hurtful. No matter how much analysts wish to exclude culturally rooted countertransferences—to be value-free psychotherapists—it is impossible. In the story "The Taxi," we see the way transference and countertransference influence both patient and therapist, simultaneously promoting and impeding the treatment. Because we cannot live outside our own experience, we should expect a racial element to exist in this case and in every case in which therapist and patient come from different backgrounds.

As painful as it is for Howard and his therapist to confront the issue of race, Howard's treatment cannot proceed without these explosive moments of truth. The issue of race, once uncovered, provides fertile ground for exploration. Nothing can be fully understood of Howard's inner world, his past experience, and his transference onto his therapist until the topic of race is engaged. Leary (2000) refers to therapeutic interactions where societal assumptions about race are replayed in the room as "racial enactments." The race-related event of being passed over by a taxi triggers a sense of outrage that reactivates Howard's warded-off feelings of humiliation and shame. His rage and contempt for his therapist thus represent an effort to redirect his own intolerable self-hatred from within himself to the outside world. At this explosive moment, his therapist becomes the embodiment of white racism: he sees her not as an individual, but as a member of the powerful and oppressive majority. We can wonder if the therapist feels a corresponding sense of shame and guilt. The author observes, *"Here I am with Howard, my patient, and I am scared. Everything I believe about myself is being challenged. What does it mean that I am suddenly aware of his fists, his size . . . his blackness?"* Though the experience of Howard's rage is terrifying and potentially destructive, we as psychotherapists consider the meaning of Howard's explosion within the context of a safe transference relationship.

Michael Lewis makes an interesting distinction between anger and rage: "Anger is the consequence of the frustration of a goal-directed action, while rage is the consequence of shame and is, therefore, a failure in the ability to maintain self-esteem" (1993, 148). Rage indicates an underlying conscious or unconscious fantasy involving a relationship between the self and another in which there is an injury to one's sense of worth. We witness Howard's rage when his therapist writes, *"His large hands clench into terrifying fists that pound once and then again into his thighs."*

To be able to think as a therapist in the midst of such a storm is extraordinarily difficult. As the author writes, *"I sit in my chair and watch, transfixed, as he glares at me in unblinking fury. A tangled knot in my stomach begins to form. I have never before seen this man in such a state of wordless rage. I watch as his blows land on the neat creases of his suit pants. I have no doubt that these blows are symbolically meant for me."* The author, suddenly acknowledging that she feels profoundly vulnerable and uncomfortable, becomes acutely aware of the racial divide. As Forrest Hamer remarks, "Complicating the resistance to an easy and meaningful discussion of race is the fact that race implicates matters of domination and subjugation or submission between people, of potential conflict, and of the sexual attractions and fears coded within ideas of race. Thus, we may often resist talking about race because race is not simply a *difference*, but one freighted with particular social and psychological history" (2002, 1225, emphasis in original). Race can serve any number of defensive purposes or take on any number of transference manifestations, disguising issues of class, power and control, and sexuality and aggression.

The most frequent psychoanalytic explanation for racism is based on the concept of projection. Projection is the unconscious process through which we deny our own unwanted attributes, thoughts, and emotions and instead ascribe them to outside persons or groups. The concept of the "other"—a person defined by his or her difference in relationship to us—becomes a container for our own frightening and unwanted impulses and fantasies. Dalal explains that "difficulties arising in the internal world of an individual . . . are split off from consciousness, repressed and projected into some object or person in the external world" (2007, 134). Smith writes, "It is around difference, real and imagined, that our earliest and most primitive defenses gather to split our objects into them and us, the feared and the safe, the loved and the hated, the privileged and the excluded, the envied and the denigrated—the different" (2007, 11). In other words, we project onto the "other" all we hate and despise in ourselves. The result of this dehumanizing process is evident in our story "The Taxi." Howard introjects (takes into himself) the societal projection of being a denigrated black man shamed by the color of his skin and then seeks to rid himself of the feeling by projecting it onto his therapist.

Projected thoughts do not dissipate; rather, they are taken in by individuals and the culture at large. Altman (2006) addresses the power of societal projections on groups, showing how projections can influence a person's sense of self and become a self-fulfilling prophecy; thus, the stereotypes can be defensively used to legitimize racist beliefs. One of the ways we can understand this pernicious process is by examining the development of children's self-awareness. Young children learn about themselves by gradually coming to know how they are perceived and held in mind by others, a process that Peter Fonagy and Mary Target (1998) refer to as "mentalization." If a child grows up swimming in a sea of cultural negative attributes, he is likely to experience himself as negatively as society perceives him. Holmes contends that those individuals whose self-images are "linked to racism and classism are apt to find that the disavowing messages take hold in the mind in a primary way" (2006, 219). In our story, we can imagine how the taxis that passed Howard compelled him suddenly to see himself as he imagined the drivers see him—as a frightening black man to be feared and scorned.

This type of searing experience corrodes the heart, just as the humiliation of the racial divide is seared into Howard's unconscious. It is no accident that he describes his shame thus: *"The black man cries tears of white-hot humiliation."* Howard is trapped, unable to free himself from ugly projections relating to his identity and his worth. He cannot extricate himself from the perception that he is to be denigrated because of the color of his skin. These perceptions of inferiority have clearly damaged his sense of self and are readily reactivated in subsequent interactions.

We often define ourselves in light of what we are not—what Harry Stack Sullivan (1953) refers to as the "not me"—that is, those attributes of another that one believes to be in sharp contrast to oneself. This is a useful concept when we consider the origin of racial prejudices. Altman offers a compelling explanation for the use of the terms *white* and *black* as racial descriptors that "characterize people whose skin color tends to vary somewhere along the pink-brown continuum" (2006, 61). He points out that in our culture the term *white* has historically represented the majority group and the de facto standard to which all other groups are compared. *Black*, then, as the contrasting term, becomes a way to disavow physical and psychological qualities that the majority culture would prefer to dis-own. Nonetheless, such disavowed attributes are actually universal. Thus, with racial prejudice "psychological similarity is denied" (61). *Black* and *white* are concretized and then maintained as a simplistic binary concept; what is good in one cannot by definition exist in the other. Thus, one is *black* only in contrast to someone who is *white*. As Altman points out, our dichotomized mindset is literally "*black* and *white* thinking" (2000, 589). Dalal says, "The naming of people as *black* or *white* is not so much a descriptive act as an *othering* process—a racializing process" (2007, 156, emphasis in original). This process provides the perfect milieu for projection.

Regardless of our ethnicity, all therapists need to acknowledge the reality of racism and at the same time seek to understand its in-dividual meaning for our patients and ourselves. In Howard's story, we see how internal and external realities collide explosively. For Howard, the racial taunting and humiliation became linked with *"years of beatings at the hands of his mentally ill mother . . . and [the] often violent sexual abuse by his white babysitter."*

Past wounds were compounded as Howard stood *"outside his office today, the cold drizzle slowly drenching his suit, while taxi after taxi passed him by, preferring to stop up the block for the white fares waving their arms."* His fragile and hard-won identity as a professional was severely rattled by the humiliation of being treated as invisible and left out in the rain. His status, position, and dignity were assaulted. Howard's rageful attack on his therapist is an attempt to restore an intact sense of self by an assertion of his authority and power. Rage has become a way to eliminate the dan-ger and to seek revenge for injury. In that dramatic moment, he is driven by the need to see his therapist suffer the same humiliation that he has experienced—more than anything, he longs to have the same kind of power over her that his tormentors had over him. Anna Freud ([1936] 1954) referred to this feeling as "identification with the aggressor."

For Howard, the shameful experience of being ignored by cab after cab is linked to his need to see his therapist that day. His fragile inner world is shaken, and he can no longer hold on to any semblance of a positive self-representation. The wish to relieve his internalized self-hatred and restore his sense of himself as a powerful person is accomplished in his fantasy of "murdering" his therapist: "*With a slow, guttural voice, he spits out, 'I hope that someday I get to watch you get hit by a car. And, most of all, I want you to know that I am there, just watching. I want you to see me as you die. In the moment when the light fades from your eyes, I want you to recognize that although I could have helped,* I . . . do . . . nothing, *and that the last thing you ever know is that* I . . . just . . . let it happen!' " With the rage now alive in the transference, both patient and therapist begin to appreciate the feelings of humiliation and powerlessness that underlie his conflicts in other areas of his life.

For authentic understanding between patient and therapist, they must consider both the internal significance and the external reality that forms the backdrop against which identity is constructed and expressed. Issues of race should not remain unaddressed, an unspoken presence in the room. When these issues are ignored and go underground, they exert hidden influences that gather force and may ultimately undermine or destroy the treatment. In contrast, struggling directly with these complex experiences can lead to deep and enduring change for both therapist and patient.

19 MY BEST FRIEND, FIONA

A therapist's misconduct derails the patient's treatment.

My best friend, Fiona, exuded an air of confidence that I associated with loving and being loved. I was convinced that the thing about Fiona was Dr. Stein, her analyst. I pictured him transforming her into the person with whom I was so enthralled. I thought of Fiona's relationship with him as this secret delight that she carried with her. I desperately wanted that for myself. But Dr. Stein, as my best friend's analyst, was not available to me, so he referred me to Dr. Bowman.

As a psychology graduate student, I was filled with a romantic view of the psychoanalytic process on which I was embarking. When I met Dr. Bowman, I saw immediately that I had gotten the silver, and Fiona the gold. Dr. Stein, whom I had met on several occasions, was from Argentina, tall and handsome, with a graying beard and piercing eyes. Dr. Bowman was an ordinary American, utterly lacking in glamour. I knew he'd be a painfully poor substitute, and I was sure Fiona knew it, too.

I tried to make Dr. Bowman into a romantic figure like Dr. Stein. I dreamed that I was kneeling at his feet and that he was stroking my long hair. The image rang hollow because I still longed for Dr. Stein. I was clearly obsessed and continued to hope that someday I would become his patient.

Dr. Stein eventually agreed to take me into analysis the year that Fiona was terminating in preparation for a move to another city. I unfolded my inner life to him. He would offer me words that seemed to reach deep inside of me. I imagined that I was special to him.

Soon after Fiona moved away, I went to visit her. In her house, I was suddenly overcome by a powerful sense of Dr. Stein's presence: here, a calendar from Argentina that Dr. Stein had given to her; there, a note pinned to the bulletin board above her desk that said, "Remember me." I preferred to remain confused a bit longer and said nothing, but on my return to analysis that Monday I spoke about feeling perplexed and agitated. An understanding was relentlessly dawning on me, but I fended it off until Fiona came to visit me a few weeks later. We went to a diner, and she told me that she and Dr. Stein were in love and that he was leaving his wife. The next day, in a rage, I went to see Dr. Stein, not sure what to say. Finally I blurted out, "She's a patient, I'm your patient, you can't love her like that. I won't see you anymore; you're not to be trusted." All this time, way inside of me, another tiny voice was crying, "You love her? You don't love me?" He said something about psychoanalysis being in conflict with reality and tried to persuade me to return. After that session, however, I left and never saw him or Fiona again.

Wanting to continue my treatment, I consulted with an analyst who confirmed that I should never return to Dr. Stein. He tried to find me a new analyst. In short order, I enlisted the help of friends, colleagues, teachers, and supervisors, coming away with two or three more names of suitable analysts and the same advice, "Stay with it. I really think she (he) could help." Over the next year and a half, I had many consultations with different therapists, telling my story again and again. Yet I never mentioned Dr. Stein's name. Some thought I was perversely protecting him, but I was ashamed, too, ashamed of my own longings and secretly ashamed that I wasn't the one he chose. I was trapped and alone in a transference love that had no exit.

During each consultation, I searched for the fantasy of fulfillment that I had lost, but it eluded me, and I grew increasingly desperate. Insignificant details about each analyst elicited my contempt. One took off her shoes and folded her bare feet beneath her. Another had fake flowers in her office. One was too old; one was too short; one had red hair and a squint. One time, after a good start with a kind man, I sat in the waiting room considering whether I wanted to come back. He came out of his office and, seeing me there, said, "Oh, by the way, the john's down the hall." That comment chased me away. And so it went.

The last person I saw was Dr. Lowry. Her office was small and cramped and piled high with papers and folders. There was barely room to sit on the couch. She was smart and direct and a bit arch. She listened to my story, and when I finished describing my many consultations, she said, "Well, one thing's clear. You have to stay here." She said that I was acting out my rage by broadcasting my story around town; I was razing the fields. She thought I was very angry indeed. She told me that she didn't particularly care if I liked her or not, but that she knew she could help.

So I stayed. I never loved her or even especially liked her. I weighed every comment against an image of perfection that existed only in my mind. Although she came up woefully short, I had to admit she was smart and she was tough. I hated her for not providing me with the fantasized contentment that I longed for. I tirelessly made fun of her to my boyfriend, speaking derisively of her pointy nose, her ugly hair, and her take-it-or-leave it attitude. Deep inside, a part of me wanted to stay lost, loving only Dr. Stein. I didn't realize until I left the area and Dr. Lowry far behind that indeed a healing process had begun.

Analysts Reflect on Boundary Violations in Treatment

There are no words to express fully the destruction that occurs when clinicians violate the boundaries of their profession. The psychotherapeutic relationship often elicits strong romantic feelings—such feelings may be the focus of treatment. They are to be discussed, though, not acted out. Because of the huge disparity in power, any sexual relationship that takes place between therapist and patient is abusive. "My Best Friend, Fiona" explores the powerful impact of a psychoanalyst's emotional seduction of two young female patients and his sexual seduction of one. Boundary violations, large and small, abound in Dr. Stein's relationships with his two young patients. The story highlights some of the cascading damaging effects of such transgressions.

When a therapist is exploitative, the impact damages patients as well as the entire profession. As John Ross writes, "Boundary violations . . . [are] 'collective traumas,' reverberating and sending shockwaves out that include relatives, colleagues and friends and the lives of generations to come" (1995, 961). Freud clearly articulated the danger of boundary violations in his paper "Observations on Transference Love": "If the patient's advances were returned it would be a great triumph for her, but a complete defeat for the treatment" ([1915] 1955f, 166). When an analyst violates a boundary, he or she destroys the relationship, the treatment, and the trust.

Boundary violations are frequent in therapy and in our everyday world. Their occurrences can both frighten and titillate us. Yet their power comes in part from the recognition that we all have the potential to transgress and violate a boundary. Under enough personal stress and trauma, even the most well-respected therapists can violate the boundaries of treatment. As Glen Gabbard points out, "There is a rather thin line between the desperately needy analyst using the patient for his own gratification and all the rest of us who regard ourselves as ethical and competent practitioners" (1998, 784). Gabbard and his colleague Eva Lester (1995) were the first contemporary analysts to look closely at the topic of boundary violations. They describe a multitude of reasons why an analyst succumbs to intense erotic longings—"love sickness" and masochistic surrender being the two primary causes. Therapists often experience romantic and sexual feelings during the course of treatment. However, through self-analysis, consultation, and supervision, they must ensure that these feelings are understood within the transference and countertransference and not acted out.

Gabbard and Lester (1995) distinguish between the crossing of a boundary, which can be benign, and a boundary violation, which is damaging to the patient. They describe a paradoxical state in which the therapist simultaneously needs a "thick" internal boundary—a clear sense of the beginning and end of one's inner self—and a "thin" outer boundary that allows for empathy—a porousness that lets in another's emotional experience. Therapy has an implicit as well as an explicit moral code in which boundary violations are unethical and illegal.

In treatment, it is with their words, not their actions, that therapists "touch" their patients. A boundary violation, whether an actual sexual transgression or a more subtle breach of trust, moves the treatment away from the realm of language and into the world of action. When this happens, the treatment can be at risk. Yet Gabbard and Lester suggest that bending the rules and violating them are not the same.

As professionals, how can we best understand the line between a subtle enactment and a serious boundary violation? The most egregious boundary violations between therapist and patient are easily recognizable. Rule breaking more often falls on a continuum, however, where the line of demarcation is less apparent. When does an action that may seem humane and caring, such as a comforting touch, go too far? As Gabbard and Lester describe, the slope is slippery. When clinicians hold on to the unquestioning conviction that what they do is always therapeutic, they are in danger of confusing their needs and wishes for gratification with what is in their patients' best interest. All therapists, regardless of gender, background, and theoretical orientation, have blind spots. This fact underscores the importance of self-analysis and ongoing professional consultation.

Early in his practice, Freud's treatment involved putting his hands on his patient's head to encourage free association. He subsequently adopted a different approach in which he believed that a detached stance, known as "analytic abstinence," was necessary to allow the patient's feelings and urges to be put into words. Yet Freud's theory often did not coincide with his actual clinical work. We see numerous examples of his extra-analytic warmth toward his patients—a number of gestures that we might question or completely avoid today. Gabbard (1995) illustrates the unavoidable gap between how we present our work to others and what we actually do with our patients.

Within the psychoanalytic profession, Freud's abstinence model became not just a therapeutic stance, but also an inviolate rule. All deviations were viewed as suspect. At times, this code of behavior was interpreted within the profession to mean that responding to patients with warmth fell outside of appropriate analytic conduct. Today we pay increasing attention to the meaning of the "real" relationship between patient and therapist, in which the ordinary rules of social engagement play a part. This "real relationship" exists alongside the powerful transference relationship.

If we are truly to engage with our patients, we cannot present ourselves as blank slates. Yet many therapists experience discomfort in the face of a patient's loving and erotic feelings. These feelings can become problematic if they result in seduction or, conversely, in the therapist's defensive flight behind a cold, distant facade. Both stances interfere with the patient's ability to fantasize and play. Analysts thus face a dilemma: How can they "fall in love" with their patient without the risk of action or the breaking of boundaries?

We find the answer to these dilemmas in a reliance on the "analytic frame." Adhering to the analytic frame—the structure and boundaries of treatment—gives the therapist the freedom to experience intense feelings toward her patients. This frame keeps in check some of the ambiguities inherent in the intimacy of a long-term therapeutic relationship. The therapeutic work relies on the consistency of the setting and the predictability of time boundaries, confidentiality, and non-physical contact. The patient learns that he can say whatever comes to mind, and the therapist will respond thoughtfully. Such aspects of the frame provide a feeling of safety, allowing the patient to share all of his thoughts, feelings, and experiences. Thus, the frame facilitates the therapeutic process by protecting the patient from exploitation, whether emotional, sexual, or financial. Likewise, boundaries permit the therapist to do the work of therapy consistently. She relies on the boundaries to protect them both from the intrusion of her needs and vulnerabilities into the therapeutic relationship.

In a panel discussion on boundary violations, Elizabeth Mayer questioned the established assumption that boundary violations result from a breach of abstinence (described and cited in Keenan 1995). She argued that boundary violations might instead result from an overly strict adherence to an idealized view of the therapist's neutrality. According to Mayer, most therapists feel pressured to conform to these ideals, but in private they work quite differently with their patients. She suggested that the frequency with which boundary violations occur may be a result of the split between how therapeutic abstinence is taught in theory and what actually happens in the consulting room. The consequence of this split "is that many analysts start subtly to dissociate their private analytic conduct from the models of analytic conduct they publicly espouse, write about, and teach" (qtd. in Keenan 1995, 856). Mayer's thesis highlights that when we don't openly discuss the real struggles and potential pitfalls inherent in our work, we are more prone to act them out.

The therapeutic relationship thus forms the scaffolding around which transference and countertransference can develop and unfold. These conditions create a regressive pull for the patient that requires a safe and containing environment. Yet this relationship is also uniquely susceptible to sexual transgressions because of the isolation in which it takes place and the power differential between the two parties. When a therapist is unable to preserve and safeguard the treatment, as in the story told here, the patient finds himself in an emotional tailspin.

We can imagine how a sexual relationship between a patient and therapist might start. Like most violations, it likely begins with small transgressions that move along Gabbard's "slippery slope"—extended sessions, a hug at the end of an hour, or long evening phone calls. Perhaps a lonely therapist confides in the patient about her own life and problems, thus flattering the patient with attention and intimacy. We can envision how gratifying this scenario might be for any vulnerable patient or therapist. For example, in our story a narcissistic collusion existed between the patient and Dr. Stein that kept the patient dangerously entrenched in the fantasy that he was the perfect love object.

In "My Best Friend, Fiona," the patient's idealization of Dr. Stein as well as Dr. Stein's poor boundaries and narcissistic indulgence set the stage for a highly destructive drama in which the transference love is exploited. The therapeutic frame deteriorates incrementally as external events overtake the analysis. The narrator describes her initial idealization of her best friend: *"My best friend, Fiona, exuded an air of confidence that I associated with loving and being loved."* The author attributes Fiona's "specialness" to her analyst: *"I pictured him transforming her into the person with whom I was so enthralled. I thought of Fiona's relationship with him as this secret delight that she carried with her. I desperately wanted that for myself."*

At the beginning of any treatment, patients often have the unconscious fantasy that they will recapture the early, idealized love they felt for a parent. Our narrator yearns for an illusory, perfect union with Dr. Stein. She imagines that he will know her completely and without words. In a summary of Melanie Klein's 1975 work, Dale Ortmeyer states, "Envy is the wish to destroy what the other person has that one doesn't have. . . . Idealization, thus, defends against instinctual aggression and is part of [an] early normal stage of development. It is universal" (1987, 222). Thus, the narrator's glowing idealization of Fiona and Dr. Stein serves to defend against the envy that can potentially destroy either or both of these important relationships. When idealization is the leading edge of the transference, the therapist is at risk for boundary violations. As in this story, unanalyzed narcissism and defensive denial on the part of either the patient or the therapist can be an explosive combination.

The writer has the fantasy that analysis with Dr. Stein will allow her to attain Fiona's "perfection." She writes: *"I desperately wanted that for myself. But Dr. Stein, as my best friend's analyst, was not available to me."* She imagines that Dr. Stein will be able to see below the surface to discover her unique specialness. She is intoxicated with the fantasy that analysis with him will provide all that is missing in her life.

Idealizations are by their nature false. As Harry Stack Sullivan has observed, "In idealizing, one projects upon another personality a body of desirable characteristics that exist within the self as a stereotype" (1965, 202). When a person is idealized, his or her real qualities are neither perceived nor acknowledged. Nor can they be until the spell is broken. Freud described such idealization as a form of seeking one's own wishes for magical completion in the other: "The loved object enjoys a certain amount of freedom from criticism, and . . . all its characteristics are valued more highly than those of people who are not loved. . . . The tendency which falsifies judgment in this respect is that of idealization. . . . We love it on account of the perfections, which we have striven to reach" ([1922] 1955c, 112).

Entering treatment often reawakens childhood yearnings for the perfect love of the still idealized parents. The author writes: *"During each consultation, I searched for the fantasy of fulfillment that I had lost, but it eluded me, and I grew increasingly desperate."* Idealization in the treatment, when not exploited by the therapist, can help carry the patient through scary and uncertain terrain. The narrator wishes that Dr. Stein's understanding and love will magically heal her and guarantee her the future she wants. It is the therapist's job to understand and interpret such wishes and fears and to support the patient's development. By contrast, when a therapist takes advantage of this position of power and enacts the incestuous relationship, he or she becomes the perpetrator of abuse.

The classical idea of transference is based on an Oedipal configuration in which the patient "falls in love" with the therapist. In this view, the female patient falls in love with her male therapist and thus reworks her earlier wishes and longings for her father within the transference. As a consequence of this working through, she gradually relinquishes the incestuous therapist–father in favor of a new, more appropriate love object. In contemporary theory, we now understand that these therapeutic dyads can involve twosomes of any gender constellation. Although some analysts such as Harold Searles (1959) acknowledge the analyst's reciprocal "falling in love," it is the analyst's responsibility and ethical mandate not to act on these feelings.

We do not learn in the story what Fiona's relationship with Dr. Stein means to her, nor do we know how their relationship transpired. We know this story only from the author's point of view. When Fiona realizes the "Oedipal fantasy" and becomes sexually involved with her analyst, the narrator is excluded and becomes locked in an actualized Oedipal situation. In her fury, she cries: " *'She's a patient, I'm your patient, you can't love her like that. I won't see you anymore; you're not to be trusted.' All this time, way inside of me, another tiny voice was crying, 'You love her? You don't love me?'* " She feels betrayed and desolate, aware that someone else, not she, has successfully enticed Dr. Stein. With this transgression, Dr. Stein renounces his role as her analyst. He can no longer help her make sense of her envy and rage at being excluded, nor can he help her relinquish and mourn the Oedipal fantasy and the transference love.

Sexual relations between therapist and patient are taboo and invasive. As in situations of child abuse, boundary violations between therapist and patient are highly destructive, have lasting repercussions, and can damage the patient's capacity to form trusting, intimate relationships in the future. In both situations, there is often disavowal or denial on the part of those involved. There is the wish to preserve the idealization and position of the authority figure, whether parent, therapist, or other trusted person.

Additional trauma occurs when there is denial from other patients, colleagues, and professional organizations, such as training institutes. For example, Gabbard and Lester (1995) describe a long history of analytic institutes' failure to respond to reports of analysts' transgressions. Such denial can be rooted in the wish to protect well-respected colleagues and the profession as a whole. In addition, psychotherapists are trained to understand and therefore can be hesitant to judge and condemn. Because of their identification with other therapists and their idealization of their profession, they may wish to protect the larger group's reputation even at the expense of the victims (Wallace 2007).

Jody Davies has suggested that when there are violations within the therapeutic setting—which are similar to childhood sexual abuse—the ongoing psychological damage is even more destructive than the physical assault. It is "the violent penetration and co-opting of mind that occurs when one is emotionally and physically dependent on another who violates and exploits . . . [and] is granted the authority to control and define the other's reality." She adds that the "ultimate boundary violation becomes the coercive superimposing of one individual's reality into the mental integrity of another, less powerful individual" (2000, 219, 220). The dilemma is that the patient's necessary regression and dependency, which allow for the potency of the therapeutic process, also create the circumstances in which the power differential between therapist and patient can be disastrously exploited.

In our story, the writer describes her confusion and inability to think or even to see what has actually happened. As she writes, *"I was suddenly overcome by a powerful sense of Dr. Stein's presence: here, a calendar from Argentina that Dr. Stein had given to her; there, a note pinned to the bulletin board above her desk that said, 'Remember me.' I preferred to remain confused a bit longer and said nothing. . . . An understanding was relentlessly dawning on me, but I fended it off."* Her wish is to protect Dr. Stein, Fiona, and, most especially, herself from the inescapable truth.

What is the legacy when hopes of Oedipal love are actualized? Describing parental abuse, Christopher Bollas has written: "The child can no longer play with her [parent] in her mind" (1989, 180). In other words, fantasy is inhibited by the intrusion of painful reality. Similarly, when boundary violations occur in therapy, the therapist is no longer available as a safe object in the patient's mind. When the therapy is derailed by a violation, successful resolution of the transference is also derailed. As a consequence, the patient is unable to mourn: *"I was trapped and alone in a transference love that had no exit."* Our author is left longing for the imagined perfection, yet she remains inevitably disappointed and angry. Rather than being able to work gradually through her idealization of Dr. Stein with him, she is traumatically disillusioned by his real flaws, unable to move on after the crushing blow. She writes, *"I was ashamed, too, ashamed of my own longings and secretly ashamed that I wasn't the one he chose."*

In her subsequent quest to find a new analyst, the author is like the unsatisfied Goldilocks: *"One was too old; one was too short; one had red hair and a squint."* Her inability to replace her analyst is understandable. She only begins to form a new attachment to Dr. Lowry after she understands that her multiple consultations were an attempt to regain her power and enact her revenge: *"Dr. Lowry said that I was acting out my rage by trying to broadcast my story around town; I was razing the fields. She thought I was very angry indeed."*

One can hope that within a new treatment a patient who has experienced a boundary violation will move toward a more mature love—one that includes real intimacy and admiration as well as the recognition of others' imperfections. Indeed, the work of analysis can proceed only when inevitable disappointments are integrated and made meaningful over the course of the treatment.

PART FIVE

When the World Shatters

20 INTO THE KITCHEN

A little girl responds to sexual abuse by splitting her life into before and after.

It was Christmas time, and she loved Christmas. Her house, like all the other houses on the cul-de-sac, was decorated with a tree and a wreath on the door. The smell of freshly baked banana bread permeated the house. Everything was just the same as before, except nothing felt the same. What she had once looked forward to now caused her to recoil. The memory of the night before was a frozen, icy ball in the pit of her stomach. As she made her way into the kitchen toward her mother, her older sister, and her baby brother, she waited for someone to ask what was wrong, but no one did. Why did no one notice? Didn't anyone care? Her little-girl mind couldn't grasp that even though everything felt turned upside down on the inside, she looked exactly the same on the outside as she had the day before.

After several years in therapy, Susan has come to recognize that at that moment she drove a wedge into her inner world, dividing it into two realms, an unbridgeable chasm between them. She was now utterly alone on one side, and everyone else—everyone she loved then, everyone she would know in the future—would be on the other. It just seemed safer that way.

As the story spills out into the stillness of my office, she describes the textures, smells, tastes, and sounds around her as she numbly made her way into the kitchen so many years ago. Listening, I fight the tendency to "go away," to dissociate during the session, lured by the siren call of almost anything else. With a deep breath, I settle into the story and note that my body's rigidity matches hers. Like her, I am warding off the assault that comes from experiencing her story. My mind sketches the images that unfold until it feels as if I am also there, horrified again by the brutality of the betrayal.

She recounts how she sat down at the table while life spun around her. Her legs dangled from the chair, not touching the floor, as she stirred the warm oatmeal her mother placed before her. The plump raisins and brown sugar that swirled in her bowl mesmerized her. Slowly, carefully she poured the milk out of her favorite creamer, the one shaped like a cow where the milk flowed out of its mouth, the one that her mother put out for her every weekend morning. Susan carefully poured the milk over her oatmeal, trying not to splash. She willed herself to disappear, to blend into the cereal along with the milk. Maybe, just maybe, she could blot out the memory that threatened to overwhelm her. Every time she put the spoon into her mouth, she felt her throat tighten and her stomach churn. She might as well have been eating sawdust. Even now, as she painfully recalls that day—a retelling that has taken place again and again in the past few months—her eyes water, a sour taste rises from the back of her throat, and a feeling of nausea overtakes her. Lying on the couch in my office, she stirs in discomfort.

Before that morning, Susan was a free-spirited little girl. A tomboy, she rode her bike, swam on the neighborhood Tadpoles swim team, and followed the older kids wherever she could. Feminine and fashion conscious, her mother and older sister despaired that Susan's hair was always tousled. Her tights had holes, and there were bruises on her knees and shins. The photos in her childhood album show an impish little girl with a bright smile and colorful, unmatched clothing.

As the story unfolds, I struggle to focus on the image of "that" Susan so that she can come alive in the sessions. Much of what the trauma stole from her will be unknowable unless I can hold that image in mind. From time to time, her childhood liveliness lights up our session for a moment, but then the light sputters, leaving just a faint outline. Even the afterimages sometimes fade, and Susan once again sinks into darkness.

Today I'm struck once again by the contrast between the messy-haired, exuberant child and the conservative, cautious woman in my office. She is attractive but seems largely unaware of it. Slightly over-weight she wears no makeup, has a "no-nonsense" hairdo, and is dressed in casual clothes and comfortable clogs. She dons her "soccer mom" persona as a cloak of invisibility. Her dress and personality keep any sexual energy or interest muted, even from herself. Traces of that lively little girl are now hazy. It is as if Susan exists only in pastels. Gone are her vibrant colors. That is the cost of living on the other side of the wedge.

Over time, Susan allows both of us to inhabit her childhood memories. In the shorthand that characterizes any long-term relationship, we refer to these memories as "before" and "after" she "came into the kitchen." We know now that "before," she had craved the attention of her grandparents when they visited during the holidays. She always felt just a little lonely in her family—a sense that she didn't fit in with the others. She tells me about how her grandfather would hold her, read books to her, and tickle her and about how special she felt to have his attention. She liked seeing the envy in her siblings' faces, even though she knew she shouldn't.

Susan haltingly tells me how confusing it was when her grandfather came upstairs that night—the first of many nights—into the room that she shared with her little brother whenever the family had company. She recalls the heavy creak of the bed as he quietly sat down beside her. In tears, she tells me how confused she was, how she pretended to be asleep and tried so hard to stay perfectly still. No matter how hard she tried, though, Susan couldn't block out the changes in her grandfather's breathing or the ways his hands became rough and insistent as he touched her body. How she could not will him away, no matter what she told herself. How helpless, utterly helpless, she felt.

It is clear that at this point in the retelling Susan has left the safe confines of my office and is once again a little girl of five intently staring down at the tips of the white bunny slippers that peek out from under her new red robe. As she lies there on my couch, her body reflects the rigidity with which she held herself on that morning so many years ago, as if by keeping herself perfectly still, she might simply vanish.

Analysts Reflect on a Patient's Memory of Trauma and Betrayal

As commonly quoted, Herbert Ward once stated, "Child abuse casts a shadow the length of a lifetime." In our work, we treat many patients who describe childhoods devastated by repeated experiences of abuse, neglect, and betrayal. Sexual abuse often occurs within the context of other forms of mistreatment and neglect. Such patients arrive in our offices with a wide array of symptoms but little understanding of the link between their early experiences and now. They either describe their abuse as historic "fact," divested of current emotion and meaning, or as a casual aside—almost a footnote—slipped into their story. Each abuse narrative unfolds and is understood within the context of the victimized child's internal world and his important relationships at the time of the abuse. The importance of this contextualization can be noted when the therapist in "Into the Kitchen" tells us how *the photos in her childhood album show an impish little girl with a bright smile and colorful, unmatched clothing. As the story unfolds, I struggle to focus on the image of 'that' Susan so that she can come alive in the sessions. Much of what the trauma stole from her will be unknowable unless I can hold that image in mind."*

To "focus on the image" of the child before the abuse, the therapist must understand the many influences that shaped the patient in her early life. She must consider the patient's relationships to the abuser and other family members, the developmental stages during which the abuse occurred, the child's preexisting emotional and cognitive resources, what role the child's fantasy plays in her response to this confusing reality, and a host of other issues. Over time, she can help the patient pick up the threads of her new insights and repeatedly weave, unravel, and then reweave them into an increasingly complex and textured narrative of her life. In therapy, our patients thus come to understand the multilayered meanings of their individual stories.

The role of the perpetrator in the victim's life and the availability of other people who do or do not provide support and nurture greatly influence the long-term effects of trauma. We find evidence for this assertion in epidemiological research. For example, in studies of the general population more women report abuse by perpetrators from outside the family (Briere 1988), but in clinical populations the reverse is true (Jaffe 1988). Thus, although the number of women abused by perpetrators outside their families is larger, those whose abuser is a family member suffer more emotional damage.

This profoundly negative impact is the result of several different factors. Children are highly dependent on caregivers and do not have the cognitive or physical resources to protect themselves. Therefore, if the adults charged with caring for them do not do so or are actively abusing or neglecting them, these children have little recourse. As noted in "Into the Kitchen," when the child *"made her way into the kitchen toward her mother, her older sister, and her baby brother, she waited for someone to ask what was wrong, but no one did. Why did no one notice? Didn't anyone care? Her little-girl mind couldn't grasp that even though everything felt turned upside down on the inside, she looked exactly the same on the outside as she had the day before."* A young child's understanding of how the world works is formed within the crucible of the family. If abuse is understood as normal or acceptable within the family, the young victim is often unable to understand that what was done to her is wrong.

As the child's emotional and cognitive development progresses, and as she is increasingly exposed to norms and values outside the family, her understanding of her abuse may shift. For example, one of our patients explained her great shame when in middle school she attended her first sleepover and discovered, while talking with her friends, that not every father asked his daughter to perform sexual acts as a demonstration of love. Another of our adolescent patients, whose father was arrested for uploading and selling online videos in which he sexually abused her, struggled with the treasured notion that he did so not simply because he thought she was beautiful. To fully acknowledge that what he did was exploitative and abusive would mean the loss of her belief that she was "special" to her father. Instead, she desperately sought to deny his betrayal and the commercialization in which he'd engaged. As she prepared for her father's trial, however, the reality of his abuse shattered her idealization, and she became suicidal. In therapy, we must understand the meanings that the abuse has for the patient and its resultant fantasies (Alexander and Anderson 1997).

The impact of sexual abuse is often more defined by the significance of the child's relationship with the perpetrator than by the frequency and type of abuse. For instance, when a family member who fills a caretaking role is also the perpetrator, the child is caught in an impossible dilemma. Under such conditions, the child now experiences the caregiver as simultaneously the source of and the solution to the problem (Main and Hesse 1990). Thus, the child's developmentally appropriate need to seek comfort from the caregiver (who is now no longer safe) and the equally compelling need to flee from danger are in conflict. This irresolvable tension causes the child to "freeze," or dissociate. When children cannot find refuge during times of terrible distress, they rely on dissociation to soothe and calm themselves. This defense makes it impossible, however, for them to develop the capacity to mentalize—to know their own thoughts—about this experience (Liotti 2006).

Children who are raised with unpredictable parenting and the absence of a loving, protective other do not develop a secure attachment. Such an impairment impedes the emergence of the necessary self-soothing capacities and results in cognitive and biological disruption. The betrayal that abused children experience may result in the development of a "false self" through a failure of empathic and attuned mirroring. Leonard Shengold coined the term *soul murder* to describe how a child, emotionally bound to and dependent on the perpetrator, is no longer able to feel authentic joy or self-efficacy. The resultant dilemma produces rage and helplessness—"unbearable feelings that must be suppressed for the victim to survive. . . . When it is necessary to retreat from feelings, good feelings as well as bad ones are compromised" (1989, 2). The patient in "Into the Kitchen" tells us how, on the morning after she was sexually assaulted for the first time, she felt profoundly abandoned: *"She drove a wedge into her inner world, dividing it into two realms, an unbridgeable chasm between them. She was now utterly alone on one side, and everyone else—everyone she loved then, everyone she would know in the future—would be on the other. It just seemed safer that way."*

In order to treat trauma patients successfully, we therapists must address the cognitive, emotional, and relational consequences of the abuse as those consequences play out in our offices and in patients' current lives. Our understanding of the widespread impact of child sexual abuse has come about only in the past few decades and has dramatically changed our clinical practice. Along with psychodynamic theory, our clinical approach to trauma is informed and enriched by many other perspectives and disciplines. The latter include cognitive science, which helps us conceptualize the unique ways that we store, retain, and retrieve traumatic memory (Bucci

2007); developmental psychopathology, which addresses the impact of early trauma on the subsequent trajectory of development (Cicchetti and Posner 2006); endocrinology, which assesses the effects of stress on the child's developing brain and body (Perry 2001; Putnam 2003); attachment theory and research (Anderson and Alexander 2005; Fonagy et al. [2002] 2005); and newly discovered advances in brain science. All these approaches shape our understanding and contribute to our current standard of care (Courtois and Ford 2009).

So how do we best make use of these important clinical and research findings in our treatment? We need to return to the early psychoanalytic conceptualizations of child abuse—both the reality of the abuse and how the child's understanding of it becomes integrated into fantasy. From this early model, we can explore how different theoretical orientations approach this issue.

No area of psychoanalytic theory has caused more debate than Freud's abandonment of the seduction theory, his early belief that hysterical neuroses developed out of early childhood seduction. This theory was his attempt to account for patients' reports of early childhood sexual victimizations. However, Freud later inexplicably supplanted this reality-based understanding of childhood sexual abuse with the Oedipal theory. In the latter, he maintained that adult patient's reports of childhood "seductions" were instead based in unconscious childhood wishes. With the adoption of the centrality of the Oedipal fantasy, the realities of childhood sexual abuse were thus obscured.

Since that time, many biographers and psychoanalytic theorists have explored the multiple meanings, influences, and consequences of Freud's shift in thinking. These views have coalesced around two dichotomously opposed positions. Some see Freud's shift as evidence of his rigorous adherence to self-analysis and his willingness to adopt new paradigms. Others argue that abandoning the seduction theory negatively impacts victims of childhood sexual abuse. Although this debate is important historically, our current discussion focuses primarily on the consequences of that theoretical shift for how we treat childhood abuse survivors.

Each major theoretical orientation within psychoanalytic thinking offers a unique lens through which to understand the internal realities and treatment concerns stemming from sexual victimization. Contemporary psychodynamic clinicians who treat trauma are generally clustered within three theoretical perspectives: ego psychology, self-psychology, and object relations. Within the ego psychology paradigm, childhood trauma is understood as having both reality and fantasy components. Ego psychologists are interested in the unconscious meaning that the event holds for the individual and in the myriad ways that the child's ego may have been utterly overwhelmed by the trauma (e.g., A. Freud 1967; Krystal 1988; Kramer 1991). Self-psychologists (Kohut 1971b; Schwartz and Stolorow 2001) focus on trauma's impact, which they believe occurs due to betrayal by early self-objects and the subsequent shattering of the child's ability to anticipate a predictable, safe, and stable world. Finally, the object-relations approach focuses strongly on the meaning of the child's subjective sense of helplessness and the devastating consequences of betrayal by primary attachment figures. However, the reality-based relationship between significant figures and the traumatized child is considered more central than either the unconscious fantasies or the child's feelings of being emotionally overwhelmed and engulfed. Object-relations clinicians who in particular have addressed the treatment of trauma include Ronald Fairbairn (1943), Peter Fonagy and his colleagues (1995), and Richard Kluft (2000). In treatment, most object-relations therapists adopt a less abstinent stance than do more classical therapists and deemphasize the role of verbal interpretations with severely regressed patients.

Whatever their theoretical orientation, psychodynamic therapists "understand" their patient's histories and symptoms through the theoretical lens with which they are most comfortable. Nevertheless, most therapists utilize varied treatment approaches. This flexibility allows them to best match their interventions to their patients' current needs and is especially important for vulnerable patients. Their goal is to help their patients make sense of their experiences, to find a way to bear knowing what was done, and to discover how it affected them, both then and now.

One component of "knowing" one's own history involves addressing issues around memory and self-reflection. Making and storing memories is complex: this hard-to-fathom process is compromised when there is a history of trauma. The complexity is heightened because our memories are composed of both episodic or declarative memory and implicit or emotional/body-based memory. When children experience early abuse, these two systems are typically dissociated from one another. Explicit memory, processed in the midbrain, is available for conscious, verbal recall—such word-based memories are the bedrock of talk therapies. In contrast, implicit memory is formed in the amygdala, a primitive and emotion-based area of the brain, and is unavailable to consciousness. Thus, implicit memory is encoded and recalled through emotions and behavior.

Traumatic memory exists primarily as implicit, body-based, nonverbal memory. As a result, to the extent that trauma remains unsymbolized and outside of verbal access, such memories "lie encrusted in a primitive core of unspeakable terror and . . . meaningless panic, intrusive ideation, and somatic sensation. As such, they exist outside the usual domain of recalled experience, unavailable to self-reflective processes and analytic examination" (Davies and Frawley 1994, 45).

Both memory systems are required for the patient eventually to create a coherent narrative, for it is through narrative that we humans build our self-awareness. Thus, therapy with traumatized patients requires repeatedly moving back and forth between the emotional, body-based awareness of trauma and the process of putting it into words. Patients learn how to use the therapy—and the therapist—to develop a greater capacity to manage their strong and disconcerting emotions, to move from unsymbolized trauma to the ability to link emotions and words and to engage increasingly in reflective thinking.

This process is accomplished largely by making use of the transference and countertransference that play out in our offices. When we work with patients who experienced profound interpersonal betrayals and early repeated traumas, we find ourselves pulled by the same powerful undertows that grab these patients. These pushes and pulls are expressed and understood through repeated enactments. As such, we are forced again and again to experience both our patients' and our own inner worlds from numerous perspectives. Such a clinical situation produces powerful and often disturbing countertransference reactions. In Susan's story, the therapist describes the strong countertransference: *"I fight the tendency to 'go away,' to dissociate during the session, lured by the siren call of almost anything else. With a deep breath, I settle into the story and note that my body's rigidity matches hers. Like her, I am warding off the assault that comes from experiencing her story. My mind sketches the images that unfold until it feels as if I am also there, horrified again by the brutality of the betrayal."*

As therapists, our goal during the treatment (imperfectly achieved, at best) is to maintain our curiosity, flexibility, and capacity to think while feeling the powerful emotions that threaten to overwhelm us. It is at such times that our patients can experience the potential for a new ending to an old and familiar dance. The goal with a patient such as Susan is to create a new ending to the old story—one that will enable her to recover some of what was stolen. She was a daring and mischievous child and had been cut off from aspects of herself for decades. By coming to know her own past more deeply, she will be able to free herself from the deadening constraints that once helped her survive but that now impede her ability to live fully.

2I THE BIRD BOX

A child's inner world is shaped by whispers from the past.

On my desk sits the little bird box that used to belong on my grandparents' shelf. It is an unusual, curved metal box, mostly black and bronze and somewhat tarnished. Across its top lies a bird, meant to be airborne, whose uplifted wings form the handles that open the lid. Inside there is an odd little assortment of things, photos and old cards. There is a postcard that I sent, with the words "The Windy City" written across the picture. It begins, "Dear Grandma and Grandpa, Chicago is very pretty, and I'm having a nice time." I remember neither the card nor the trip. Also, there is a faded photo of me at eight years old, in which I am smiling awkwardly—too aware of being photographed. Someone has written my name and the number "8" on the back in red ink. The box looks out of place on my desk among my disordered papers—familiar and yet foreign away from its usual resting spot on my grandparents' bookcase.

The box summons up scents and images of my grandparents' apartment. I picture the linoleum kitchen table, and, peering around the corner, I can almost see the meat grinder my grandfather affixed to the kitchen wall. I feel the sticky, stiff plastic slipcover that protected the sofa from dust and remember the feeling of my sweaty legs in summer, shifting uncomfortably as I sat and listened to the grownups talk. My grandparents showed no inclination to learn English or to teach me Yiddish, so I absorbed more of the music of their language than the meaning. From time to time, my grandfather would turn his good-humored eyes toward me and ask, "Maidele, faschteicht? A bissele? Nein?" (Sweetheart, do you understand? A little? No?). To me, Yiddish was a test of my value as a daughter, granddaughter, and first-generation American, and in all regards I feared I was a failure.

When we visited, the laughter and joke telling would go on well into the evening. My father and grandfather were animated, trading funny stories, discussing politics, remembering the past. Bored, I would look around the room. Yiddish books with yellowed pages lined the bookshelf, and I would open them randomly, searching for clues. It sometimes felt as if there were nothing in this apartment that I could understand. Sitting at the kitchen table with my grandmother while she baked *kichel* or made kreplach, I would study her exquisitely lined face, her inscrutable eyes, and marvel at her dark hair coiled into a high and elegant chignon.

What I truly knew about her life was nothing but bits and pieces, hardly enough to fill an album or even write a story. I knew she had been in the camps, as had my father and grandfather. I knew who had lived, but only some of the names of those who had died. My grandmother, separated from her husband and from my father, her oldest son, witnessed the death of her other two children, fourteen-year-old Friedele and six-year-old Yonkele. My middle name was chosen to commemorate my uncle, and it inextricably links me to him, a long-lost little boy.

I'd been told scraps I could barely understand, much less imagine. She worked in the kitchens. In the salt mines. On a tower. Day turned to night, and night into day. Too little food, no family, no warmth. Even now I can picture her face so clearly. Yet my mind draws a blank; there is a gaping empty space where history—and its stories—should be.

My father and grandfather were the lucky ones. They were together, always, throughout the terror. Each believes the other saved his life. I, my father's daughter, like to believe that he was the strong one—swifter, more astute, the one others could depend on—and I cannot understand when I am told that my father had been a *musulman*—one of the walking dead. Again, I know very little of the story. They were boot makers, then prisoners, then concentration camp inmates. Always on the move, always choosing the lucky side. My father told me one time, "We were brought to a new place, a camp. We were separated for an instant, your grandpa in one group and me in the other. Suddenly Grandpa yanked me to him. The next day all the others were gone. All gone." "Gone?" I blinked and didn't think "gas chamber." I thought, "They must have run away. Why didn't you?"

Years later, when my grandmother died, we went to their apartment to clean it out and to make space for the nurse who was now to care for my grandfather. There was a shoebox full of photographs with Polish handwriting across the back, words I could not understand written in fluid blue ink in yet another language I did not know. The apartment smelled musty and seemed forlorn. We decided to remove the plastic slipcovers—for the first time in decades, someone would be sleeping on the pullout couch. As the plastic peeled away, we saw that the fabric, in spite of its protective sheath, was moldy, yellowed, and dry. My eyes searched the room, trying to memorize its details, and my gaze landed on the funny little bird box. The same strange little bird, frozen in time, now perches on my desk while I work. Beneath its lid remain the vestiges of the faraway and incomprehensible world contained within the walls of my grandparents' apartment. Inside lies the tangible evidence that I was there, too.

Analysts Reflect on Transgenerational
Transmission of Trauma

In times of war and other human catastrophe, people experience atrocities that forever change their world. The story "The Bird Box" shows us how traumatic events are transmitted from generation to generation. Untold narratives are woven into family history and become the backdrop against which the child's emotional development unfolds and takes shape. When such events are relegated to the shadows, they often continue to exert a powerful force, a kind of aching longing, as the author describes: *"my mind draws a blank; there is a gaping empty space where history—and its stories—should be."*

History is replete with examples of unspeakable acts of genocide and atrocities born out of large-scale political and social hostilities. With many of our patients, unspeakable horror takes up silent residence in the treatment, present yet inaccessible, as if beyond language or knowing. The task of therapy with such patients is to put words to the unspeakable and make meaning where there was none. It is only then that we can thread together a past that can be integrated into the self with the promise for restoration of a historical rupture.

As in this story, children of Holocaust survivors are entangled with a past that is in their bones but not a part of their lived experiences. They themselves are survivors of a sort because, "by all odds, neither the parent nor the child were to exist" (Krell 1979, 564). Hovering in the air for many survivors is the unspoken recognition that survival in a concentration camp was nearly hopeless. The survivor's child may look upon his or her very existence as an utterly random occurrence—an accident of fate.

When a parent or grandparent has a personal history that contains a traumatic experience of such devastating proportions, the family's past becomes integrated into the child's inner life in several ways. For instance, traumatic memories shape the survivor's subsequent parenting style and the child's identification with or rejection of certain traits of their survivor parent that are linked to their traumatic experiences. Or the child has his own, developmentally informed ways of imagining his parent's painful experiences. Many children, lacking a coherent narrative of their parents' past, might fill in the gaps of what they know via conscious and unconscious elaborations in fantasy. Such gaps then become the defining edge of their experience.

For children of survivors, the knowledge that their parents survived the Holocaust, whether they are aware of specific details or not, serves as a template for all later knowledge. It acts as a set of organizing principles through which the children's ongoing experience is filtered. However, these children, even though knowledge of the Holocaust pervades their internal worlds, are simultaneously beset by confusion and despair of ever truly "knowing" the Holocaust. Such a traumatic history, coupled with a sense of "a nostalgia that has no legitimacy" (Fresno 1984, 421), can lead to particular trends and vulnerabilities in their development and functioning—including difficulties with separation and individuation; problems with guilt, aggression, and superego development; and difficulty in maintaining a clear delineation between reality and fantasy (Levine 1982).

After the Holocaust, survivors experienced the world as dangerous and unpredictable. They saw the world shatter and thereafter were acutely aware of the possibility of imminent catastrophe. For them, the threat of annihilation resided not only in fantasy, but also in real, lived experience, and it clouded every aspect of their world, shaping the way they parented their children. It is for this reason that separation and individuation take on complex meanings for survivor families. Parents may resist separation because "their losses have been so overwhelming, their very sense of integrity often rests on not allowing any further loss" (Freyberg 1980, 93).

In the course of their children's progression toward autonomy, survivor parents can have confusing and conflicted responses. Earlier fears and losses are reactivated in the face of the wish that this time things will be different. They may encourage their children to do what they were unable to do during their own childhood and adolescence. However, they also may transmit to their children a deep sense of mistrust of others and the world. As a result, children experience a dilemma: they are encouraged to pursue opportunities that their parents were denied but at the same time are cautioned to avoid risk and not venture too far.

Children of survivors grow up in a world dominated to a greater or lesser degree by their awareness—mediated through their parents—that something bad can happen at any moment. In their inner worlds, fantasy blends with history (Phillips 1978). Atrocities that should belong only to the world of children's most primitive fears and terrors are materialized in their parents' real-life experiences. As the author of this story reflects, *"My grandmother, separated from her husband and my father, her oldest son, witnessed the death of her other two children, fourteen-year-old Friedele and six-year-old Yonkele. My middle name was chosen to commemorate my uncle, and it inextricably links me to him, a long-lost little boy."*

Howard Levine emphasizes that people who undergo traumatic events have difficulty in "maintaining the 'make-believe' quality of fantasy." He goes on, "For many children of survivors, the fact that real life events concretely give actuality to what are for others just primitive fantasies contributes to an ego distortion in which there is a blurring of the distinction between fantasy and reality" (1982, 88). Children of survivors are faced with a reality that contains within it horrors that normally reside only in the realm of fantasy. This collision of reality and fantasy can swamp the child's imagination, thus collapsing the internal space needed to resolve typical childhood fears and worries. The author thus writes, *"I'd been told scraps I could barely understand, much less imagine."*

The events of the Holocaust threaten a breakdown of symbolic functioning (Auerhahn and Laub 1984; Grubich-Simitis 1984) because the overwhelming nature of the trauma is often difficult or impossible to put into words. The pact of silence maintained by many survivors upholds a barrier between their past, which is barely imaginable and profoundly extraordinary, and their ordinary, present-day life. This silence carries with it grave consequences for their children's capacity to make sense out of the past. They are left with bits and pieces they discover and cannot understand instead of with a coherent story. Some parents silently deny knowledge of the Holocaust, and others live in a sea of overwhelming and unmetabolized images and memories. By contrast, what we see in our clinical practices is that as families develop a more coherent narrative, the children can better integrate knowledge of their history. As the author of "The Bird Box" writes, *"I cannot understand when I am told that my father had been a* musulman—*one of the walking dead. Again, I know very little of their story. They were boot makers, then prisoners, then concentration camp inmates. . . . My father told me one time, 'We were brought to a new place, a camp. We were separated for an instant, your grandpa in one group and me in the other. Suddenly Grandpa yanked me to him. The next day all the others were gone. All gone.' 'Gone?' "* Such fragments are confusing for children who are trying to make sense out of the contents of their minds and can lead to, on the one hand, overstimulation of their fantasy world and, on the other, a sense that the past itself is unreal and cut off. As a consequence of both of these positions, such children are unable to play freely or to dream.

Dori Laub and Nanette Auerhahn write that those of us "who lack direct experience with the Holocaust must assimilate it through our imagination" (1985, 4). For children of survivors, the task of knowing the Holocaust is made infinitely more complicated by their experience of living in its shadow, without having access to its true dimensions. In "The Bird Box," the author tells us, *"[My grandmother] worked in the kitchens. In the salt mines. On a tower. Day turned into night, and night into day. Too little food, no family, no warmth."* In order to enter into the world of metaphor and symbolic representation, the reality of the Holocaust must be affirmed, and its historical context given meaning and shape.

However, in many families of Holocaust survivors, silence about the trauma is often the painful solution to an unbearable truth. When this occurs, children learn about the Holocaust indirectly through overheard snatches of conversation, papers found while rifling through parents' drawers in search of secret knowledge, and intense, nonverbal messages (Fogelman 1988). This acquisition of information is a form of "knowing without knowing." Our author describes a similar search: *"I would look around the room. Yiddish books with yellowed pages lined the bookshelf, and I would open them randomly, searching for clues."* In some families, as Tamar Shoshan suggests, when children are exposed early on to harrowing events of the past, they may develop "a defensive impermeability to terror" (1989, 200), in particular when parents cannot express the emotional pain that accompanies the memories. The child is left to guess the meanings behind the palpable yet implacable silence. Knowledge of the Holocaust thus takes on great importance in the fantasy lives of survivors' children.

For any child, family history—the past that he inherits from his parents—is essential for constructing a self-narrative. In order to feel whole, a child must be able to forge a connection to his historical legacy. We are continually building and reworking self-narratives throughout our lives. New experiences are assimilated into the fabric of the self. The story is transformed and takes on new dimensions while still maintaining its essential characteristics. In other words, there is a sense of self-sameness that continues over time and constantly assimilates new understandings. However, overwhelming trauma dramatically impairs the ability to construct a flexible, reality-based self-narrative, which rests on the capacity for symbolic functioning. The overwhelming, disorganizing feeling of trauma profoundly disrupt such a capacity. The ways in which survivor parents may help or inhibit their children's capacity to verbalize their experience, to understand, and to deal with these strong emotions shape how the story of trauma comes to be known across the generations.

In "The Bird Box," the author writes, *"My grandparents showed no inclination to learn English or to teach me Yiddish, so I absorbed more of the music of their language than the meaning. From time to time, my grandfather would turn his good-humored eyes toward me and ask, 'Maidele, faschteicht? A bissele? Nein?'(Sweetheart, do you understand? A little? No?). To me, Yiddish was a test of my value as a daughter, granddaughter, and first-generation American, and in all regards I feared I was a failure."* One can imagine this young girl's experience of the warmth of connection side by side with the ineffable sense of absence that can neither be bridged with words nor fully held in the present. Thus, the child's sense of her family's history, normally passed from parent to child, is frozen in time, always longed for yet never fully realized in the intergenerational relationship. The child is left with disjointed fragments and pockets of knowledge, which she is unable to integrate into a complete story of herself and her family. If symbolic processes and the capacity to create narrative are disrupted, the establishment of an ongoing sense of completeness is elusive.

Children born to Holocaust survivors are inevitably deeply affected by the legacy of their parents' trauma. They may experience "a sense that they must go back in time, become part of the parents' experience of the past, and resolve the unresolvable" (Kestenberg 1980, 781). However, the impact of the Holocaust on the next generation's psychological development and personality organization is as diverse and as personal as it is on the survivors themselves. Children of survivors thus may exist simultaneously in two worlds—that of their present-day lives and that of their parents' past—yet they feel fully grounded in neither. As the author writes, *"The same strange little bird, frozen in time, now perches on my desk while I work. Beneath its lid remain the vestiges of the faraway and incomprehensible world contained within the walls of my grandparents' apartment. Inside lies the tangible evidence that I was there, too."*

22 PHANTOM LIMB

A child dies and a mother's grief sweeps over her.

Without you, my life is a tumultuous sea. I am struggling to stay above water, to keep from drowning. I can't breathe. The waves crash down and wash over me as the water swells. There are some things I can expect . . . prepare myself for . . . brace myself against. But it is the small, ordinary moments—a word, a gesture, a song—that bring another surge of grief and suck me back into the dark morass of what lurks just below sea level: you are gone. My stomach churns, once again in knots, and sorrow ripples through my head. With you gone, the terror roars and thunders. So I wait a few minutes, a few hours, for the calm to return and for me to regain my sea legs. But even on the stillness of land, with no waves swelling, I am drowning.

I imagine I am a war veteran who lost a limb. I continue to feel pain where there is an absence. An essential part of me is missing. Sarah, you are my phantom limb. Once part of me, now I can't even hold you. An emotional amputation—I am forever maimed. There are no words for this pain. If a husband dies, you are a widow; with the death of a wife, you are a widower; when your parents die, you are an orphan. But when your child dies, there is no word for what you become. It doesn't exist in our vocabulary. It is too horrific to be named.

I continue to feel that you are there, but you are not. You still exist in every thought, every word. Even though you are gone, you haunt my days, so I seek the comfort of sleep, but you pursue me in my dreams at night. Then I realize it's not you haunting me—I haunt you. I see you around every corner, in every encounter, in every face. I search for you everywhere. I yearn for you. Although it makes no sense, I wait to hear from you or from some messenger you will surely send to me. I find myself incessantly checking every possible means of communication—scrolling my voicemail, my email, waiting eagerly for the mail to come. I am desperate for some utterance. I'm not sure from whom it will come, and, of course, it never arrives. But I cannot stop the hope from rising each time. Again and again I feel the fleeting conviction that my expectation will be met, only to feel disappointment wash over me. I know my desperate search for you inevitably brings with it another wave of inconsolability, the proof that you are truly gone. Once again it sinks me.

Analysts Reflect on Immediate Loss

Mourning is the process of grieving a significant loss. Samuel Johnson describes it as a state of wandering, lost and disconnected from the world: "I have ever since seemed to myself broken off from mankind; a kind of solitary wanderer in the wild of life, without any direction, or fixed point of view: a gloomy gazer on the world to which I have little relation" (qtd. in Boswell [1791] 2008, 264). In "Phantom Limb," the writer captures this early stage of grief—the shock, numbness, and disorganization after a significant loss. The writer's image of the sea symbolizes waves of grief in which rapidly shifting experiences of intense emotion immerse the author in unpredictable and intense bursts of inconsolability.

Grief is complex and multidetermined by the meaning and timing of the death, the significance of the person lost, the developmental timeframe, prior losses, the mourner's ego functioning, the cultural context in which the death occurred, the presence of a community able to support the mourner, and other factors. It is a painful process that can extend over a long period of time, possibly even a lifetime.

In many ways, grief is like a wound that requires time and attention to heal. Yet when focus on the loss is unremitting, grief remains unresolved and never heals. Many researchers (Klass 1996; Archer 1999; Walter 2003) show that extensive periods of rumination during mourning can lead to a deep and entrenched depression, characterized by a continual revisiting of the death. This depression prevents painful emotions from transforming or being repaired. In that case, the bereaved person remains frozen at the threshold of loss, unable to work through the death. In contrast to ruminative mourning, profound grief is a normal experience that manifests as devastating sadness. The person in an acute stage of grief may express a wide range of symptoms, including physical pain, insomnia, irritability, tearfulness, anger, fatigue, and feelings of despair. Indeed, Irvin Yalom and Morton Lieberman (1991) conclude that the experience of profound grief does not lessen the likelihood of finding meaning after the loss and subsequently of experiencing healing and personal growth.

In our profession, when we write about grief and mourning, we often begin with Freud's classic paper "Mourning and Melancholia" ([1917] 1955e). Here Freud describes the process of mourning as a gradual detachment of libido (feelings of love and attachment) from the memory of the loved one. He states that the mourner suffers because her internal attachment to the lost loved one has ruptured. The goal of mourning is thus to separate oneself from the person one has lost. Freud's idea of mourning was an intrapsychic one that emphasized the mourner's internal disorganization and gradual restoration of a sense of balance rather than addressing the actual death and the loss of the relationship.

In Freud's early view, the bereaved person can recover from the loss only when detachment from the internal object is complete. As he wrote elsewhere, "Mourning has a quite specific psychical task to perform: its function is to detach the survivor's memories and hopes from the dead" ([1913] 1955l, 65). In this view, bereaved individuals need to accept that the loved one is gone forever. Otto Fenichel (1945) later used the concept of "introjection" to describe the ongoing process in which the lost love is mentally kept close during the early phases of grief and is then given up at the end of the grieving process. In support of Freud's idea that mourning has a specific endpoint, Tammy Clewell maintains that "mourning comes to a decisive and 'spontaneous end.' . . . [W]hen the survivor has detached his or her emotional tie to the lost object and reattached the free libido to a new object, the individual can then accept consolation in the form of a substitute for what has been lost" (2004, 44).

In "Mourning and Melancholia," Freud differentiated between normal grief and mourning, on the one hand, and the more pathological, depressive state of melancholia, on the other. He described how the grieving process is compromised when there is unresolved anger at the loved one. Thus, the loss is compounded by feelings of unresolved disappointment. "In mourning," he wrote, "it is the world which has become poor and empty; in melancholia it is the ego itself" ([1917] 1955e, 246). Melancholia is a depressive state that includes guilt, self-reproach, and loss of self-esteem. In Freud's theory, we understand the mourner's self-deprecation as displaced anger and ambivalence redirected from the lost, "disappointing" loved one and turned against the self. In this scenario, instead of withdrawing their attachment from the person they lost, mourners direct the rage back toward themselves. According to Freud, when the mourner is able to acknowledge such guilt and self-reproach, he is better able to redirect his affection elsewhere. John Baker writes, "A continuing internal relationship can coexist with the development of new object relationships, which in turn enrich the inner world in their own unique ways, [leading to the] . . . coexistence of inner attachments in the mourning individual, even long after the death of the love object" (2001, 70).

Freud's theoretical stance—that loss requires detachment from the loved one and substitution of a new love object—did not describe his own experience of mourning the death of his daughter Sophie in 1920. In a 1929 letter consoling a colleague whose son had died, he wrote: "Although we know that after such a loss the acute stage of mourning will subside, we also know we shall remain inconsolable and will never find a substitute. No matter what may fill the gap, even if it be filled completely, it nevertheless remains something else. And actually this is how it should be. It is the only way of perpetuating the love which we do not want to relinquish" (2003, 386). Thus, far from experiencing detachment after Sophie's death, Freud eloquently described the enduring bond to his beloved child after her death.

Melanie Klein's (1940) object-relations theory presented a different perspective on mourning. Klein placed less emphasis on detachment from the lost loved one. In her view, death evokes painful and destructive fantasies toward the dead: the world previously experienced as good and safe is now infused with aggressive and rageful urges. Klein thought of mourning as a time of repair during which unleashed destructive fantasies are recaptured and a positive internal relationship with the lost object is reestablished.

John Bowlby (1980) also has made significant contributions to our understanding of grief and mourning in his study of attachment. In examining the impact of losing one's mother in childhood on later development, he emphasizes biology rather than psychology. According to Bowlby, attachment is a protective biological mechanism that has evolved to ensure survival. The death of the mother is a cataclysmic event that undermines the child's sense of safety in the world. For a mother who loses a child through death, there is a similar disruption in attachment. The mother's inability to protect her child from danger activates an instinctual, insatiable longing for her lost child. This process of continued yearning and searching for the lost love is movingly depicted in the story "Phantom Limb." The author writes, *"I see you around every corner, in every encounter, in every face. I search for you everywhere. I yearn for you. Although it makes no sense, I wait to hear from you or from some messenger you will surely send to me."* This yearning captures the fantasy of reunion that characterizes a significant aspect of the grief process.

Edith Jacobson ([1965] 1984) was the first to write about such reunion fantasies in adult patients who had lost their parents when they were young. Joan Didion, in her 2006 book *The Year of Magical Thinking*, describes how such fantasies continue throughout life. In spite of the finality of her husband's death, she maintains a conviction that he might still return to her. Paul Maciejewski and his colleagues (2007) more recently conducted a study with 233 people who had experienced the death of a parent, child, or spouse. They found that the predominant feeling was not depression, disbelief, or even anger, but instead yearning.

Freud's early view of mourning as gradual detachment does not hold true for most contemporary theorists and clinicians. Robert Gaines (1997) conceives of mourning not as Freud's "decathecting"—breaking the bonds between the survivor and loved one—but in terms of "creating continuity." He writes that the mourner's capacity to preserve a connection with the deceased loved one protects the mourner from melancholia, or pathological mourning. We now believe that the task of normal mourning is to preserve rather than to sever the internal relationship.

Reminiscing and sharing memories are important ways to keep the loved ones alive. In this way, painful feelings of loss can dissipate gradually and make room for an array of deep and complex feelings in relation to the person who died. In "Phantom Limb," the bereaved is in an early stage of grief. As a result, she can't yet find a way to move from feeling "haunted" to accessing richer, more resonant memories.

As psychodynamic therapists, we believe that the bereaved need to hold on to the memory of the loved one and at the same time to reinvest in new goals. We see mourning as a complicated task that requires the living to assimilate the loss, maintain a positive internal connection to the lost person, and continue to find meaning in other areas of life. Victor Frankl (1984) believes that our survival in situations of loss depends on our ability to find meaning in our grief. Through the process of mourning, we seek to become wiser, stronger, more empathic, and more compassionate.

Culture, religion, family history, and beliefs powerfully influence the bereaved individual's unique experience of mourning. For example, in some cultures grief is treated as a private event. Emotions are expected to be kept silently contained, and a high premium is placed on "moving on," "bucking up," and "putting it behind you." In other cultures, grief is highly emotional, demonstrative, and public.

Religious beliefs can be equally important in integrating traumatic loss. Religion can help people create a soothing and comprehensible narrative. For instance, some believe that they will ultimately reunite with the deceased, and others conceptualize the loved one as an omniscient spirit who watches over them. Religious beliefs must be considered within the context of a wide variability among families, even those within similar cultural and religious environments, which can effect an individual's expression of grief over time. Such variations become woven into the internal fabric of the individual's self-perceptions.

The social dimension of mourning reveals itself in the mourner's ongoing need to bring the person "to life" by remembering and sharing their memories with others. Many current psychotherapists stress the centrality of existing relationships for successfully resolving traumatic loss in both children and adults (Fowlkes 1991; Hagman 1996; Sussillo 2005). They contend that mourning is a highly social process. Meaning is thus derived in part from the relationships within which the loss is nested. Supportive others help ameliorate the feelings of stigma and isolation that stem from the unique circumstances of each death.

Despite others' support, grief and mourning are intensely personal processes. No two people grieve in the same way, and numerous variations fall within the normal range. Sadness is a universal response to loss. For people who seek therapy, it is important to differentiate predictable feelings of grief and loss from a more intractable depression. However, although one may move on with life, the pain of loss never disappears. Time does not heal all wounds. The experience of traumatic loss and bereavement can produce, at its extremes, either despair or transcendence. This struggle, which lies at the heart of our clinical work, requires us to "continue to bear witness to the struggle with meaning and meaninglessness, to bear witness to despair, and—sometimes—to bear witness to transcendence" (Landsman 2002, 28).

23 THE QUESTION

The death of a child changes everything.

"How many children do you have?"

My husband and I were dining in a New York restaurant with my in-laws and a few of their neighbors. From the moment I had entered the room, I was determined to be gracious and friendly, holding at bay the tempest within me. In the candlelight, I felt myself begin to relax and savor my first course. Then one of the women turned to me with a smile and asked that seemingly simple question.

Time stopped. My mind froze. How many children do I have? Three or four? Three or four? In that moment, I did not know. The numbers ricocheted, firing back and forth in my brain again and again and again. I could not answer the question. Speechless, I just started to weep. I felt raw, exposed, and embarrassed. Signaling toward the ladies room, I fled from the table.

Such a simple question. Two months before that dinner, I would have proudly answered, "Four." I would have happily responded to the usual flow: "How old are they?" and "Where are they in school?"

Then Sarah died.

There are moments between what was before and what is now that clash loudly. Three months after that New York dinner, a friend invited me to a book party. Holding a glass of wine, I darted between the art-filled rooms, not landing in one place. I feared where any conversation might lead, but I eventually settled down in the newly remodeled kitchen. To my great surprise, I found myself face to face with none other than the real Miss Manners. Although on another day I would have been tickled to meet her, now I was aware of just trying to stay afloat. We began chatting. Within minutes, the conversation moved in the dreaded direction. Miss Manners, in her feminine dress, hair wrapped in a bun, politely inquired, "Do you have children?" and "How many?" Without thinking, I answered "Four." Panicked and determined to avoid tears, I turned away.

I abruptly moved on to the living room in what I imagined was not at all a Miss Manners–approved style, hoping a new environment would distract me. But there are perils at every turn for a person like me. A friendly woman in her midforties soon approached, smiling warmly. She was perfectly coiffed, with a lustrous blue cashmere scarf draped around her neck. When she posed the inevitable question, I was still feeling the lingering fragility from the conversation in the kitchen. This time I chose the safer route and responded simply, "Three." *As I said the number, the image of Sarah's face lit up in my memory; at our kitchen table, she is laughing with friends. It's just months before she died; she's seventeen, her riveting blue eyes alight with the pleasure in sharing a good story, her friends and I enthralled.* A stab of pain brought me back to the present. I glanced to my left, and there stood Miss Manners, who, moments earlier, had distinctly heard me answer that I had four children. With a cocked head and a puzzled expression, she stared at me. I now wish I'd had the presence of mind to turn to her, the expert on these matters, and ask, "How should a mother like me respond to this question?" Instead, I did a quick about-face, grabbed my husband, and escaped to the safety of our home.

I feel empathy for the other person in all of these situations who, by asking such a simple and basic question, innocently becomes the perpetrator of terrible pain. They witness my grief. Picking up Sarah's younger sister at school one time, I was searching the halls when the dean of students popped out of her office and inquired in a friendly voice, "Have you lost a child?" *Another flash of Sarah. Newborn, so long ago, still safely attached by her umbilical cord, lying on my stomach. Her head turns toward me as I call her name. I am certain that amid all the voices in the room, she recognizes mine.* Standing in the school hallway, I saw the shock and horror spread across the dean's face as soon as she realized what she said. She stammered and then quickly offered to help me find my daughter's class.

Experiences like these occur almost weekly. Now, several years later, I'm a little more prepared, yet I still struggle with how to respond. I have four children. Sarah is still as constant in my heart and mind as she was before she died—my beloved daughter. If I say "three," I lose her by omission. If I say "four," I lose her all over again with the words "she died."

In each of these encounters, I long to acknowledge these unspoken thoughts. We can—we must—speak about Sarah. I know, too, that when strangers ask casually about my family, nothing can prepare them or me for the intensity of my grief. I long to have an answer, but I remain trapped between unbearable three and unreachable four.

Analysts Reflect on Memory and Grief

As indicated in the previous story, "Phantom Limb," the early stage of deep loss is chaotic and overwhelming. It is a biologically raw state. We weep, we long, we search. We are irritable, angry, and anxious. We cannot sleep, we cannot eat, we lose weight. The trauma of death can lead to extremes of heightened emotion, on the one hand, or feelings of deadness and dissociation, on the other. After the initial shock wears off and the acute grief begins to subside, there remains a lifetime of reexperiencing and bearing the pain. The need to integrate the meaning of the loss into one's self-experience is ongoing. In "The Question," each time the writer is asked, "How many children do you have?" she reexperiences an excruciating blow, abruptly reminding her that her daughter is no longer here.

The irrevocability of death makes the pain feel unbearable, as if one may not survive. Freud wrote, "Death will no longer be denied; we are forced to believe it. People really die" ([1915] 1955k, 291). Yet such awareness is psychically overwhelming and thus only transiently available. Someone can attend to all the public and social symbols of death, sign documents, plan a memorial service, and even make decisions on burial, while still not truly knowing or acknowledging the death. For protective reasons, death is accepted and integrated slowly into consciousness. In this way, the individual is better able to titrate the shock and grief that would otherwise be too overwhelming to absorb.

Joan Didion (2006) uses the term *the vortex effect* to describe how, for the bereaved, some event or interaction triggers a thought about the person who died, which leads to another thought and then another, until one is eventually awash in remembering. "The Question" captures moments in which the writer is caught unaware and unprepared for the flood of memories that follow brief, ordinary encounters in the course of simply living. These unexpected encounters lead to a cascade of feelings from which, like a vortex, one cannot escape.

Our conscious and unconscious mind work to create one established and seamless story line of our lives. Self-awareness begins in childhood as we strive to construct a cohesive narrative of the self. In fact, Freud described the aim of analysis as the creation of an "intelligible, consistent and unbroken" life story ([1905] 1953b, 18). Old memories and previous views of ourselves are dyed in the color of the current mindset. It is as if the mind has effortlessly integrated present-day knowledge into prior memory. To achieve some synchrony, the mind matches the remembered "truth" with the current affect, so it re-creates the memory in terms of the emotion we feel now. The author of the story writes, *"Two months before that dinner, I would have proudly answered, 'Four.' I would have happily responded to the usual flow: 'How old are they?' and 'Where are they in school?'"* In this way, memories are continuously constructed and reconstructed. Thus, the mind that retrieves a memory is not the same as the one that initially formed the memory.

We think of memories as emerging out of our latest draft of our life story. They can never be viewed in isolation from one another. If we consider memories to be narratives based on a blend of real events from the past and present-day feelings and wishes, they illustrate current trends of thought about the self and others. The altering of memory builds a predictable and secure understanding of the world, a way of weaving the threads of one's life into a coherent pattern. The mind in this case wants to think: "It was always like that." The creation of a cohesive narrative allows us to feel whole and intact. Richard Powers, in his novel *The Echo Maker*, states, "The job of consciousness is to make sure that all of the distributed molecules of the brain seem integrated. That we always seem familiar to ourselves" (2006, 363).

Yet there is a difference between the impact of a normal developmental progression on one's evolving sense of self and the impact of a traumatic event that shatters one's world. When an event cannot be woven neatly into one's identity and memory, the mind refuses to accept or integrate such an occurrence. As the author writes, *"My mind froze. How many children do I have? Three or four? Three or four? In that moment, I did not know. The numbers ricocheted, firing back and forth in my brain again and again and again. I could not answer the question. Speechless, I just started to weep. I felt raw, exposed, and embarrassed."* At her core, the author of "The Question" and "Phantom Limb" knows herself to be the mother of four children. After such a shattering death, how can she once again feel whole and intact without a cohesive narrative that includes her daughter? With each repetition of the question, the assault on her identity and sense of self is repeated.

When a person loses someone who has played a significant role in defining and sustaining important aspects of her internal and external worlds, then she is faced with the task of restructuring a meaningful self-narrative and sense of identity. In "The Question," the death of the author's daughter must be woven into her revised self-narrative. As the author recalls, *"I now wish I'd had the presence of mind to turn to her, the expert on these matters, and ask, 'How should a mother like me respond to this question?' Instead, I did a quick about-face, grabbed my husband, and escaped to the safety of our home."* Throughout this process, the profound sense of dislocation is unremitting. History becomes disjointed, not allowing the mind to right itself.

Yet, as Lucy Grealy states in remembering her own experience of losing one-third of her jaw to cancer at age nine, "sooner or later we all have to learn the words with which to name our own private losses" (1994, 52). Over time, the task of mourning is to integrate one's prior sense of self with the current experience of loss and subsequent narratives of the self. We catch the author of "The Question" in the midst of this process as she tries to integrate early memory into present reality: *"When she posed the inevitable question, I was still feeling the lingering fragility from the conversation in the kitchen. This time I chose the safer route and responded simply, 'Three.'* As I said the number, the image of Sarah's face lit up in my memory; at our kitchen table, she is laughing with friends. It's just months before she died; she's seventeen, her riveting blue eyes alight with the pleasure in sharing a good story, her friends and I enthralled. *A stab of pain brought me back to the present."* What gradually emerges is a newly revised and more cohesive view of oneself that contains the full range of affect, memories, and hopes for the future.

Although death is a singular and discrete event, coping with the aftermath is a gradually evolving process that unfolds over a period of months and years. As C. S. Lewis said, grief "needs not a map but a history." And as "The Question" conveys, the author engages in an ongoing struggle to span the chasm between "before" and "after" the death of her child. She writes: *"I long to have an answer, but I remain trapped between unbearable three and unreachable four."* The question that continuously confronts her—*"How many children do you have?"*—reminds her that the world has been irrevocably changed, although she remains fundamentally herself. Her journey toward reintegration will last a lifetime.

CONCLUSION

As analysts and as writers, we continually seek ways to put words to experience and to communicate our thoughts and feelings. We hope to capture the essence of what makes us human, what makes us unique, and what defines us. Our patients come to us because they, too, are engaged in a struggle to find their voices. When we listen to our patients, we try to understand what lies beneath their words and find our own words to forge a connection with them. Over the course of treatment, patient and analyst develop a shared vocabulary, one that is meaningful and unique to each dyad. As we come to know a patient, we learn to listen in a complex way to words and silence, to breathing, to bodily communications, to shifts in tone and emotion. Like a dreamscape, the therapeutic conversation sometimes takes unexpected images and links them together to form a new picture, which may be incongruous until we gradually begin to see its meaning. In therapy, as in our writing, we treat our words with care, paying attention to their impact and their potential to wound—to the power they have to touch others.

Yet, as Daniel Stern has pointed out, language can be viewed as a "double-edged sword" because although it "makes parts of our known experience more shareable with others . . . [and] permits two people to create mutual experiences of meaning that had been unknown before and could never have existed until fashioned by words," it can also separate us from others. Stern explains that language "makes some parts of our experience less shareable with ourselves and with others. It drives a wedge between two simultaneous forms of interpersonal experience: as it is lived and as it is verbally represented" (1985, 161).

Stern points out that before the infant develops verbal abilities, the shared understanding between mother and infant, which grows out of multiple experiences of responding and being responded to, creates a feeling of mutual, preverbal attunement. This attunement allows for a sense of absolute union—even though we understand that the attunement actually consists of a perpetual dance of aligning and realigning with the other. With language, however, we introduce the possibility of misunderstanding and miscommunication. This process is similar to that of therapy. Words provide an entryway to our patients' inner worlds but also demand that we attend to those experiences that cannot be put into words. Thus, we must work to weave together the shared verbal domain with the realm of inner experiences.

Throughout the process of writing this book, we were struck by how storytelling and psychotherapy originate from the same creative wellspring. When we write personal essays, we revisit our past. The act of writing invites us to explore the complicated interplay of our unique history, memory, and current-day feelings. The work of psychodynamic psychotherapy involves understanding the connection between memories and inchoate feelings. Both writing and therapy entail reminiscing through time and memory and offer opportunities to explore our thoughts, wishes, and fears. Each seeks a personal, deeper truth, or what we call a "psychical truth." We often find that these "truths" are continuously reworked to match our longings and fantasies. Yet, as we discussed in chapter 1 on screen memories, it is hard to know what is actually "true" memory because to some degree we are constantly engaged in creating and rewriting our pasts. As Rainer Maria Rilke wrote, "And still it is not enough to have memories. One must be able to forget them when they are many, and one must have the great patience to wait until they come again. For it is not yet the memories themselves. Not until they have turned to blood within us, to glance, to gesture, nameless and no longer to be distinguished from ourselves—not until then can it happen that in a most rare hour the first word of a verse arises in their midst and goes forth from them" ([1910] 2008, xii).

In our stories and reflections, an overriding theme has emerged. Throughout our lives, we look for ways to construct our personal narrative. The mind organizes memories in search of an unbroken and cohesive storyline. We seek a narrative that fits with our ideas about who we are and what matters most to us at a given moment in time. After events transpire, we weave narratives around them that draw on language, metaphor, and images and thus form a tapestry from the wisps of our memory. We try to put our many thoughts and feelings into words, no matter how eloquent, raw, or unformed. One word follows another, and for a period of time we often find ourselves frustrated because we do not know the pattern the words are creating. We long for certainty, yet we find that as soon as we have one story line, it slips through our fingers and another appears in its place. What was once in the foreground becomes the background, which shifts the focus of our life story. Then suddenly we discover yet another new thread.

In other words, the process of simply living life revises our earlier memories. Consider, for example, this memory: A blue-eyed child dances at a wedding. In the memory, she is at the center, surrounded by other dancers. She sways to the music. In your mind's eye, you see the child glide across the floor, twirling, a wide smile spread across her face. Years later you run into the bride at this wedding, and you both recall the dancing child. She mentions that it's her tenth wedding anniversary and you are momentarily puzzled. You do a quick calculation and suddenly realize the child was only eleven months old at the wedding, far too young to dance and twirl across the floor. Now the memory is revised, and a new one appears, just as real as the one before: an infant, sitting on the floor, rocks to the beat.

So why does your memory have her gracefully dancing on two firm legs? Here, the memory is altered to better fit one's current understanding of the world. The long-ago memory of the child has become consolidated with a present-day image. In this way, memories are both timeless and changeable. We rescript our history in order to ensure that our self-narrative keeps pace with our current emotional state. We unconsciously synchronize external events with our internal experience so that our memories are consistent with the emotions we feel now.

Despite the complex processes through which memory is altered, we are predisposed to dichotomize memory as either true or false, as if we were not continually revising our own stories. It is like writing an internal memoir: we seek a version of the truth—an emotional truth—rather than a factual one. Similar to the process of writing, a memory goes through many revisions. When we return to it later, it no longer looks the same to us. Hence, we typically need not decide if a memory is veridical truth or fiction. It is always the "truth" as seen through the current slant of one's life and always looks different from afar. When we write, it is the same: we can only hope to evoke, through words, the many meanings that lie beneath the surface.

One of the challenges of writing this book was finding our own voices as individuals and coauthors. As analysts, we have struggled throughout our careers to integrate the multiple contributions to our work made by teachers, therapists and analysts, mentors, and psychodynamic thinkers and, perhaps most important, to utilize the insights and wisdom we have garnered from our patients. In the course of writing this book together, we sought to distill what we believe to be the liveliness of psychoanalytic theory and the myriad ways it enriches our thinking. This process is similar to what happens between patient and therapist. Over time, we find a common language.

As we wrote this book, a striking parallel emerged: just as treatment changes our patients, so, too, writing or the process of putting words to our ideas has changed us. Our own understanding of theory has evolved and deepened over the course of this joint project. A wonderful and unexpected outgrowth of our writing was that the creative process affected us in personal ways beyond what we ever anticipated. As our project took shape, our stories became more articulated, and themes emerged that had shared meanings and resonated within each of us in different ways. We were continually surprised by the power of words to evoke new understanding.

We see that in stories, as with patients, the points of entry and change are through affect. If we can engage our patients in meaningful ways, then the process of healing can begin. When a new insight or understanding is developed, its power lies in reawakening old feelings that now become available for reworking and repair. It is through an enlivened connection with the therapist that a patient can resume the process of development and growth. When stories touch us the most, it is likewise because they reach us in an affectively alive way.

Stories have the potential not only to surprise and delight us, but also to disturb, confuse, or even dismay us. Being surprised by new insight is both exciting and scary. It is not always easy to listen to the stories of our patients, especially when they can cause us to cringe or want to turn away. Like traumatic memory, which can be disconnected, affectively deadened, or incomprehensible, narratives of trauma can jolt the reader. Yet as readers we know that what is most disturbing can also be most important, and it is the same with clinicians. Our most potent tool as therapists is our ability to strive for meaning, to find some part of us that can hold on to what is broken in our patients—to not turn away.

Because we recognize that the clinician's task is complicated and challenging, we are convinced that it is crucial for clinicians to discuss their work openly. There are many reasons why this task challenges us. It is difficult to shake off the internal supervisors who sit on our shoulder, ready to judge, criticize, or take issue with our work. Beyond that, however, we struggle to recapture in language all that transpires with our patients—even though the sum of the work is exponentially greater than even the most diligent of our process notes can convey.

As writers and psychoanalysts, we believe we share strands of meaning and commonalities in life. We express our commonalities through our stories. As you see in our book, and as we know from our work with patients, our narratives vary widely in details, yet the themes are the same. We love, we hate, we want, we grieve for what we've lost, and we celebrate what is to come.

REFERENCES

Adatto, C. P. 1966. "On the Metamorphosis from Adolescence Into Adulthood." *Journal of American Psychoanalytic Association* 14:485–509.

Alexander, P. C. and C. L. Anderson. 1997. "Incest, Attachment, and Developmental Psychopathology." In D. Cicchetti and S. Toth, eds., *Developmental Perspectives on Trauma: Theory, Research, and Clinical Applications*, vol. 8 of *Rochester Symposium on Developmental Psychopathology*, 343–78. Rochester, N.Y.: University of Rochester.

Altman, N. 2000. "Black and White Thinking: A Psychoanalyst Reconsiders Race." *Psychoanalytic Dialogue* 10:589–605.

——. 2006. "Whiteness." *Psychoanalytic Quarterly* 75:45–72.

Anderson, C. L. and P. C. Alexander. 2005. "The Effect of Abuse on Children's Development." In P. F. Talley, ed., *Handbook for the Treatment of Abused and Neglected Children*, 3–23. Binghamton, N.Y.: Haworth Press.

Archer, J. 1999. *The Nature of Grief*. New York: Routledge Press.

Auerhahn, N. and D. Laub. 1984. "Annihilation and Restoration: Posttraumatic Memory as Pathway and Obstacle to Recovery." *International Review of Psychoanalysis* 11:327–44.

Bach, S. 2006. *Getting from Here to There: Analytic Love, Analytic Practice*. Hillsdale, N.J.: Analytic Press.

Baker, J. E. 2001. "Mourning and the Transformation of Object Relationships: Evidence for the Persistence of Internal Attachments." *Psychoanalytic Psychology* 18:55–73.

Balint, M. 1950. "On the Termination of Analysis." *International Journal of Psychoanalysis* 31:196–99.

Barkin, L. 1978. "The Concept of the Transitional Object." In S. Grolnick, L. Barkin, and W. Muensterberger, eds., *Between Fantasy and Reality: Transitional Objects and Phenomena*, 511–37. New York: Jason Aronson.

Bartlett, A. 2005. "Maternal Sexuality and Breastfeeding." *Sex Education* 5, no. 1: 67–77.

Beebe, B. and F. M. Lachmann. 2002. *Infant Research and Adult Treatment: Co-constructing Interactions*. Hillsdale, N.J.: Analytic Press.

Behrends, R. and S. Blatt. 1985. "Internalization and Psychological Development Throughout the Life Cycle." *Psychoanalytic Studies of the Child* 40:11–39.

Benedek, T. 1959. "Parenthood as a Developmental Phase—A Contribution to the Libido Theory." *Journal of American Psychoanalytic Association* 7:389–417.

Benjamin, J. 1991. "Father and Daughter: Identification with Difference—a Contribution to Gender Heterodoxy." *Psychoanalytic Dialogues* 1, no. 3: 277–99.

——. 2004. "Beyond Doer and Done to: An Intersubjective View of Thirdness." *Psychoanalytic Quarterly* 73:5–46.

Bergman, A. 1993. "To Be or Not to Be Separate: The Meaning of Hide-and-Seek in Forming Interpretations." *Psychoanalytic Review* 80:361–75.

Bergmann, M. S. 1997. "Termination: The Achilles' Heel of Psychoanalytic Technique." *Psychoanalytic Psychology* 14:163–74.

Bettelheim, B. 1977. *The Uses of Enchantment: The Meaning and Importance of Fairy Tales*. New York: Vintage Books.

Bibring, E. 1937. "Therapeutic Results of Psychoanalysis." *International Journal of Psychoanalysis* 18:170–89.

Bion, W. R. 1962. *Learning from Experience.* London: Heinemann.

Bird, B. 1972. "Notes on Transference: Universal Phenomenon and Hardest Part of Analysis." *Journal of American Psychoanalytic Association* 20:267–301.

Blos, P. 1967. "The Second Individuation Process of Adolescence." *Psychoanalytic Study of the Child* 22:162–86.

Blum, H. P. 1997. "Clinical and Developmental Dimensions of Hate." *Journal of the American Psychoanalytic Association* 45:359–75.

Bollas, C. 1989. *Forces of Destiny: Psychoanalysis and Human Idiom.* London: Free Association Books.

Boswell, James. [1791] 2008. *The Life of Samuel Johnson.* New York: Penguin Classics.

Bowlby, J. 1969. *Attachment.* Vol. 1 of *Attachment and Loss.* London: Hogarth Press and Institute of Psycho-Analysis.

——. 1980. *Loss, Sadness, and Depression.* Vol. 3 of *Attachment and Loss.* New York: Basic Books.

Briere, J. 1988. The Long-Term Clinical Correlates of Childhood Sexual Victimization. *Annals of the New York Academy of Sciences* 528: 327–34.

Brockman, D. D. 2003. *Reflections on Clinical Theory: From Late Adolescence to Adulthood.* Madison, Conn.: International Universities Press.

Bucci, W. 2007. "Dissociation from the Perspective of Multiple Code Theory. Part I: Psychological Roots and Implications for Psychoanalytic Treatment." *Contemporary Psychoanalysis* 43:305–26.

——. 2010. "Converging Evidence for the Referential Process from Psychoanalysis, Cognitive Science, and Neuroscience." Paper presented at the New Directions conference, Pentagon City Residence Inn, Arlington, Va., February 5–7.

Chasseguet-Smirgel, J. 1988. "From the Archaic Matrix of the Oedipus Complex to the Fully Developed Oedipus Complex—Theoretical

Perspective in Relation to Clinical Experience and Technique." *Psychoanalytic Quarterly* 57:505–27.

Chused, J. F. 1991. "The Evocative Power of Enactments." *Journal of American Psychoanalytic Association* 39:615–39.

——. 1996. "The Therapeutic Action of Psychoanalysis: Abstinence and Informative Experiences." *Journal of American Psychoanalytic Association* 44:1047–71.

Cicchetti, D. and M. I. Posner. 2006. "Editorial: Cognitive and Affective Neuroscience and Developmental Psychopathology." *Development and Psychopathology* 17, no. 3: 569–75.

Clewell, T. 2004. "Mourning Beyond Melancholia: Freud's Psychoanalysis of Loss." *Journal of the American Psychoanalytic Association* 52:43–67.

Courtois, C. and J. Ford. 2009. *Treating Complex Traumatic Stress Disorders: An Evidence-Based Guide.* New York: Guilford Press.

Dahl, K. 2002. "In Her Mother's Voice: Reflections on 'Femininity' and the Superego." *Psychoanalytic Study of the Child* 57:3–23.

——. 2004. " 'Last Night I Dreamed I Went to Manderly Again': Vicissitudes of Maternal Identifications in Late Female Adolescence." *Psychoanalytic Inquiry* 24:657–79.

Dalal, F. 2007. "Racism: Processes of Detachment, Dehumanization, and Hatred." *Psychoanalytic Quarterly* 75:131–62.

Davies, J. M. 2000. "Descending the Therapeutic Slopes—Slippery, Slipperier, Slipperiest: Commentary on Papers by Barbara Pizer and Glen Gabbard." *Psychoanalytic Dialogue* 10: 219–29.

Davies, J. M. and M. G. Frawley. 1994. *Treating the Adult Survivor of Childhood Sexual Abuse: A Psychoanalytic Perspective.* New York: Basic Books.

Davis, M. and D. Wallbridge. 1987. *Boundary and Space.* London: Karnac Press.

DiAmbrosio, P. E. 2006. "Weeble Wobbles: Resilience Within the Psychoanalytic Situation." *International Journal of Psychoanalytic Self Psychology* 1:263–84.

Didion, J. 2006. *The Year of Magical Thinking*. New York: Random House.

Eissler, K. R. 1958. "Notes on Problems of Technique in the Psychoanalytic Treatment of Adolescents—with Some Remarks on Perversions." *Psychoanalytic Study of the Child* 13:223–54.

Ellis, B. and J. Garber. 2000. "Psychosocial Antecedents of Variation in Girls' Pubertal Timing: Maternal Depression, Stepfather Presence, and Marital and Family Stress." *Child Development* 71, no. 2: 485–501.

Erikson, E. H. 1956. "The Problem of Ego Identity." *Journal of the American Psychoanalytic Association* 4:56–121.

Fairbairn, W. R. D. [1943] 1952. "The Repression and the Return of Bad Objects (with Special Reference to the 'War Neuroses')." In *Psychoanalytic Studies of the Personality*, 59–81. London: Tavistock.

Fenichel, O. 1945. *The Psychoanalytic Theory of Neurosis*. New York: Norton.

Ferenczi, S. 1949. "Confusion of Tongues Between Adults and the Child." *International Journal of Psychoanalysis* 30:225–30.

Fogelman, E. 1988. "Intergenerational Group Therapy: Child Survivors of the Holocaust and Offspring of Survivors." *Psychoanalytic Review* 75, no. 4: 619–40.

Fonagy, P., G. Gergeley, E. Jurist, and M. Target. [2002] 2005. *Affect Regulation, Mentalization, and the Development of the Self*. New York: Other Press.

Fonagy, P., T. Leigh, R. Kennedy, G. Mattoon, H. Steele, M. Target, M. Steele, and A. Higgitt. 1995. "Attachment, Borderline States, and the Representation of Emotions and Cognitions in Self and Other." In D. Cicchetti and S. Toth, eds., *Rochester Symposium on Developmental Psychopathology*, 6:371–414. Rochester, N.Y.: University of Rochester Press.

Fonagy, P. and M. Target. 1996. "Playing with Reality: I. Theory of Mind and the Normal Development of Psychic Reality." *International Journal of Psychoanalysis* 77:217–33.

——. 1998. "Mentalization and the Changing Aims of Child Psychoanalysis." *Psychoanalytic Dialogue* 8:87–114.

Fosshage, J. L. 1994. "Toward Reconceptualising Transference: Theoretical and Clinical Considerations." *International Journal of Psychoanalysis* 75:265–80.

———. 1997. "The Organizing Function of Dream Mentation." *Contemporary Psychoanalysis* 33:429–55.

Fowlkes, M. R. 1991. "The Morality of Loss—The Social Construction of Mourning and Melancholia." *Contemporary Psychoanalysis* 27:529–51.

Fraiberg, S. H., E. Adelson, and V. Shapiro. 1975. "Ghosts in the Nursery: A Psychoanalytic Approach to the Problem of Impaired Infant–Mother Relationships." *Journal of the American Academy of Child Psychiatry* 14:387–422.

Frank, G. 2000. "Transference Revisited / Transference Revisioned." *Psychoanalytic Contemporary Thought* 23:459–78.

Frankl, V. E. 1984. *Man's Search for Meaning: An Introduction to Logotherapy.* 3rd ed. New York: Simon and Shuster.

Fresno, N. 1984. "Remembering the Unknown." *International Review of Psychoanalysis* 11:417–27.

Freud, A. [1936] 1954. *The Ego and the Mechanism of Defence.* New York: International Universities Press.

———. 1963. "The Concept of Developmental Lines." *Psychoanalytic Study of the Child* 18:245–65.

———. 1967. "Comments on Trauma." In S. S. Furst, ed., *Psychic Trauma,* 235–45. New York: Basic Books.

Freud, S. [1910] 1953a. "Five Lectures on Psychoanalysis." In *Five Lectures on Psychoanalysis, Leonardo da Vinci, and Other Works,* vol. 11 of *The Standard Edition of the Complete Psychological Works of Sigmund Freud,* 5–55. London: Hogarth Press.

———. [1905] 1953b. *Fragment of an Analysis of a Case of Hysteria.* In *Three Essays on Sexuality and Other Writings,* vol. 7 of *The Standard Edition of the Complete Psychological Works of Sigmund Freud,* 1–122. London: Hogarth Press.

———. [1910] 1953c. "The Future Prospects of Psychoanalytic Therapy." In *Five Lectures on Psychoanalysis, Leonardo da Vinci, and Other*

Works, vol. 11 of *The Standard Edition of the Complete Psychological Works of Sigmund Freud*, 139–52. London: Hogarth Press.

———. [1900] 1953d. *The Interpretation of Dreams.* In *The Interpretation of Dreams*, vol. 4 of *The Standard Edition of the Complete Psychological Works of Sigmund Freud*, 1–626. London: Hogarth Press.

———. [1901] 1953e. *The Psychopathology of Everyday Life.* In *The Psychopathology of Everyday Life*, vol. 6 of *The Standard Edition of the Complete Psychological Works of Sigmund Freud*, 1–289. London: Hogarth Press.

———. [1899] 1953f. "Screen Memories." In *Early Psycho-Analytic Publications*, vol. 3 of *The Standard Edition of the Complete Psychological Works of Sigmund Freud*, 301–22. London: Hogarth Press.

———. [1905] 1953g. *Three Essays on the Theory of Sexuality.* In *Three Essays on Sexuality and Other Writings*, vol. 7 of *The Standard Edition of the Complete Psychological Works of Sigmund Freud*, 123–246. London: Hogarth Press.

———. [1917] 1955a. "Analytic Therapy." In *Introductory Lectures on Psychoanalysis, Part III*, vol. 16 of *The Standard Edition of the Complete Psychological Works of Sigmund Freud*, 448–63. London: Hogarth Press.

———. [1918] 1955b. *From the History of an Infantile Neurosis.* In *An Infantile Neurosis and Other Works*, vol. 17 of *The Standard Edition of the Complete Psychological Works of Sigmund Freud*, 1–124. London: Hogarth Press, 1955.

———. [1922] 1955c. "Group Psychology and the Analysis of the Ego." In *Beyond the Pleasure Principle, Group Psychology, and Other Works*, vol. 18 of *The Standard Edition of the Complete Psychological Works of Sigmund Freud*, 69–144. London: Hogarth Press.

———. [1911] 1955d. "The Handling of Dream-Interpretation in Psychoanalysis." In *"The Case of Schreber," "Papers on Technique," and Other Works*, vol. 12 of *The Standard Edition of the Complete Psychological Works of Sigmund Freud*, 91–96. London: Hogarth Press.

———. [1917] 1955e. "Mourning and Melancholia." In *On the History of the Psycho-analytic Movement, Papers on Metapsychology, and Other*

Works, vol. 14 of *The Standard Edition of the Complete Psychological Works of Sigmund Freud*, 237–58. London: Hogarth Press.

——. [1915] 1955f. "Observations on Transference Love." In *"The Case of Schreber," "Papers on Technique," and Other Works*, vol. 12 of *The Standard Edition of the Complete Psychological Works of Sigmund Freud*, 159–71. London: Hogarth Press.

——. [1913] 1955g. "On Beginning the Treatment." In *"The Case of Schreber," "Papers on Technique," and Other Works*, vol. 12 of *The Standard Edition of the Complete Psychological Works of Sigmund Freud*, 123–44. London: Hogarth Press.

——. [1938] 1955h. "An Outline of Psycho-Analysis." In *"Moses and Monotheism," "An Outline of Psycho-Analysis," and Other Works*, vol. 23 of *The Standard Edition of the Complete Psychological Works of Sigmund Freud*, 139–207. London: Hogarth Press

——. [1912] 1955i. "Recommendations to Physicians Practicing Psychoanalysis." In *"The Case of Schreber," "Papers on Technique," and Other Works*, vol. 12 of *The Standard Edition of the Complete Psychological Works of Sigmund Freud*, 109–20. London: Hogarth Press.

——. [1914] 1955j. "Remembering, Repeating, and Working-Through." In *"The Case of Schreber," "Papers on Technique," and Other Works*, vol. 12 of *The Standard Edition of the Complete Psychological Works of Sigmund Freud*, 145–56. London: Hogarth.

——. [1915] 1955k. "Thoughts for the Times on War and Death." In *On the History of the Psycho-analytic Movement, Papers on Metapsychology, and Other Works*, vol. 14 of *The Standard Edition of the Complete Psychological Works of Sigmund Freud*, 274–300. London: Hogarth Press.

——. [1913] 1955l. *Totem and Taboo*. In *Totem and Taboo and Other Works*, vol. 13 of *The Standard Edition of the Complete Psychological Works of Sigmund Freud*, 1–161. London: Hogarth Press.

——. 1974. Sigmund Freud to C. G. Jung, November 21, 1909. In *The Freud/Jung Letters: The Correspondence Between Sigmund Freud and C. G. Jung*, 265–67. Princeton, N.J.: Princeton University Press.

———. 2000. Sigmund Freud to Sándor Ferenczi, May 21, 1911. In *1908–1914*, vol. 1 of *The Correspondence of Sigmund Freud and Sándor Ferenczi*, 280–82. Cambridge, Mass.: Belknap Press of Harvard University Press.

———. 2003. Sigmund Freud to Ludwig Binswanger, April 11, 1929. In E. L. Freud, ed., *Letters of Sigmund Freud, 1873–1939*, translated by Thomas Roberts, 386. New York: Other Press.

Freyberg, J. 1980. "Difficulties in Separation–Individuation as Experienced by Offspring of Nazi Holocaust Survivors." *American Journal of Orthopsychiatry* 50, no. 1: 87–95.

Gabbard, G. O. 1995. "The Early History of Boundary Violations in Psychoanalysis." *Journal of the American Psychoanalytic Association* 43:1115–36.

———. 1998. "Commentary on Paper by Jody Messler Davies." *Psychoanalytic Dialogue* 8:781–90.

Gabbard, G. O. and E. P. Lester. 1995. *Boundaries and Boundary Violations*. New York: Basic Books.

Gaines, R. 1997. "Detachment and Continuity." *Contemporary Psychoanalysis* 33:549–71.

Garmezy, N. 1987. "Stress, Competence, and Development: Continuing in the Study of Schizophrenia in Adults, Children Vulnerable to Psychopathology, and the Search for Stress Resilient Children." *American Journal of Orthopsychiatry* 57:159–74.

Ginot, E. 2001. "The Holding Environment and Intersubjectivity." *Psychoanalytic Quarterly* 70:417–45.

Grealy, L. 1994. *Autobiography of a Face*. Boston: Harper/Perennial Press.

Greenacre, P. 1958. "Early Physical Determinants in the Development of the Sense of Identity." *Journal of the American Psychoanalytic Association* 6:612–27.

Grubich-Simitis, I. 1984. "From Concretism to Metaphor: Thoughts on Some Theoretical and Technical Aspects of the Psychoanalytic Work with Children of Holocaust Survivors." *Psychoanalytic Study of the Child* 39:301–19.

Hagman, G. 1996. "The Role of the Other in Mourning." *Psychoanalytic Quarterly* 65:327–52.

Hamer, F. M. 2002. "Guards at the Gate: Race, Resistance, and Psychic Reality." *Journal of the American Psychoanalytic Association* 50:1219–37.

Hetherington, E. M. and J. Kelly. 2003. *For Better: Divorce Reconsidered.* New York: W. W. Norton.

Hirsch, I. 1997. "On Men's Preference for Men." *Gender and Psychoanalysis* 2:469–86.

Holmes, D. E. 2006. "The Wrecking Effects of Race and Social Class on Self and Success." *Psychoanalytic Quarterly* 75:215–36.

Holtzman, D. and N. Kulish. 2003. "The Femininization of the Female Oedipal Complex, Part II: Aggression Reconsidered." *Journal of the American Psychoanalytic Association* 51:1127–51.

Hong, K. M. 1978. "Transitional Phenomena—a Theoretical Integration." *Psychoanalytic Study of the Child* 33:47–79.

Jacobs, T. 1986. "On Countertransference Enactments." *Journal of the American Psychoanalytic Association* 334:289–307.

Jacobson, E. [1965] 1984. "The Return of the Lost Parent." In R. V. Frankie, ed., *Essential Papers on Object Loss,* 233–90. New York: New York University Press.

Jaffe, D. S. 1988. "Psychoanalytic Principles and Principle Deviations." *Psychoanalysis* 16:5–79.

Joseph, B. 1985. "Transference: The Total Situation." *International Journal of Psychoanalysis* 66:447–54.

——. [1981] 1989. "Defense Mechanism and Phantasy in the Psychoanalytic Process." In M. Feldman and E. B. Spillius, eds., *Psychic Equilibrium and Psychic Change: Selected Papers of Betty Joseph,* 116–26. London: Routledge.

Kaplan, L. 1984. *Adolescence: The Farewell to Childhood.* New York: Simon and Shuster.

Katz, G. A. 1998. "Where the Action Is: The Enacted Dimension of Analytic Process." *Journal of the American Psychoanalytic Association* 46:1129–67.

Keenan, M. C. 1995. "Enactments of Boundary Violations." *Journal of the American Psychoanalytic Association* 43:853–68.

Kellerman, H. 2008. *The Psychoanalysis of Symptom Formation.* New York: Springer Science.

Kestenberg, J. 1980. "Psychoanalyses of Children of Survivors of the Holocaust: Case Presentations and Assessment." *Journal of the American Psychoanalytic Association* 28:775–804.

Klass, D. 1996. "Grief in Eastern Culture: Japanese Ancestor Worship." In D. Klass. P. R. Silverman, and S. L. Nickman, eds., *Continuing Bonds: New Understandings of Grief,* 59–70. Washington, D.C.: Taylor and Francis.

Klauber, J. 1977. "Analyses That Cannot Be Terminated." *International Journal of Psychoanalysis* 58:473–77.

Klein, M. 1940. "Mourning and Its Relation to Manic-Depressive States." *International Journal of Psychoanalysis* 21:125–53.

——. 1945. "The Oedipus Complex in the Light of Early Anxieties." *International Journal of Psychoanalysis* 26:11–33.

——. 1946. "Notes on Some Schizoid Mechanisms." *International Journal of Psychoanalysis* 27:99–110.

——. 1975. *Envy and Gratitude and Other Works 1946–1963.* New York: Delta.

Kluft, R. P. 2000. "The Psychoanalytic Psychotherapy of Dissociative Identity Disorder in the Context of Trauma Therapy." *Psychoanalytic Inquiry* 20:259–86.

Kohut, H. 1971a. *The Analysis of the Self.* New York: International Universities Press.

——. 1971b. Peace Prize 1969 Laudation. *Journal of the American Psychoanalytic Association* 19:806–18.

——. 1977. *Restoration of the Self.* New York: International Universities Press.

Kramer, S. 1991. "Psychopathological Effects of Incest." In S. Kramer and S. Aktar, eds., *The Trauma of Transgression: Psychotherapy of Incest Victims,* 1–22. Northvale, N.J.: Jason Aronson.

Krell, R. 1979. "Holocaust Families: The Survivors and Their Children." *Comprehensive Psychiatry* 20:560–67.

Krystal, H. 1988. *Integration and Self-Healing: Affect, Trauma, Alexithymia*. Hillsdale, N.J.: Analytic Press.

Landsman, I. S. 2002. "Crises of Meaning in Trauma and Loss." In J. Kauffman, ed., *Loss of the Assumptive World: A Theory of Traumatic Loss*, 13–30. New York: Brunner-Routledge.

Laub, D. and N. Auerhahn. 1985. Prologue. *Psychoanalytic Inquiry* 5, no. 1: 1–8.

Leary, K. 1997a. "Race in Psychoanalytic Space." *Gender and Psychoanalysis* 2:157–72.

——. 1997b. "Race, Self-Disclosure, and 'Forbidden Talk': Race and Ethnicity in Contemporary Clinical Practice." *Psychoanalytic Quarterly* 66:163–89.

——. 2000. "Racial Enactments in Dynamic Treatment." *Psychoanalytic Dialogue* 10:639–54.

Lester, E. P. and M. T. Notman. 1986. "Pregnancy, Developmental Crisis, and Object Relations: Psychoanalytic Considerations." *International Journal of Psychoanalysis* 67:357–65.

Levine, H. 1982. "Toward a Psychoanalytic Understanding of Children of Survivors of the Holocaust." *Psychoanalytic Quarterly* 51:70–92.

Levy-Warren, M. 1996. *The Adolescent Journey: Development, Identity Formation, and Psychotherapy*. Northvale, N.J.: Jason Aronson.

Lewis, M. 1993. "The Development of Anger and Rage." In R. A. Glick and S. P. Roose, eds., *Rage, Power, and Aggression*, 148–67. New Haven, Conn.: Yale University Press.

Lictenberg, J. D. 1999. "Listening, Understanding, and Interpreting: Reflections." *International Journal of Psychoanalysis* 80:719–37.

Liegner, E. 1977. "The First Interview in Modern Psychoanalysis." *Modern Psychoanalysis* 2:55–66.

Liotti, G. 2006. "A Model of Dissociation Based on Attachment Theory and Research." *Journal of Trauma and Dissociation* 7, no. 4: 55–73.

Loewald, E. 1982. "The Baby in Mother's Therapy." *Psychoanalytic Study of the Child* 37:381–404.

Loewald, H. W. 1960. "On the Therapeutic Action of Psycho-Analysis." *International Journal of Psychoanalysis* 41:16–33.

——. 1962. "Internalization, Separation, Mourning, and the Superego." *Psychoanalytic Quarterly* 31:483–504.

——. 1970. "Psychoanalytic Theory and the Psychoanalytic Process." *Psychoanalytic Study of the Child* 25:45–68.

——. 1989. "Internalization, Separation, Mourning, and the Superego." In *Papers on Psychoanalysis*, 257–76. New Haven, Conn.: Yale University Press.

Maciejewski, P. K., B. Zhang, S. D. Block, and H. G. Prigerson. 2007. "An Empirical Examination of the Stage Theory of Grief." *Journal of the American Medical Association* 297, no. 7 (February 21): 716–23.

Mahler, M. S. 1972. "Rapprochement Subphase of the Separation–Individuation Process." *International Journal of Psychoanalysis* 41: 487–506.

Mahler, M. S., F. Pine, and A. Bergman. 1975. *The Psychological Birth of the Human Infant.* New York: Basic Books.

Main, M. and E. Hesse. 1990. "Parents' Unresolved Traumatic Experiences Are Related to Infant Disorganized Attachment Status: Is Frightened and/or Frightening Parental Behavior the Linking Mechanism?" In M. Greenberg, D. Cicchetti, and E. M. Cummings, eds., *Attachment in the Preschool Years: Theory, Research, and Intervention*, 161–84. Chicago: University of Chicago Press.

Main, M., K. Kaplan, and J. Cassidy. 1985. "Security in Infancy, Childhood, and Adulthood: A Move to the Level of Representation." In I. Bretherton and E. Waters, eds., *Growing Points of Attachment Theory and Research*, 66–104, Monographs of the Society for Research in Child Development, vol. 50, nos. 1–2. Chicago: University of Chicago Press.

Malawista, K. 2007. "Memory." *Voices: The Art and Science of Psychotherapy* 43, no. 1: 70–72.

Malawista, K. L. and P. Malawista. 1999. "The Opening Phase of the Analysis of Mr. B: A Dramatic Transference Phenomenon." In J. Edwards and E. Rose, eds., *The Social Work Psychoanalyst's Case Book: Essays in Honor of Jean Sanville*, 23–46. Hillsdale, N.J.: Analytic Press.

Mayer, E. L. 1985. "'Everybody Must Be Just Like Me': Observations on Female Castration Anxiety." *International Journal of Psychoanalysis* 66:331–47.

———. 1995. "The Phallic Castration Complex and Primary Femininity: Paired Development." *Journal of the American Psychoanalytic Association* 43:17–38.

Mayes, L. C. and D. J. Cohen. 1993. "Playing and Therapeutic Action in Child Analysis." *International Journal of Psychoanalysis* 74:1235–44.

Mayman, M. 1967. "Object-Representations and Object Relationships in Rorschach Responses." *Journal of Projective Techniques* 31: 17–24.

Meadow, P. W. 1990. "Treatment Beginnings." *Modern Psychoanalysis* 15:3–10.

Meissner, W. W. 2000. "Reflections on Psychic Reality." *International Journal of Psychoanalysis* 81:1117–38.

Milrod, D. 2002. "The Superego: Its Formation, Structure, and Functioning." *Psychoanalytic Study of the Child* 57:131–48.

Mitchell, S. A. 1988. *Relational Concepts in Psychoanalysis: An Integration.* Cambridge, Mass.: Harvard University Press.

Modell, A. H. 1976. "The Holding Environment and the Therapeutic Action of Psychoanalysis." *Journal of the American Psychoanalytic Association* 24:285–307.

———. 1988. "Changing Psychic Structure Through Treatment: Preconditions for the Resolution of the Transference." *Journal of the American Psychoanalytic Association* 36 (suppl.): 225–39.

Novick, J. 1982. "Termination: Themes and Issues." *Psychoanalytic Inquiry* 2:329–65.

Novick, J. and K. K. Novick. 1991. "Some Comments on Masochism and the Delusion of Omnipotence from a Developmental Perspective." *Journal of the American Psychoanalytic Association* 39:307–31.

———. 2006. *Good Goodbyes: Knowing How to End in Psychotherapy and Psychoanalysis.* Lanham, Md.: Rowman and Littlefield.

Orgel, S. 2000. "Letting Go: Some Thoughts About Termination." *Journal of the American Psychoanalytic Association* 48:719–38.

Ortmeyer, D. H. 1987. "Idealization and Entitlement: Clinical Approaches to 'Narcissistic' Transferences (a Symposium)." *Contemporary Psychoanalysis* 23:221–29.

Perry, B. 2001. "The Neurodevelopmental Impact of Violence in Childhood." In D. Schetky and E. Benedek, eds., *Textbook of Child and Adolescent Psychiatry*, 221–38. Washington, D.C.: American Psychiatric Press.

Philips, H. 2002. "Paranormal Beliefs Linked to Brain Chemistry." *The New Scientist* (July): 19–26.

Phillips, A. 1988. *Winnicott*. Cambridge, Mass.: Harvard University Press.

Phillips, R. 1978. "Impact of the Nazi Holocaust on Children of Survivors." *American Journal of Psychotherapy* 32:370–77.

Pine, F. 1992. "From Technique to a Theory of Psychic Change." *International Journal of Psychoanalysis* 73:251–54.

Poland, W. S. 1984. "The Analyst's Words: Empathy and Countertransference." *Psychoanalytic Quarterly* 53:421–24.

——. 2002. "The Interpretive Attitude." *Journal of the American Psychoanalytic Association* 50:807–26.

Powers, R. 2006. *The Echo Maker*. New York: Farrar, Straus, and Giroux.

Provence, S. and R. C. Lipton. 1962. *Infants in Institutions*. New York: International Universities Press.

Putnam, F. W. 2003. "Ten-Year Research Update Review: Child Sexual Abuse." *Journal of the American Academy of Child and Adolescent Psychiatry* 42, no. 3: 269–78.

Renik, O. 2004. "Intersubjectivity in Psychoanalysis." *International Journal of Psychoanalysis* 85:1053–56.

Richards, A. K. 1996. "What Is New with Women." *Journal of the American Psychoanalytic Association* 44:1227–41.

Rilke, R. M. [1910] 2008. *The Notebooks of Malte Laurids Brigge: A Novel*. Trans. Burton Pike. Urbana: University of Illinois Press.

Ritvo, S. 1971. "Late Adolescence—Developmental and Clinical Considerations." *Psychoanalytic Studies of the Child* 26:241–63.

——. 1976. "Adolescent to Woman." *Journal of the American Psychoanalytic Association* 24S:127–37.

Ross, J. M. 1995. "The Fate of Relatives and Colleagues in the Aftermath of Boundary Violations." *Journal of the American Psychoanalytic Association* 43:959–61.

Sandler, J. and B. Rosenblatt. 1962. "The Concept of the Representational World." *Psychoanalytic Study of the Child* 17:128–45.

Sandler, J. and A. M. Sandler. 1983. "The 'Second Censorship': The 'Three Box Model' and Some Technical Implications." *International Journal of Psychoanalysis* 64:413–25.

Schwartz, J. M. and R. D. Stolorow. 2001. "Trauma in a Presymbolic World." *Psychoanalytic Psychology* 18:380–87.

Searles, H. F. 1959. "Oedipal Love in the Counter Transference." *International Journal of Psychoanalysis* 40:180–90.

Shengold, L. 1989. *Soul Murder*. New York: Random House.

Shoshan, T. 1989. "Mourning and Longing from Generation to Generation." *American Journal of Psychotherapy* 43, no. 2: 193–207.

Slochower, J. 1991. "Variations in the Analytic Holding Environment." *International Journal of Psychoanalysis* 72:709–17.

Smith, B. [1943] 1989. *A Tree Grows in Brooklyn*. New York: Mass Market Paperback.

Smith, H. 2006. "Countertransference, Conflictual Listening, and the Analytic Object Relationship." In A. Cooper, ed., *Contemporary Psychoanalysis in America: Leading Analysts Present Their Work*, 619–37. Washington, D.C.: American Psychiatric Publishing.

——. 2007. "Invisible Racism." *Psychoanalytic Quarterly* 75:3–20.

——. Forthcoming. "Continuous Enactment and the Analyst's Thinking." *Psychoanalytic Quarterly*.

Solnit, A. J. 1998. "Beyond Play and Playfullness Superego." *Psychoanalytic Study of the Child* 53:102–10.

Stern, D. N. 1985. *The Interpersonal World of the Infant: A View from Psychoanalysis and Development*. New York: Basic Books.

Stolorow, R. D. and G. E. Atwood. 1992. *Contexts of Being: The Intersubjective Foundations of Psychological Life*. Psychoanalytic Inquiry Book Series, vol. 12. Hillsdale, N.J.: Analytic Press.

Strauch, B. 2003. *The Primal Teen: What the New Discoveries about the Teenage Brain Tell Us About Our Kids.* New York: First Anchor Books.

Sullivan, H. S. 1953. *The Interpersonal Theory of Psychiatry.* New York: Norton Press.

——. 1965. *Personal Psychopathology.* New York: W. W. Norton.

Sussillo, M. V. 2005. "Beyond the Grave—Adolescent Parental Loss: Letting Go and Holding." *Psychoanalytic Dialogue* 15:499–527.

Tessman, L. H. 2003. *The Analyst's Analyst Within.* Hillsdale, N.J.: Analytic Press.

Tolpin, M. 1971. "On the Beginnings of a Cohesive Self—An Application of the Concept of Transmuting Internalization to the Study of the Transitional Object and Signal Anxiety." *Psychoanalytic Study of the Child* 26:316–52.

Tronick, E. Z. 2003. "Of Course All Relationships Are Unique: How Co-creative Processes Generate Unique Mother–Infant and Patient–Therapist Relationships and Change Other Relationships." *Psychoanalytic Inquiry* 23:473–91.

Tyson, P. 2003. "Some Psychoanalytic Perspectives on Women." *Journal of the American Psychoanalytic Association* 51:1119–26.

Viorst, J. 1982. "Experiences of Loss at the End of Analysis: The Patient's Response to Termination." *Psychoanalytic Inquiry* 2:399–418.

Wallace, E. M. 2007. "Losing a Training Analyst for Ethical Violations: A Candidate's Perspective." *International Journal of Psychoanalysis* 88:1275–88.

Wallerstein, R. S. and S. J. Coen. 1994. "Impasses in Psychoanalysis." *Journal of the American Psychoanalytic Association* 42:1225–35.

Walter, C. A. 2003. *The Loss of a Life Partner: Narratives of the Bereaved.* New York: Columbia University Press.

Weiss, S. S. and J. Fleming. 1980. "On the Teaching and Learning of Termination in Psychoanalysis." *Annual of Psychoanalysis* 8:37–55.

Willoughby, R. 2001. "The Dungeon of Thyself: The Claustrum as Pathological Container." *International Journal of Psychoanalysis* 82:917–31.

Winnicott, D. W. 1949. "Hate in the Counter-Transference." *International Journal of Psychoanalysis* 30:69–74.

——. 1953. "Transitional Objects and Transitional Phenomena." *International Journal of Psychoanalysis* 34:89–97.

——. 1960. "The Theory of the Parent–Infant Relationship." *International Journal of Psychoanalysis* 41:585–95.

——. [1958] 1965a. "The Capacity to Be Alone." In *The Maturational Process and the Facilitating Environment*, 29–36. New York: International Universities Press.

——. [1958] 1965b. "From Dependence Towards Independence in the Development of the Individual." In *The Maturational Process and the Facilitating Environment*, 83–92. New York: International Universities Press.

——. [1963] 1965c. "Psychiatric Disorders in Terms of Infantile Maturational Processes." In *The Maturational Process and the Facilitating Environment*, 230–41. New York: International Universities Press.

——. 1967. "The Location of Cultural Experience." *International Journal of Psychoanalysis* 48, no. 3: 213–31.

——. 1968. "Playing: Its Theoretical Status in the Clinical Situation." *International Journal of Psychoanalysis* 49:591–99.

——. 1969. "The Use of an Object." *International Journal of Psychoanalysis* 50:711–16.

——. 1971. *Playing and Reality*. London: Tavistock.

Yalom, I. D. and M. A. Lieberman. 1991. "Bereavement and Heightened Existential Awareness." *Psychiatry* 54:334–45.

Zusne, L. and W. H. Jones. 1989. *Anomalistic Psychology: A Study of Magical Thinking*. 2d ed.. Hillsdale, N.J.: Lawrence Erlbaum.

INDEX